(PAOLO BENI)

A Biographical and Critical Study

P. B. DIFFLEY

CLARENDON PRESS · OXFORD

1988

Oxford University Press, Walton Street, Oxford OX2 6DP
Oxford New York Toronto
Delhi Bombay Calcutta Madras Karachi
Petaling Jaya Singapore Hong Kong Tokyo
Nairobi Dar es Salaam Cape Town
Melbourne Auckland
and associated companies in

Beirut Berlin Ibadan Nicosia
Oxford is a trade mark of Oxford University Press

Published in the United States
by Oxford Univeristy Press, New York

© P. B. Diffley 1988

British Library Cataloguing in Publication Data
Diffley, P. B.
Paolo Beni: a biographical and critical study.
1. Beni, Paolo
I. Title
850.9   PQ4610.B3/
ISBN 0–19–815855–6

Library of Congress Cataloging in Publication Data
Data available

Set by Promenade Graphics Ltd., Cheltenham
Printed and bound in
Great Britain by Biddles Ltd,
Guildford and King's Lynn

CONTENTS

PC1064
.B46
.D5
1988

ABBREVIATIONS

A.	*L'Anticrusca, Parte II, III, IV* (1982)
AI	*L'Anticrusca*, Part I (1612)
ABSFG	Gubbio, Archivio del Convento di S. Francesco
ARSJ	Rome, Archivum Romanum Societatis Jesu
ASGA	Gubbio, Archivio di Stato, Fondo Armanni
ASGN	Gubbio, Archivio di Stato, Fondo Notarile
ASVB	Archivio Segreto Vaticano, Archivio Beni
Atti	'Atti dell'Accademia dei Ricovrati' (MS)
BB	'Beniana bibliotheca' (MS)
BN	Paris, Bibliothèque Nationale
Cav.	*Il Cavalcanti* (1614)
Comp.	*Comparatione di Homero, Virgilio e Torquato* (1612)
DBA	*De Ecclesiasticis Baronii . . . Annalibus disputatio* (1596)
DH	*De historia libri quatuor* (1611)
DHS	*De humanitatis studiis oratio* (1600)
DIQO	*Disputatio in qua ostenditur . . .* (1600)
DSIT	*Discorsi sopra l'inondation del Tevere* (1599)
G	*Il Goffredo* (1616)
MA	Milan, Biblioteca Ambrosiana
ME	Modena, Biblioteca Estense
MT	Milan, Biblioteca Trivulziana
OD	*Oratoriae disputationes* (1624)
OQ	*Orationes quinquaginta* (1613)
OQS	*Orationes quinque et septuaginta* (1625)
P.	*In Aristotelis Poeticam commentarii* (1613)
PO	Pesaro, Biblioteca Oliveriana
PU	Padua, Biblioteca Universitaria
R.	*In Aristotelis libros rhetoricorum commentarii* (1624–5)
Risp.	*Risposta* (to Malacreta) (1738)
RV	*Rime varie* (1614)
S.	*In Sallustii Catilinariam commentarii* (1622)
VA	Città del Vaticano, Biblioteca Apostolica
VM	Venice, Biblioteca Marciana

All references (except the first) to Beni's works are in the form of title followed by arabic numerals (for page numbers). In other references I have used (for authors of several works quoted in this study) the terms 'op. cit.', 'art. cit.' and 'ed. cit.'. In using these I distinguished between 'op. cit.' (a complete volume by one author) and 'art. cit.' (an article in a periodical or book).

ACKNOWLEDGEMENTS

In the course of writing this book I have contracted many debts to institutions and individuals, which it is my pleasure to acknowledge. I should like to thank the British Academy and the Curators of the Taylor Institution (Oxford) for generous financial assistance towards the cost of visits to Italian libraries and archives. I am particularly grateful to the President and Fellows of Magdalen College for electing me first to a Prize Fellowship and then to a Supernumerary Fellowship, thereby affording me a long undisturbed period for research and composition. I am deeply grateful to Professor Cecil Grayson, who has guided and encouraged me with all his unfailing tact and good sense; to Professor Uberto Limentani and Dr John Woodhouse, who, as my D. Phil. examiners, read an earlier draft of this book and offered many constructive comments and suggestions; to Dr Alan Raitt, for all his friendly encouragement over the years. Finally, I am happy to record my thanks for various suggestions, comments, and material help to the late Father Georges Bottereau, SJ, Professor Martino Capucci, Mr Peter Hainsworth, Dr Anthony Kenny, Father E. Lamalle, SJ, Dr Valerio Lucchesi, Dr Christina Roaf, Mr David Robey, Dr Gillian Thompson, and my wife, Caroline.

P. B. D.

To Cecil Grayson

INTRODUCTION

In his day Beni was known as a theologian, a philosopher, a humanist scholar, minor poet, linguist, and historian. Benedetto Fioretti described him as worthy 'd'essere annoverato fra' primi litterati d'Italia', and Pierre Bayle later allowed that his works showed 'beaucoup de lecture et beaucoup d'érudition, et même bien du génie'.[1] Yet today, if anyone remembers the name of Paolo Beni, it is usually in connection with his anti-Cruscan campaign or with his supposed Baroque distortion of the *Poetics*: he is seen, in short, as foremost amongst the Moderns in the *Querelle des anciens et des modernes* in the early seventeenth century. His life and works enter into several learned articles and books which discuss, usually as part of some larger project—the Italian language, the *Poetics*, the Baroque, historiography, Dante, Boccaccio, Tasso, and so on—this or that isolated aspect of his prodigious activity. His reputation rests, therefore, on very scanty and occasional examination of his work; and all too often it is apparent that the critics who discuss his works have not actually read them, and are content to reiterate the sweeping generalizations of previous generations of critics. And no one has ever attempted to examine within one volume the identity of, and relationship between, Beni's various literary and cultural activities.

As for his life, little has been discovered since his death. The currently 'standard' work on the subject, Mazzacurati's article of 1966 in the *Dizionario biografico degli Italiani*, despite its real merits as a synthesis, owes most of its few dates and facts to the substantial article on Beni published as long ago as 1760 by Mazzuchelli. Since 1966 no serious work has been undertaken on the subject; and critics (such as Paparelli, Dell'Aquila, Casagrande, Landoni, and others) have mostly been content to summarize Mazzacurati's article. In order to put my findings in perspective, and in order to avoid constant repetition and refutation of Mazzacurati and others in the present work, I should

---

[1] [B. Fioretti], *Proginnasmi poetici di Udeno Nisiely da Vernio, accademico apatista*, 5 vols. (Florence, 1620–39), i (1620), 46; P. Bayle, *Dictionaire historique et critique*, 1st edn., 2 vols. (Rotterdam, 1697), i. 541.

like here to summarize the 'facts' about Beni's life which Maz-zacurati offers: Beni was born around 1552–3, possibly on Crete. His younger brother Giacomo was born in Gubbio, where Beni was brought up and educated. He was in Padua around 1574, and there met Tasso in the Animosi. Between about 1580 and 1590 he received a doctorate in theology in Padua and worked for Cardinal C. Madruzzo in Rome, and then for the Duke of Urbino. Also between 1580 and 1590 he became a Jesuit. From about 1590 to 1593 he taught theology at Perugia, and in 1594 he was called by Clement VIII to teach philosophy at the Sapienza in Rome. Around 1596 he was dismissed from the Jesuits for unknown reasons. In November 1599 he was elected to the chair of humanities in Padua, from which he retired, with half his salary, in 1623. He died on 12 February 1625. No one has attempted to go beyond these few vague facts to find out what Beni actually did, when he did it, and why.

The fact that Beni has undergone a premature fossilization over the years is attributable to several causes. First, the sub-ject-matter of his works is now often considered to be of minor importance, and at best incidental to the mainstream of Italian vernacular culture. Yet what may seem minor to us was major to Beni and to many of his contemporaries. His contributions to knowledge in the areas in which he chose to exercise himself are amongst the very best of his age. And to understand Beni is to understand a large portion of the culture of his times, the cul-ture of Tasso, of the Italian Counter-Reformation, of the acade-mies and of the universities. In this way he is of inestimable historical importance.

Secondly, the intractable bulk, prolixity, and scholastic Latin of most of his works have in large measure contributed to our neglect of him. Even his Italian works are apt to seem pedantic, verbose, and stylistically dull. Here again, this was no dis-advantage to many of his contemporaries: indeed it was a merit. However, more recent critics have taken one look at his output and have shied away, preferring to repeat earlier views and verdicts rather than to examine afresh the evidence for a reassessment.

Thirdly, Beni's later unpopularity is due to his own (in many ways) unfortunate personality. In his own lifetime he showed a curious capacity for inspiring dislike and even hatred in others;

and, as a man, he showed a considerable lack of charm. This characteristic occasionally comes through in his writings, but only in a very small proportion of his massive output, and that mostly of a minor polemical nature. Thus it is that his personality, which spilled over occasionally into some of his writings, has earned for him the reputation of an inconsistent and belligerent polemicist, more full of venom than truth. This is an unjust verdict on his major scholarly works.

Finally, Beni and his works have suffered that neglect and misjudgement which his period in general has also suffered. He has been linked (especially in the early part of the present century) with the decline in Italy following the Renaissance and with the decadence of the late sixteenth and early seventeenth centuries. From this a negative judgement on his work has automatically ensued.

The aim of the present work is to fill these various gaps in our knowledge and appreciation of Beni's life and works. This has been made possible not just through a careful examination of his often neglected publications but also through the fortunate discovery of a large number of his unpublished works (mostly presumed lost), as well as of previously unused archival and other MS material pertaining to his life and works in Gubbio, the Archivio Segreto Vaticano (which houses the hitherto unnoticed and by far the richest collection of Beniana), the Archivum Romanum Societatis Jesu, Milan, Padua, Vicenza, Venice, Pesaro, and elsewhere. As my researches progressed, letters, contracts, lost works, important testimonies all began to unfold a clearer picture not only of Beni's activities and actions but also (in some cases) of his motivation. Some biographical problems were solved quite quickly (his birthplace, his teaching career, his ancestry), while others (especially his Jesuit career, and some details of his relationship with his family) required longer and more patient research. Clearly there are still parts of his personality (the sexual, for instance) which have not emerged and which we could hardly expect to have emerged from the available evidence. Yet, within these limitations, it is remarkable how much of his personality has emerged, and how far it has been possible (through an inevitable interpretation of bare facts and figures) to discover what motivated him on this or that occasion, or in this or that relationship.

I have not found it possible, in the scope of this work, to discuss in equal detail the whole of his output, published and
unpublished. He wrote an enormous number of words, as he
was fond of pointing out, and nobody could hope to cover them
all here. In my treatment of his writings I have tried to work
empirically, outwards from the texts, rather than inwards from
ex post facto views and opinions about cultural trends in the
Renaissance and the Baroque. I have done this in the belief that,
until we have individual studies of a large number of individual writers, we cannot hope to be able to write a literary or cultural history of any period. What we need, to understand a
period and the major writers in it, are reliable and full studies of
secondary writers and figures who stand in the background,
and from whom the major writers emerge or detach themselves.
In the course of my work I have come across the opposite
approach and have found it mostly unsatisfactory (Weinberg on
literary criticism, Cochrane on historiography, and so on). And
it is clearly dangerous, as well as pointless, to see Beni as a link
in some prejudged cultural chain, rather than as an individual
with an individual voice: such an approach has led many Italian
critics (including Toffanin, Jannaco, and Mazzacurati) to mis-
read him.

My choice of focus is thus biographical and critical. In Part
One these two approaches run parallel: for up to about 1604 all
Beni's works were inextricably bound up with his biography,
and some of them are almost incomprehensible without reference to it. Part Two is primarily biographical, and consists of an
account of his life (divorced from detailed discussion of his
works) from about 1604 to his death. After 1604 (by which time
he had settled down for good in Padua) the previously close
links between his life and works were broken: he no longer
published his works as soon as they were written; many were
not published until his final years, when he began to collect
together works for his *Opera omnia*; and many were never published. To have treated these in chronological order of publication (a treatment which well suited his earlier works) would
have falsified the true picture of his activities in Padua, and
would, incidentally, have necessitated much repetition (for
many of the works overlap in subject-matter). Part Three is
therefore reserved for his major Paduan works, grouped accord-

ing to subject-matter. My aim has been to give of them as full a critical assessment as possible in the space available: to examine the issues which they treat, and to see them in their historical background in so far as that can be established. In this way I hope both to provide a fuller and more reliable account of Beni's life and works, and to contribute in some way to the long overdue reassessment of his cultural and historical importance.

Part One

THE YEARS OF PREPARATION

1

THE EARLY YEARS

I

The city of Gubbio climbs from the floor of a small fertile depression up the foothills of the Apennines. It is dominated by three dome-shaped hills; and this overshadowing of it, together with its medieval appearance, still gives the city a stern uncompromising bleak air. With its steep roads, it remains remote, often uncannily so; and its people and institutions show a certain moderation and cautious temperance. It has altered very little since Beni's time. Its character, its hilliness, its severity are all built into his nature: he was born there.[1]

His early biographers claim that he was born in Gubbio.[2] But in 1690 this tradition was quietly shaken by the Abbé de Charnes who, in his *Vie du Tasse*, writes of 'le sentiment de Paul Beni. Ce sçavant Grec transplanté en Italie'.[3] At first this— Beni's Greek origin—was not universally accepted: Bayle argues against it in the first edition (1697) of his *Dictionaire*; 'Il n'étoit point Grec de nation'; but in the second edition (1702) he agrees that the Abbé de Charnes was right after all, and that Beni was Greek.[4]

Bayle's acceptance of Candia as Beni's birthplace was a turning-point, and from then until now all Beni's biographers (except Papadopoli and Facciolati)[5] have thought him to be

---

[1] See my 'A Note on Paolo Beni's Birthplace', *Studi secenteschi*, 24 (1983), 51–5.

[2] I. Ph. Tomasini, *Illustrium virorum elogia iconibus exornata* (Padua, 1630), 350; G. Ghilini, *Teatro d'uomini letterati*, 2 vols. (Venice, 1647), i. 184; L. Crasso, *Elogii d'huomini letterati*, 2 vols. (Venice 1666), ii. 79; L. Moréri, *Le Grand Dictionnaire historique*, 2nd edn., 2 vols. (Lyons, 1681), i. 562; D. P. Freherus, *Theatrum virorum eruditione clarorum*, 2 vols. (Nuremberg, 1688), ii. 1518. This list is not exhaustive.

[3] [J. A. de Charnes], *La Vie du Tasse* (Paris, 1690), 'Lettre à MG A.D.M.'

[4] P. Bayle, *Dictionaire historique et critique*, 1st edn., i. 541; 2nd ed., 3 vols. (Rotterdam, 1702), i. 553.

[5] N. C. Papadopoli, *Historia Gymnasii patavini*, 2 vols. (Venice, 1726), i. 350; I. Facciolati, *Fasti Gymnasii patavini* (Padua, 1757), p. lix.

Greek. In the eighteenth century we have the authority of Moréri, Mazzuchelli ('nacque di civile famiglia circa il 1552, non già in Gubbio, come molti hanno affermato, ma in Candia per testimonianza di lui medesimo, donde ancor giovanetto venne trasferito in Gubbio e quivi allevato'), Tiraboschi, as well as Vecchietti and Moro.[6] And Beni's twentieth-century biographers, basing their work on Mazzuchelli for the most part, more or less accept his Greek origin: Belloni, Jannaco, Mazzacurati, Paparelli, M. L. Doglio, Weinberg, and Casagrande.[7]

This tradition, which was solidly established and confirmed by the large dictionaries of Bayle and Mazzuchelli, is founded upon one piece of evidence. It is this piece of evidence which persuaded Bayle to change his mind about Beni's birthplace. It comes from the opening of the *Comparatione*, in which the Accademico Nomista (alias Beni?) expatiates on his love of Italy and her poets:

Io non saprei ridire, Uditori generosissimi, il contento e dolcezza che provai nel mio cuore allhor che ancor fanciullo posi il pargoletto piede ne' fortunati e cari liti d'Italia; con far mio albergo prima in quella Città laqual non lungi siede felicissima Reina d'Adria: et indi poscia in questa nuova e famosa Athene. E sebene non mai porrò in oblio il mio Greco terreno, e 'l mio caro e natio paese, famoso al presente per mille doni di Natura, non meno che ne gli antichi tempi foss'anco per certo Città illustre e chiaro [sic], nondimeno con cento e mille catene d'amore ho sentito e sento annodarmi il cuore in questo felice seno che tra gli Euganei colli et il mar d'Adria giace ristretto. Che certo il temperamento del Cielo e dolcezza dell'aria, la piacevolezza de' colli e fertilità

---

[6] L. Moréri, *Le Grand Dictionnaire historique*, 10 vols. (Paris, 1759), ii. 354; G. M. Mazzuchelli, *Gli scrittori d'Italia* (Brescia, 1760), ii/2. 842; G. Tiraboschi, *Storia della letteratura italiana*, 8 vols. (Modena, 1787–94), vii (1791), 1059; F. Vecchietti and T. Moro, *Biblioteca picena*, 5 vols. (Osimo, 1790–6), ii (1791), 169.

[7] A. Belloni, 'Beni, Paolo', in *Enciclopedia italiana*, vi (1930), 640; C. Jannaco, *Il Seicento* (Milan, 1963), 66; G. Mazzacurati, 'Beni, Paolo', in *Dizionario biografico degli Italiani*, viii (1966), 494; G. Paparelli, 'Paolo Beni e l'*Anticrusca*', in *Da Ariosto a Quasimodo* (Naples, 1977), 48 and n. 1; M. L. Doglio, 'Beni, Paolo', in *Dizionario critico della letteratura italiana*, ed. V. Branca, 3 vols. (Turin, 1973), i. 273; B. Weinberg (ed.), *Trattati di poetica e retorica del Cinquecento*, 4 vols. (Bari, 1970–4), iv (1974), 435; G. Casagrande, 'Introduzione', in P. Beni, *L'Anticrusca parte II, III, IV* (Florence, 1982), p. xi. E. Landoni has recently hinted that Beni was probably not born in Greece, but has not further explored the problem, admitting that 'la questione, come si nota dai pochi indizi a disposizione, è tutt'altro che risolta' ('A proposito della vita e delle opere di Paolo Beni (1552–1625)', *Rendiconti dell'Istituto lombardo*, 113 (1979), 29).

de' campi, la varietà dell'arti e l'industria maravigliosa, la nobilità rara et illustre, la gentilezza, cortesia e bellezza delle genti, e sopra tutto la virtù, la dottrina e l'ingegno che a maraviglia splende e riluce in queste parti, sono per me invisibili catene e lacci di benevolenza e d'amore.

Con tutto ciò, se debbo confessarne il vero, una cosa è quella che sopra tutte mi riempie quasi d'infinita dolcezza in queste parti, e mi fa benedir'il giorno nel qual mi esposi a solcar mari così perigliosi e lunghi. Ma qual cosa fia questa? dirà alcuno. La gentilezza Signori e felicità de gl'Italiani poeti: i quali nel vero così dolci e soavi sembrano al mio gusto, così vaghi e leggiadri, et in somma così pieni d'ogni gratia e bellezza, che mentre con questi passo l'hore et i giorni, parmi in certa maniera di poter dire col Toscano Poeta Lirico,

Che Ambrosia o Nettar non invidio a Giove[8]

This eloquent and apparently sincere eulogy suggests (and has suggested to all Beni's most authoritative biographers) that Nomista is here acting as Beni's *portavoce*. But can this complete identification of Nomista and Beni be accepted?

A reading of Beni's other works has revealed in fact that this piece of evidence is inconclusive as far as Beni's birthplace is concerned. For the Accademico Nomista can be shown to represent, not a fictional authorial *persona* as has long been thought, but an historical personality who corresponds in every way to what he is made to tell us about himself in the above quotation from the *Comparatione*. Beni supplies the clues to Nomista's identity when, in the *Cavalcanti*, he tells us that the name Nomista is an anagram of Simone Stamini who was destined to become Rettore of the University of Padua.[9] The same information is offered in the *Goffredo* when Beni expounds Tasso's anagrammatical Ismeno (=Simon Mago):

Così noi nella nostra Comparatione racchiudemmo nel nome di Nomista (che così vien chiamato l'Academico introdotto a ragionar nel primo Discorso) Simon 'e [*sic*] Stamino, che fu quegli il quale nell'Academia de' Ricovrati recitò il Discorso di ch'io parlava, e fu generosissimo a splendidissimo Rettore dello Studio di Padova.[10]

---

[8] *Comparatione di Homero, Virgilio e Torquato* (Padua, 1607), 1–2. All future references to the *Comparatione* will be to the 2nd enlarged edn. (Padua, 1612), hereafter *Comp.*

[9] *Il Cavalcanti: overo la difesa dell'Anticrusca* (Padua, 1614) (hereafter *Cav.*), 53–4.

[10] *Il Goffredo, overo la Gierusalemme liberata, del Tasso, col commento del Beni* (Padua, 1616) (hereafter *G.*), 252.

It has fortunately been possible to verify the truth of Beni's picture of Stamini both as member of the Accademia dei Ricovrati who once read a paper in praise of Tasso, and as Rettore of the Studio. Furthermore, it has been possible to discover that Stamini was indeed Greek, born in Crete (or Candia as it then was). In the first place, Beni's testimony (quoted above from the *Goffredo*) as to the identity of the speaker in *Comparatione I* is corroborated by the following note, penned by Toldo Costantini,[11] in the unpublished 'Atti' of the Ricovrati Academy in Padua:

A gli 8 di Aprile l'anno M.DCIV l'Academia stete dolcemente occupata nell'ascoltare il Signor Simone Stamini candiotto, il quale con lingua italiana sì, ma con greca eloquenza, spiegò un dottissimo paralello [*sic*] fra la Gerusalemme di Torquato Tasso, et li due Poemi d'Homero, et l'Eneide di Virgilio.[12]

Secondly, that in 1607 and 1608 the same Stamini was Rettore at Padua is confirmed by Tomasini when he records 'Simeon Phtaminus Cretensis' as 'Iuristarum Rector' for the year 1607, and by Papadopoli who lists 'Simeon Phtaminius Cretensis I.C.R.' under 'Gymnasiarchae Patavini ad Annum MDCCXXIII' for the years 1607 and 1608.[13]

It is clear from all this that the one piece of evidence in favour of Beni's Greek origin can no longer be relied upon since it can be proven to refer to a separate historical personality. By using the figure of Nomista in the *Comparatione*, and by lending him an individual and separate identity, Beni initiated the method he was later to develop in the *Cavalcanti*. For there the fictional author and narrator (Michelangelo Fonte) is given the historical personality of Bartolomeo Cavalcanti (1503–62); and the many details about the authorial *persona* which emerge clearly refer to

[11] On him see U. Limentani, 'La fortuna di Dante nel Seicento', *Studi secenteschi*, 5 (1965), 7, 26, and 40; and V. Lettere, 'Costantini, Toldo', in *Dizionario biografico degli Italiani*, xxx (1984), 304–6, who, however, fails to relate that Costantini was a secretary to the Ricovrati.

[12] 'Atti dell'Accademia dei Ricovrati', Giornale A (hereafter Atti), fo. 92ᵛ. From this source it also appears that Stamini was elected a member of the Ricovrati on 29 January 1604 (Atti, fo. 87ʳ). I am grateful to the Librarian and staff of the Biblioteca dell'Accademia Patavina di Scienze, Lettere ed Arti for allowing me to consult these records.

[13] I. Ph. Tomasini, *Gymnasium patavinum* (Udine, 1654), 439; Papadopoli, i. 98–9.

B. Cavalcanti's, and evidently not to P. Beni's, biography. It is true that Beni felt close to Stamini (in his admiration for Tasso) and to Cavalcanti (in his presumed anti-Florentinity), yet his sympathy is not in itself proof that he was either Greek or Florentine.[14]

And, if he were of Greek origin, it is indeed surprising that he almost always signed himself *Eugubinus*, that he clearly looked on Gubbio as his *patria*,[15] and that his vituperative linguistic opponents in the *Crusca* debate made slighting reference, not to his Greek, but to his Gubbian provenance.[16] It is only recently that Beni's presumed Greek origin has been thought to have exercised a psychological influence on his polemical nature. Giorgio Spini has written of him (almost certainly mistakenly) as follows:

Come il Patrizi, il Davila, il Biondi—e come d'altronde il Vergerio, il Flaccio Illirico, il De Dominis—anche il Beni era un veneto di provenienza trasmarina, invece che un veneto di terraferma come lo Speroni, il Robortello, il Riccoboni. E come questi altri veneti dai mari di Dalmazia o del Levante, invece del composto e togato tradizionalismo di terraferma, portava nelle vene il germe della irrequietudine spirituale, della eterodosia [*sic*] religiosa, della iconoclastia irriverente.[17]

There is no evidence to prove that Beni was Greek, and it can safely be assumed that he was born in Gubbio and, indeed, that he never left Italian soil.[18]

But when was he born? Traditionally the period 1552–3 has

[14] Indeed, throughout his career, Beni showed a remarkable willingness to write speeches, sermons, letters, and prefaces on behalf of his friends and colleagues. See his *Orationes quinquaginta* (Padua, 1613) (hereafter *OQ*), and his *Orationes quinque et septuaginta* (Venice 1625) (hereafter *OQS*).

[15] See the extensive laudatory description of Gubbio and its achievements in *Cav.* 110–14. In a letter to his nephew Francesco Beni, dated 15 July 1616, Beni sees this description of Gubbio as 'azza o pegno della mia ottima volontà et affettione verso la patria' (Archivio Segreto Vaticano, Archivio Beni (hereafter ASVB), 36).

[16] See, for example, O. Pescetti, *Risposta all'Anticrusca* (Verona, 1613), 110, where it is thought ludicrous that 'un'Agubbino dar voglia legge al Boccaccio intorno al suo parlar naturale'.

[17] G. Spini, 'I trattatisti dell'arte storica nella Controriforma italiana', in *Contributi alla storia del Concilio di Trento e della Controriforma* (Florence, 1948), 121.

[18] See Beni's unfavourable review of the anonymous *Squitinio della libertà veneta* (Mirandola, 1612). During the course of this review (which forms the second, and largest, part of his unpublished treatise 'Della veneta libertà') Beni casts doubt on the assumed Italian identity of the author of the *Squitinio*, and

been given (for example by Mazzacurati, art. cit., p. 494). Casa-grande has recently tried to dispel this vagueness; and, by quot-ing Beni's unpublished 'Beniana bibliotheca' (where, in 1621, he said he 'annum sexagesimum nonum ageret'), Casagrande con-cludes that Beni 'nacque sicuramente nel 1552' (ed. cit., p. xi).[19] But this conclusion is open to the following objections: first, if Beni was sixty-nine (as Casagrande believes) at some point in 1621, he could nevertheless have been born in 1551; secondly, Beni's Latin expression could well mean that he was in his sixty-ninth year, and therefore sixty-eight, when he wrote. This does not therefore help much. Neither does another indication from Beni, also from the year 1621: in a letter, dated 30 April 1621, to his nephew Francesco Beni, Beni describes himself as 'poco meno che settuagenario' (ASVB 36). But this is easily seen as the special pleading of an old man who, in this case, is asking for assistance. More helpful and reliable is Beni's will of the same year, dated 1 October, in which he describes himself as 'nel-l'anno sessantesimo nono',[20] which I take to mean that he was in his sixty-ninth year. Further clarification comes from the Jesuit Archives in Rome. The oldest catalogue of Jesuits, and the most reliable (for it depends on the verbal testimony of candidates), states that 'Paolo Beni, a di 4 de maggio 1581, venne a Sant'An-drea. Anni 28'.[21] All this leaves us with the hypothesis that he was born after 1 October 1552 and before 4 May 1553.

But we can go further here. In a short biography of Beni in Gubbio's Archivio di Stato, which was written during the pon-tificate of Urban VIII (1623–44, but obviously after Beni's death

---

incidentally sheds light on his own birthplace: 'Seben vo io sospettando che tanto siate Italiano voi, quanto son Tedesco io che nacqui nel centro d'Italia, e fuor d'Italia giamai non posi il piede' (Padua, Biblioteca Universitaria (hereafter PU), MS 412, p. 357).

[19] See 'Beniana bibliotheca' (hereafter BB), Venice, Biblioteca Marciana (here-after VM), MS Lat. xiii. 87 (=3998), p. 244.

[20] Gubbio, Archivio di Stato, Fondo Armanni (hereafter ASGA), ii. d. 27, fo. 1[r].

[21] Rome, Archivum Romanum Societatis Jesu (hereafter ARSJ), MS Rom. 171. c, 198. Other Jesuit MS catalogues, which are generally less reliable, are clearly wrong when they would have him born in 1554 and 1558 (ARSJ MS Rom. 53. i, fo. 73[v] and MS Ven. 37, fo. 32[v] respectively). I am most grateful to the late Father Georges Bottereau, SJ, Assistant Archivist in the Jesuit Archives in Rome, for his unfailing assistance in discovering the truth about Beni's Jesuit career.

c.1625), the writer states that Beni was born on 10 January 1553.[22] This biography, though it contains a few bibliographical errors, has more specific circumstantial detail than any other, and clearly has benefited from inside local information. Not only does it provide some sparse details about Beni's education—particulars which it would have been pointless to invent in an unpublished biography—but it also contains precise and reliable references to Beni's unpublished works, which are otherwise mentioned nowhere outside his own 'Beniana bibliotheca'. For these reasons we cannot lightly disregard the specific birthdate of 10 January 1553, the more so since it falls between our hypothetical 1 October 1552 and 4 May 1553. And, for want of better evidence, I accept it as a working hypothesis in what follows.

Beni was born into a family which had noble Gubbian ancestry on both sides.[23] His mother was Modesta, daughter of Federico Panfili (or sometimes Pamfili), and his father was Francesco, son of Giovanni Bernardino Beni.[24] The Panfili are mentioned in archival documents as early as 1114 (ASGA I. B. 12, fo. 58ʳ), and they had held key positions of power in the city since the twelfth century (Lucarelli, pp. 307–10). They evidently possessed some (limited) literary talent; in the *Cavalcanti* (p. 113) Beni alludes vaguely to an uncle on his mother's side

[22] ASGA II. E. 9, Sect. 145. This is a later copy of the seventeenth-century original which is conserved, in its damaged and partly indecipherable state, in ASGA I. D. 3, fos. 82ʳ–83ᵛ. Future reference will be made to the later copy. The original seventeenth-century biography formed part of a series of biographies of famous Gubbian writers collected by the indefatigable Gubbian scholar and local historian, Vincenzo Armanni (1608–84). It is tempting to assume that Armanni himself wrote this MS biography of Paolo Beni; but it is unlikely because Armanni did not return to Gubbio, and devote himself to local history, until after Urban VIII's death (in 1644), and therefore after this biography was written (see U. Coldagelli, 'Armanni, Vincenzo', in *Dizionario biografico degli Italiani*, iv (1962), 223 for details about Armanni's return to Gubbio). However, the biography in question must have satisfied Armanni's very high standards of scholarship and accuracy; and this is another good reason for attending to it.

[23] Apart from the MSS in the Fondo Armanni of Gubbio's Archivio di Stato, I have found the following publications useful for the history of Beni's ancestors: V. Armanni, *Delle lettere*, 3 vols. (Rome, 1663–74), i (1663), 700–34; ii (1674), 'A Mons. Odoardo Cybo', 587–90; id., *Della famiglia Bentivoglia* (Bologna, 1682), 106–7; O. Lucarelli, *Memorie e guida storica di Gubbio* (Città di Castello, 1888), 233–4 (on the Beni family) and 370–1 (on P. Beni, but very inaccurately).

[24] Gubbio, Archivio della Biblioteca del Convento di S. Francesco (hereafter ABSFG), 17. G. 7, p. 46 (a short biography of Giacomo Beni).

who was a poet, we do not know his name, but it was possibly
Federico Panfili (ASGA I. B. 10, fo. 5^v).

As for the Beni, they are first mentioned in records dating
back to 1049 (ASGA II. D. 31, p. 43; Armanni, *Bentivoglia*, p. 106;
Lucarelli, pp. 233–4). After that not much is recorded about
them until the thirteenth century when, as the Conti di Serra,
they gradually acquired wealth, esteem, civic privileges, and
ecclesiastical honours.[25] They were Ghibellines; and when
power was seized by the Guelphs in 1315 the Beni were prohibited from public office. They retired to their Castello della
Serra di S. Abbondio, near Gubbio, where they owned much
land. There they remained and increased until one of them,
Luca, was recalled to Gubbio around 1390, after the end of the
civil discord in the city (ASGA II. D. 31, pp. 45–6 and 82). Luca
was one of the most gifted and popular members of the family.
The Archives in Gubbio contain many glowing accounts of
him. On his return to Gubbio he acquired land and property
(thirty-four farms, ninety-eight plots of land, three castles,
houses, mills, vineyards, and a mausoleum (ASGA II. A. 17)).
And, after 1384 when Gubbio ceased to be a free commune and
was passed to the Duchy of Urbino, Luca was soon (in 1406)
appointed Cancelliere of the city; and so began a close relationship between the Beni and Urbino, which continued into Paolo's time (ASGA I. F. 10). Luca was a soldier, with a respect for
learning (ASGA I. B. 15, fos. 34^r and 51^r). A monument to his
stature and enterprise still stands in the vast, imposing, grim
Palazzo Beni which dominates Piazza Bosone in Gubbio. But,
for us, his chief importance lies in the fact that he founded the
three branches of the Beni family which were alive in Paolo's
day. Luca's eldest son, Federico, served both the Duke of
Urbino (in 1481 and 1482) and the pope (in 1478) (ASGA I. B. 15,
fos. 87^r and 168^r; ASGA I. D. 17, fo. 104^v). He began the wealth-
iest branch of the family which, in Paolo's day, inhabited the
Palazzo Beni, was known as the Conti Beni, and displayed the
family coat of arms (two halves divided horizontally: the upper
half containing a crown above an eagle on a yellow ground; the
lower half containing four gold diamonds on a blue diagonal

---

[25] Amongst the many records of them in this period we can cite, for example:
ASGA I. B. 12, fos. 72^r and 108^v; ASGA I. B. 13, fos. 18^v, 118^r, 142^r, 149^v, 151^r, 174^r,
193^r, 194^r and 202^r; ASGA I. B. 14, fo. 16^v etc.

stripe on a white ground (as illustrated in ASGA I. F. 3, fo. 10^r, No. 39)). Another of Luca's sons, Battista, began the second branch, which was also talented and wealthy, and which eventually bore the subject of this study. A third branch, begun by Galasso, another of Luca's sons, was the least important and fruitful of all (ASGA II. D. 10, fo. 130^v).[26]

Luca began a tradition of public service to the city which was passed down through his son, Battista (ASGA I. F. 11(6), fos. 9^v–10^r) and thence, via Baldo Beni, to Paolo's grandfather, Giovanni Bernardino, who was Gonfaloniere of the city five times, and finally to Paolo's father, Francesco, who held that office eight times from 1539 to 1580 (ASGA II. D. 31, pp. 71–3). Francesco was not without wealth and property, as we shall discover from his will of 1586; and he must have been a strict and powerful father, with high ideals for his children as for his *patria*. A good idea of his character and standing can be gathered from a document which states that, in 1561, he, with seven others, was elected to put into practice various new measures designed to curb both excessive dowries and 'il soverchio vestire delli huomini maxime de' gioveni' (ASGA I. C. 13, Fasc. 9). This puritanical attitude, which is as much a part of Gubbio as it is of the Beni family,[27] was later to evince itself in his son Paolo.

Francesco and Modesta had six children: two girls (Theodora who married Dottor Giulio Montegranelli in 1569 (ASGA II. D. 31) and Eleonora who took the veil and seems to have been recorded nowhere save in her father's will of 1586).[28] Of the four sons, Giacomo, the eldest, was clearly his father's favourite. He will figure largely in Paolo's future, and mentions his brother briefly in his *De privilegiis I[uris] consultorum*.[29] He was born

[26] It should be noted here that the archival material does not agree unanimously on this ancestry: in some documents Luca is shown to have begun only one branch of the family (the Conti Beni), for example ASGA II. D. 31, 79–80; others show doubt on this score, for example ASGA I. F. 11(6), fos. 9^v–10^r, where a correction (which looks like a contemporary afterthought) shows Battista as Luca's son. But most documents are in line with my interpretation, for example ASGA II. D. 10, fo. 130^v; ABSFG in an uncatalogued bundle of 52 documents relating to the Beni family of Gubbio; and Armanni, *Bentivoglia*, 106–7.

[27] Interestingly it was Vincenzo Armanni who provided an expurgated version of the *Adone*, for details of which see his *Bentivoglia*, 193 and U. Coldagelli, art. cit., 222.

[28] Gubbio, Archivio di Stato, Fondo Notarile (hereafter ASGN), 554, fos. 141–5.

[29] Venice, 1602, fo. 47^r.

around 1550, and studied jurisprudence in Rome. He returned
to Gubbio, and was seven times Gonfaloniere. He found favour
with the Duke of Urbino, who appointed him Podestà of
Urbino in 1606 and 1607, and Residente in Venice for the period
3 November 1607 to 6 August 1610 (ASVB 31). Not only did Giacomo write on jurisprudence, but he also reformed in 1616 the
antiquated fourteenth-century Statutes of Gubbio. The new
Statutes were published in 1624, and remained in force in the
city until the end of the eighteenth century.[30] Paolo, Federico,
and Giulio were born after Giacomo; it is not known in what
order. Federico does not seem to have distinguished himself in
any way, and he died quite young, though not before producing heirs; Giulio followed a successful ecclesiastical career
and became Proposto of the cathedral of Fano, and was otherwise famous in his native city for having donated to the Padri
della Congregazione Lateranense a vineyard which had once
belonged to St Ubaldo in Gubbio (ASGA II. D. 31).

II

Although Beni was destined not to tolerate, or to be tolerated
by, his family, he does seem to have had a happy childhood in
what he calls, albeit through a haze of literary artifice, his 'natio
ricetto amato'.[31] At the age of five he went (it is not recorded
where), with Giacomo, to take lessons with Timocrate Aloigi, a
doctor of law, who had before him a distinguished career as
Avvocato Concistoriale and Agente for the Duke of Urbino in
Rome, where he was to remain for forty years, ending his days
as Bishop of Cagli, a position he held from 17 May 1607 to his
death on 17 May 1610.[32] For a talented and spiritual boy, the
education available in Gubbio at that time was not ideal: in
1552 a Jesuit school had been established, but it was soon closed
(in 1554) because of the warlike rather than literary and spiritual

[30] *Statuta civitatis Eugubii, auctoritate Serenissimi Francisci Mariae II Ducis nostri confirmata et edita* (Gubbio, 1624). The best source of information on Giacomo
is ABSFG 17. G. 7, pp. 46–8; see also ASGA II. D. 31, p. 56.

[31] *Rime varie* (Padua, 1614) (hereafter *RV*), *Canzone* to the Duke of Urbino, pp.
6–11 (p. 7).

[32] ASGA II. E. 9, Sect. 145. On Aloigi see D. A. Tarducci, *De' vescovi di Cagli*
(Cagli, 1896), 97–8.

inclinations of its pupils.[33] It is not surprising, therefore, that some time afterwards, and probably as soon as he could read and write, Beni was sent to study in Rome. The unpublished biography (ASGA II. E. 9, Sect. 145), which I mentioned earlier, records that Beni became a boarder (*convittore*) at the Jesuit Collegio Germanico in Rome. At first sight this seems unlikely, for that college was reserved for the pupils of the German countries. But the Collegio Germanico was principally a boarding establishment: unlike other Jesuit colleges for non-Italian pupils, all its classes and lessons were held at the famous Collegio Romano (Farrell, p. 433).

At this time (1558–65) the Collegio Romano was still at an experimental stage. In 1551 it had one hundred pupils; by 1565 it had almost one thousand (Farrell, p. 86). Its lessons were for the most part in Latin, and they concentrated upon grammar and rhetoric in the first instance, later building on to these a knowledge of logic, mathematics, physics, metaphysics, and ethics. Such was the curriculum from 1553 (Farrell, pp. 75 and 104–5). But the main concern of the college was with the humanities, of which rhetoric was given first place: much attention was paid to the composition and improvisation of orations in Latin or Greek, as well as to exercises in Latin debate (Farrell, p. 80). The cultivation of Latin style through imitation of Cicero was far more important at this pre-university level than the serious study of theology, philosophy, science, and mathematics (Farrell, pp. 141 and 144–5).

However, Beni was forced to leave Rome, and his literary studies, some time before 1566. In a later poem to the Duke of Urbino (*RV* 6–11) he gives a poetic description of the occasion of his departure:

> E havendo Circe nobilmente a sdegno
> Cercai d'ornar l'ingegno,
> De l'arti a Palla più gradite e care.
> Ma mentre m'ergo a così degna spene
> Giunone intenta a far mia vita trista
> Sorse turbata in vista,
> E mi contese il desiato bene,

[33] See A. P. Farrell, SJ, *The Jesuit Code of Liberal Education: Development and Scope of the 'Ratio Studiorum'* (Milwaukee, 1938), 92 and 103.

Talche astretto da sorte acerba e dura
Tornai dolente a le paterne mura.   (p. 7)

What had happened here? The situation is clarified by a Latin
letter from the young Beni to Paolo Manuzio (1512–74), dated
Perugia 15 January 1566.[34] Allowing for some degree of exaggeration in both the poem (quoted above) and the letter, it is easy
to divine the bare facts. Beni's father had decided that Paolo
should give up literary studies and devote himself to civil law,
like his elder brother Giacomo. Paolo sadly returned to Gubbio,
and in due course was sent to Perugia to study law. From there
he wrote to Manuzio in terms of extreme admiration, even
hero-worship, and grief at his own disappointed ambition. He
says in the letter that he had been set to study civil law, but (and
here he is like so many Italian literary men) he rebelled and
turned, guided by the shining example of Manuzio, to literary
studies. Manuzio represented everything Paolo wanted to be:
an editor of Latin classics (especially the works of Cicero), a
printer supervising the printing of 'correct' versions of the
Church Fathers for anti-Protestant purposes, and, above all, a
writer of elegant Latin letters and prefaces. Beni's letter shows
how prodigiously talented and accomplished (at barely thirteen) he was in Latin composition according to the Ciceronian
model, as well as in his knowledge of Greek. It is an astonish-
ingly mature letter, wise and elegant, despite more than an
occasional hint of ostentatious and impulsive youth. And Beni
refers to himself—no doubt with some refractory adolescent
pride—as *Urbinas* rather than *Eugubinus*. We see him here
stretching out beyond his town and family, dismissing both, in
a quest for humanism, for learning, for literary achievement
(and here his rejection of *Eugubinus* is symbolic). His letter,
finally, gives us a pattern for three successive developments in
his life and work. First, and most important, his latching onto
the long established Italian humanistic tradition. This, more
than his later acquaintance with Tasso, was decisive in shaping
his future career. Second, his rebellion against his father and

[34] Città del Vaticano, Biblioteca Apostolica (hereafter VA), Vat.lat. 3435, fo. 44
contains the autograph. There is a sixteenth-century copy in Modena, Biblioteca
Estense (hereafter ME), MS It. 1827=Beta. 1. 3. 1. c, fos. 71^v–72^r. Beni's letter has
recently been published in *Inedita manutiana 1502–1597*, ed. by E. Pastorello
(Florence, 1960), 255–7.

his home, which will become a constant in his attitude to these. Third, and more obliquely here, his resentment against his brother Giacomo, who, as far as his father was concerned, followed the right career. Paolo could never do right.

III

His rebellion against civil law must have been successful; and he was allowed (perhaps as a compromise with his father) to study philosophy and theology at Bologna, probably in 1566. There he eventually fell very ill and came close to death (probably in 1572 or 1573); and, after leaving Bologna, he went to Padua in 1573 to continue his theological studies. This date can be deduced from the exordium to a lecture, dated 1503 (obviously wrongly), and clearly delivered in 1600, in which Beni says, on his return to Padua in 1600, that he originally came to the Studio twenty-seven years earlier in order to complete his theological studies.[35]

In Padua he came under the spell of Girolamo Quaino. Beni later remembered him as a theologian who, in contrast to all the other Paduan teachers of theology, jurisprudence, philosophy, and medicine, combined wisdom and eloquence (*OQS* 43). Quaino was a Paduan and a famous preacher, who belonged to the Ordine dei Servi. He possessed a thorough knowledge of classical Latin and Greek; and this, together with his achievement of a balance in his lectures between *res* and *verba*, furnished Beni with yet another influential model of scholarship. Quaino began teaching at the Studio in 1561 or 1571, and died at the age of fifty-eight in 1582.[36]

Beni later recalled this period of his life as undisturbed: 'Sic sane huic [*i.e.* Quaino] diligenter operam dedi triennio toto donec importuna pestilentiae vi in Bononiam aufugere, mox etiam ad Urbem remigrare, coactus sum' (*OQS* 43). And yet, it

---

[35] For the lecture see *OQS* 45. Information about his education at Bologna and Padua is supplied by him in *OQS* 45, *RV* 8, and by his anonymous biographer in ASGA II. E. 9, Sect. 145.

[36] On him see A. Portenari, *Della felicità di Padova* (Padua, 1623), 461; Tomasini, *Gymnasium patavinum*, 286; G. Cinelli Calvoli, *Biblioteca volante*, 2nd edn., 4 vols. (Venice, 1734–47), iv (1747), 106–7, who lists two small works by Quaino; and G. Vedova, *Biografia degli scrittori padovani*, 2 vols. (Padua, 1832–6), i (1832), 131–3. These works do not agree on when he began teaching at the Studio.

would seem that, by April 1574, Beni was installed in Rome as Procuratore to Carlo Borromeo (1538–84). This would seem to be proved by two letters, dated 3 and 17 April, in which a certain Paulo Beni, writing to Gio. Battista Borromeo in Milan, signs himself as Procuratore in Rome to Carlo Borromeo.[37] It is clear from these letters that Paulo Beni (Procuratore) had taken up his post in Rome well before 3 April, and that he was by that time proficient in ecclesiastical legal jargon and the ways of ecclesiastical law. Nor was he writing as a secretary under dictation: he writes with an independent forthrightness and as someone closely involved in the preparation of the case with which the two letters deal. Instead, he was acting under the instructions of his superior, Cesare Speciano (1539–1607), who was at that time C. Borromeo's Agente in Rome. Speciano was a highly respected and learned ecclesiastic, later to become a Jesuit noted for his zeal and uprightness. His early success with C. Borromeo led him through the offices of Procuratore, Referendario Apostolico, and Secretary to the Cardinals. He was sent on various foreign missions, and he wrote a book of *Proposizioni morali e civili*.[38]

Though I previously assumed that these letters (along with some later ones) were the work of our Paolo Beni, I am now convinced that we are here dealing with a different figure. The reasons for my change of mind can be summarized as follows. First, the skilled work in Rome impinges chronologically on Paolo Beni's university career in Padua. Second, the existence in the Archivio Segreto Vaticano's Fondo Borghese (Serie I, 649, fo. 278) of a further letter, dated Madrid 18 June 1599, from Paulo Beni (Procuratore) is absolutely inconsistent with our Paolo Beni's later claim that he had never left Italian soil.[39] Third, by 1599 Beni would have been reluctant to leave his prestigious post at the Sapienza in Rome to act in Madrid as Procuratore. Fourth, the signature of Paulo Beni (Procuratore) on all the ecclesiastical legal letters is at odds with our Paolo Beni's autograph: Paulo Beni (Procuratore) invariably signed 'Paulo Beni' neatly separating the two words; our Paolo Beni

---

[37] Milan, Biblioteca Trivulziana (hereafter MT), MS N. 1. 127. 14.

[38] First published in an edition by N. Mosconi (Brescia, 1961). On Speciano see F. Arisi, *Cremona literata*, 3 vols. (i and ii: Parma, 1702–26; iii: Cremona, 1741), ii (1726), 420–3.

[39] See above Chapter 1, Note 18.

signed 'Pauolo Beni' (in the 1580s) and 'Paolo Beni' (from the 1590s) always joining the two words and with the 'P' of Paolo in the lower case. Fifth, it is clear, on examination, that the hand in all the ecclesiastical legal letters is different from Paolo Beni's authenticated hand. We can therefore assume that Beni was busy studying theology in Padua during these years until the invitation came for him to join the Accademia degli Animosi.

When did he join the Animosi and when did he meet Tasso? The Animosi was established in 1573 and first met in March of that year. Its members included many leading lights of Padua and Venice. Beni would no doubt have met all of these; and his description of the Academy and its members in the *Cavalcanti* (pp. 52–3) has been used by the Academy's later historians[40] (none of the original *Atti* have survived):

Et in questo numero vi era in particolare lo Sperone, il Piccolomini, il Tomitano, il Querengo, l'Arnigio, Torquato Tasso; e di tale Academia fu anco il Beni, il quale, ancorchè giovanetto, era udito volentieri: tanto che etiandio a' tempi più celebri gli fu incaricato di ragionare.

This was of course a great honour: clearly Beni was showing immense promise and confidence at this time. What he most cherished in his memory of all this was his friendship with Tasso about which he wrote in the *Cavalcanti* (pp. 114–15): 'havendo havuto amistà e famigliarità con Torquato Tasso di cui nell'Academia degli Animosi di Padova fin del 74 fu collega'.[41] Now Tasso's biographers, notably Serassi and Solerti, have disputed Beni's date (1574) on the grounds that Tasso was not in Padua during that year; and they have concluded that Beni mistakenly and forgetfully wrote 1574 for 1575, during which year (in March and April) Tasso visited Padua, as we shall see.[42] But have they interpreted Beni's words correctly? Is not Beni making two *separate* points in the above quotation: first, that he had been a friend of Tasso for a long time; and

---

[40] On the Animosi see G. Gennari, 'Saggio storico sopra le Accademie di Padova', in *Saggi scientifici e letterari dell'Accademia di Padova*, 3 vols. (Padua, 1786–94), i (1786), pp. xli–liii; and M. Maylender, *Storia delle accademie d'Italia*, 5 vols. (Bologna, 1926–30), i (1926), 197–200.

[41] The same information, but without dates, is to be found in the preface to the 1607 edition, and in the dedicatory of the 1612 edition, of the *Comparatione*.

[42] See P. A. Serassi, *Vita di Torquato Tasso* (Rome, 1785), 201, n. 4; C. Guasti (ed.), *Le lettere di Torquato Tasso*, 5 vols. (Florence, 1852–5), i (1852), 51; A. Solerti, *Vita di Torquato Tasso*, 3 vols. (Turin–Rome, 1895), i. 202 n. 4.

second, that he became Tasso's colleague in the Animosi in 1574? He is not saying, therefore, that Tasso joined the Academy in 1574, or, indeed, that Tasso attended any meetings in that year. All he is saying is that he (Beni) joined in 1574. It may be that Tasso was made an honorary member (in his absence) from the start in 1573; and it is surely more likely that Tasso, rather than the inexperienced Beni, should be a founder member. Various other factors make my interpretation likely. First, Beni says elsewhere (in the Dedicatory Letter in the *Comparatione* (1612)) that he heard Tasso read and recite in the Accademia degli Infiammati. This would obviously have preceded any meeting in the Animosi. Secondly, as we have seen, Beni returned to Padua in 1574, very probably in order to become a member. It is, of course, not impossible that Tasso visited Padua during his stay in Venice late in 1574,[43] but what Beni says is not, and is not intended to be, proof or testimony that he did so. Critics (such as Maylender, Mazzacurati, and Dell'Aquila)[44] who, unlike Serassi and Solerti, have taken Beni's evidence as proof that Tasso did in fact join the Animosi in 1574 have been on the wrong track.

There is a further general misapprehension concerning Beni's relationship with Tasso. Several of Tasso's biographers have asserted that part of the purpose of his visit in 1575 to Padua (where he stayed with G. V. Pinelli) was to seek advice about the *Liberata* from (amongst others) Paolo Beni.[45] But there seems to be no documentary evidence for this, and it appears to be an absolute hypothesis based (one supposes) on what Beni says in the *Cavalcanti* (quoted above). On examination, it seems unlikely for two reasons that Beni helped with the revision of the *Liberata*. First, because Tasso nowhere mentions Beni's name in connection with the revision in any of the numerous letters on the subject (and he does mention the names— frequently in some cases—of the other revisers). Secondly, Beni never refers to his role in the revision: if he had played such a role it is inconceivable that he would not have used it later as ammunition in the *Crusca* debate, and on other occasions when

---

[43] See F. Pittorru, *Torquato Tasso: l'uomo, il poeta, il cortegiano* (Milan, 1982), 109–10.

[44] Maylender, i. 198; Mazzacurati, art. cit., 494; M. Dell'Aquila, *La polemica anticruscante di Paolo Beni* (Bari, 1970), 40.

[45] See, for example, E. Mazzali (ed.), in T. Tasso, *Prose* (Milan–Naples, 1959), 761 n. 4; Pittorru, 116.

his authority to judge of poetry was called into question. The most we can say, therefore, is that Beni and Tasso were friends around this time.

It was at this time, also, that Beni first turned his hand to writing poetry. The occasion for this was the doctorate in Padua of Giuseppe Spinelli at the very beginning of 1575. A celebratory volume of Italian poetry was prepared and dedicated, by Giovanni Fratta (an Animoso), to Alberto Lavezola on 12 May 1575.[46] It is a small rare attractively produced book with contributions from (amongst others) Giovanni Fratta himself, Arnigio, Giovanni Vida, Giacomo Dolce, Veronica Franco (probably the most famous), Ludovico Fracastorio [sic] and a host of other now mostly forgotten names. Many of the contributors were Animosi, and Beni published his six poems as an 'Academico Animoso'. All the poems in the collection centre on Spinelli and his doctorate, from which it understandably proved difficult to extract much significance, poetic or otherwise. Beni's contributions are by far the most ambitious in the collection: he is the only poet who attempts any form as extensive as a *canzone* (fos. 20^r–22^v); and in that form he goes beyond the narrow boundaries of the pastoral idyll to which Spinelli's name all too readily lent itself (*spina* ='thorn'), and bravely enters the world of classical mythology. None the less, his poems bear an inordinately heavy debt to Petrarch; and it is clear that his often rigid Petrarchism (which already marks him off from rebels like Tassoni) has little to do with Spinelli's doctorate:

> Vaghe, novelle, amorosette fronde,
> Herbette fresche, et odorati fiori,
> Vezzose Ninfe, e pargoletti Amori,
> Ch'ornate al bel Medoaco ambe le sponde:
>
> Naiadi sante, arene pure, e monde,
> Aura gentil, che dolcemente fuori
> Spirando, scherzi intorno al grembo a Clori,
> Chiare, pure, correnti, e lucid'onde:

<hr/>

[46] *Panegirico nel felice dottorato dell'illustre, et eccellentissimo signor Giuseppe Spinelli, dignissimo rettor de legisti, et cavalier splendidissimo. Raccolto da Giovanni Fratta gentil'huomo veronese, et academico animoso* (Padua, 1575). For Beni's poems see fos. 20–4 and 31^v–32^r. These were reprinted with some alterations in *RV* 1–5 and 32–5. In addition a sonnet on Spinelli appears in *RV* 34 ('Hor che fra [. . .] bello') which was not in the *Panegirico*. From the same period date two Latin poems by Beni on Spinelli, printed in 'Epitaphia et elogia', in *OQS* 73.

Cedano a voi del più fecondo Aprile.
E del più temperato Arabe seno
Aure, fior, herbe, frondi, Amori, e Ninfe;

E del'Indo, e del Tago arene, e linfe.
Poscia che al Po mal fido ha posto il freno
Il cortese SPINELLI, almo e gentile.[47]

No doubt Beni saw himself after this as a poet; and he will still see these compositions as evidence of his poetic talent in 1614, when heavily involved in linguistic wrangles (hence the publication of the *Rime varie* together with the *Cavalcanti*). But there was little future for him in this branch of literature. Clearly he was held back by a lack of inventive imagination (and he was not alone in his age in being thus limited). He never wrote anything without a practical purpose: a poem about an event or a person, a treatise for or against this or that, and so on. It is not difficult to imagine the disastrous results that might have followed any more ambitious attempts on his part. In many ways one would expect him to have tried an epic in the manner and spirit of Trissino or Luigi Alamanni: he certainly had the requisite industry and knowledge, both literary and historical; but it is to his credit that he did not try to exploit his limited poetic talent beyond the odd occasional piece.

In any case, he was soon to turn his mind to other matters. At some point before March 1576 he received his doctorate in theology from Padua; and then, around March and April, he was offered a lectureship in philosophy, again in Padua, which the advent of the plague forced him to decline (ASGA II. E. 9, Sect. 145). This was the devastating plague which caused Tasso to put off a visit to Venice, as he says in one of his letters, dated 12 March 1576, to Luca Scalabrino (*Prose*, ed. cit., p. 771).[48] At first, Beni fled to Bologna (*OQS* 43), and thence very briefly to Gubbio. Finally, still in 1576, he returned to Rome 'con gl'occhi molli' (*RV* 9). It is easy to imagine his bitter disappointment at having to leave Padua and such an opportunity just when he

---

[47] *Panegirico*, fo. 23ʳ. Reprinted in *RV* 33 with some minor alterations of spelling and punctuation, and with the last two lines altered to 'Hor che calca del Po l'orgoglio, e'l Rheno/Frena, il nostro SPINELLI almo e gentile'.

[48] On this outbreak of the plague see Portenari, 459 and Facciolati, ii. 213.

was coming into his own. He had now to support himself, and could not wait idly by until the plague receded from the Veneto. He had to do something. He went to Gubbio to find support with his family. But it is easily to be imagined how the already strained relationship with his father and brothers could not sustain such a visit; and, in any case, Beni was impatient, now as always, to break free from the narrow horizons of Gubbio, and to make a more than local name for himself. Hence his decision in 1576 to return to the 'superbe alme contrade' (*RV* 9).

IV

Once in Rome he took up free-lance literary work. He was secretary to Cardinal Cristoforo Madruzzo from around this time until the latter's death, as we shall see (ASGA II. E. 9, Sect. 145; ASVB 35). It is not clear in what his work for Madruzzo consisted, but at least part of it involved him in the composition of occasional celebratory verse, for which the earlier poetry in praise of Spinelli had no doubt prepared him. As testimony of this, there appear in the *Rime varie* a sonnet in praise of Madruzzo's fountain at Soriano (p. 29) and a dialogue between the Muses and Echo on the occasion of the Cardinal d'Este's visit to Soriano (p. 30).

In 1577 we find him working, probably again in a secretarial capacity, for the great French humanist, Marc-Antoine Muret (1526–85), who had fled to Italy around 1554 under something of a cloud, had been teaching in Rome since 1563, and who had taken holy orders in 1576.[49] Beni later writes of this episode:

Etenim cum M. Antonium Muretum, cui sane operam dederam adolescens officii causa, domi convenissem aliquando: ac post multa, ut fieri solet, quid de questione hac gravissima sentiret ex eo sciscitarer; ecce tibi nunciatur adventare, ac iam iam adesse duo florentissima eius aetatis ingenia, ac splendidissima lumina. Erat autem ex iis unum Carolus Sigonius [c.*1520–84*], vir sane cum omni fere doctrinarum laude ornatus, tum maxime eximia quadam rerum gestarum ac totius antiquitatis scientia excultus et perpolitus. Venerat enim Romam per eos dies, ut Gregorio XIII pulcherrimos offerret, quos de Occidentalis

---

[49] These details are taken from C. Déjob, *Marc-Antoine Muret: un professeur français en Italie dans la seconde moitié du XVIe siècle* (Paris, 1881), 46–61, 167, etc.

imperio scripserat commentarios. Alter erat Achilles Statius [1524–81], vir a forensi strepitu ac popularibus concertationibus remotus ille quidem: quique in praesentia a publicis ingeniorum theatris abhorreret, et vulgari luce [. . .]. Nam praeterquam quod in Hebraeis Graecisque literis (ut de Latinis taceam) apprime versatus erat et eruditus: Poetarum vero ac Rhetorum studia magna cum laude coluerat sacrae profanaeque Philosophiae instituta atque praecepta callebat non mediocriter.[50]

There is no reason to disbelieve this. Sigonio's work, which Beni mentions in the passage quoted above, was first published in Bologna in 1577, when, as we have seen, Beni was working in Rome. And the relationship amongst the three scholars was close, as other independent evidence testifies.[51] The influence on Beni's development of these three humanists should not be underestimated. In the first place, their erudition (that of an earlier generation) and especially their knowledge of rhetoric impressed him for the rest of his life. This humanistic influence helped to shape his own *forma mentis*, especially as we see it in his Latin commentaries. Second, like Beni, Muret and Sigonio combined religion with rhetoric; indeed, Sigonio was to become a Jesuit in September 1580.[52]

Nothing is known of how long Beni spent in Muret's service. But on 20 March 1578 he assumed yet another office, that of Miles Pius in some (unspecified) military and religious order. From the papal contract (the office was bestowed by Gregory XIII) (ASVB 35), we learn that Beni was already in some (religious?) order before this time: for he is described as from the same order as the previous incumbent, Johannes Baptista Lomellimus ('devotus illius ordinis Paulus Benius Laicus Eugubinus'). What this was we do not know. This *cavalierato pio* (as

[50] *Oratoriae disputationes seu rhetoricae controversiae* (Venice, 1624) (hereafter *OD*), 3.

[51] See, for example, *Pontificum Rom. epistolae XXX . . . .Epistolae XXV M. Antonii Mureti et ad Muretum* (Rome, 1758), which contains one letter to Muret from Stazio (pp. 435–7) and two to Muret from Sigonio (pp. 437–41).

[52] On him see L. A. Muratori, 'Vita Caroli Sigonii mutinensis', in Sigonio, *Opera omnia*, 6 vols. (Milan, 1732–7), i (1732), pp. i–xxii, and Io. Ph. Krebs, *Vitam Caroli Sigonii . . . ad imitandum iuventuti exposuit . . . Io. Phil. Krebsius* (Weilburgi, 1837).

Beni will later call it in the 1620s) was purchased by his father Francesco, who was allowed by the terms of the contract to dispose of it whenever he wished (except in the event of Paolo's illness). Paolo had absolutely no control over it: it was to remain the property of Francesco, though Paolo was to retain the 'honores, onera, salaria et emolumenta' deriving from it. There was a fixed income form this *cavalierato pio*, which Beni was to enjoy for the rest of his life, even after he had left the duties of the office behind. What those duties were can only be conjectured. Perhaps, as a Cavaliere Pio, Beni was required to act as companion to the pope or to some other less lofty but important ecclesiastic in Rome: in short, it seems likely that he became part of the retinue of some ecclesiastical dignitary.[53]

Whatever Beni's duties as Miles Pius, they cannot have taken up much of his time. For he served Madruzzo until the latter's death on 5 July 1578. The Cardinal, who had been ill off and on since 1572, retired from Rome to Tivoli in June 1578, at the age of seventy-five. On the journey to Tivoli he fell ill, his tongue swelled up, and his breathing became difficult. After much misery and suffering, he died in the afternoon of 5 July.[54] Perhaps Beni accompanied him on his last journey; perhaps he did not. But he was loyal to him until his death, and bitterly lamented his own subsequent desolation in Rome.

Shortly after 10 January 1579 (if the birthdate of 10 January 1553 be accepted) Beni sought employment with the Duke of Urbino, to whom he addressed for the purpose a poetic account of his plight (from which I have already quoted). Beni was twenty-six as he wrote ('Giunto a riva [. . .] al second'anno/Del sesto lustro di mia stanca vita' (*RV* 6)). In this *Canzone* he bewails (amongst other things) the recent loss of his Roman mentor and guide whom he does not name:

---

[53] Extensive researches in ecclesiastical histories, dictionaries of military and religious orders, etc. have yielded no information on this *cavalierato pio*. Father E. Lamalle, SJ, Director of the Jesuit Archives in Rome, to whom I am most grateful, has also investigated the matter on my behalf, but has found nothing. He suggests that *cavaliere* might here mean 'accompagnatore', which seems to be the best interpretation in the circumstances.

[54] On this episode see E. Tessadri, *Il grande cardinale Cristoforo Madruzzo* (Milan–Rome, 1953), 162–3. This biography is, however, more a religious evocation of the spirit of Madruzzo than a work of scholarship.

Questi a mia vita acerba
Con la man soccorendo, e coi consigli
Temprava in parte l'aspro mio tormento:
Quando rea parca, in cui pietate è spenta,
(Con sospir mi rammenta)
Troncolli il fatal crine in un momento;
Ond'io fui giunto a tal ch'apena crede
L'alma ch'io mi sia in vita, e pur sel vede.   (*RV* 10)

This sort of complaint, here obviously exaggerated for effect, is part and parcel of Beni's depressive personality. It was present in a mild way in his letter of 1566 to Manuzio. But this is the first strong evidence we have of it. From now on it will recur at increasingly frequent intervals in his correspondence.

His plaintive poem achieved its result, and at some point between 1579 and May 1581 (when he entered the Jesuit Order) Beni became secretary to the Duke of Urbino (ASGA II. E. 9, Sect. 145; *RV* 6). On 4 February 1580 he was in Pesaro, whence he wrote on some legal matter to an uncle, Baldo Beni, in Gubbio (ASVB 36). The most probable explanation for his presence in Pesaro is that he was working there for the Duke. But there is no proof of that. Though he stayed in the Duke's service for only a short time, their relationship was always to remain amicable. This can hardly be said for his relationship with the Jesuits which we must now bring to the surface.

2

THE JESUIT INTERLUDE

On 4 May 1581 Beni entered the Jesuit novitiate at Sant'Andrea del Quirinale in Rome (ARSJ Rom. 171A, fo. 74^v). This event, and the episode in Beni's life which followed it, which can now be delineated in some detail, has always been the subject of rumours; and, as is the way with rumours, they have gradually assumed more and more the appearance of solid fact. Many of Beni's early biographers did not mention his relationship with the Jesuits. Imperiale (1640) seems to have been the first to do so in print, and, without giving any dates, he attributed Beni's departure from the Order to his desire to publish an obscene commentary on the *Symposium*.[1] The same information was repeated by (amongst others) Freherus in 1688 (ii. 1518), Bayle in 1702 (p. 553), most authoritatively by Mazzuchelli in 1760 (ii/2. 842), and by Tiraboschi in 1791 (vii. 1059). This tradition eventually found its way into Mazzacurati's article in the *Dizionario biografico degli Italiani* (p. 495), but there other hypotheses are more cautiously advanced: Beni may have divulged some of his future theological work on divine grace; or his work on the *Timaeus* may somehow have been the cause of his break with the Jesuits. Mazzacurati adds to the 'facts' by tentatively assigning his departure from the Jesuits to 1596 (according to the same authority Beni had joined the Order between 1580 and 1590). The date of 1596, which was hypothetical in Mazzacurati, becomes certain fact in the later works of Dell'Aquila (p. 43) and Casagrande (ed. cit., p. xiii), who otherwise shed no new light on this biographical problem.

To some extent, the problem has been the result of the inaccessibility of the relevant documents, which I have been fortunate enough to discover. Furthermore, Beni himself drew a veil over this ghastly period of his life (for reasons which will become clear); and this has made it difficult but exciting to

---

[1] G. Imperiale, *Musaeum historicum et physicum* (Venice, 1640), 160.

reveal. And finally, Beni's biographers have been too willing to
accept second-hand rumours and have paid insufficient attention to the evidence of Beni's own writings of this period.

His entry to the novitiate is described vividly in the Jesuit
Archives (ARSJ Rom. 171A, fo. 74ᵛ):

Paolo Beni d'Augubio venne alli 4 de maggio 1581 e portò seco un
ferraiolo de teletta, casacca e calzoni di capriolo, una ciamarra de
mocheano trinata con bottoni, calzetti di stame, gioppone di tela
bianca con bambace, duoe camice, un paro di fazzoletti; duoi para di
scarpini et una scuffia et una beretta di velluto riccio. Una cassa di
abete con alcuni libri et scritture come apparre in una polisa che è
dentro essa cassa. Li panni tutti usati.²

A note in the margin puts the value of all this at a mere 'dieci
scudi'. So it was as a relatively poor ecclesiastic that Beni began
his new existence as a Jesuit. From now on there was to be no
personal liberty, no physical affectation or vanity, no scope for
the ego. The 1583 edition of the Jesuit *Constitutiones*³ makes
clear some of the conditions which are relevant to Beni's case:
first, all family ties were to be severed for the novitiate period
(two years) so as to ward off possible distractions (p. 21);
second, no Jesuit was allowed to give money to his family:
instead it should be given to the poor who were not members of
his family (pp. 19–20); third, before taking final vows (usually
after a long period of training, from between ten to fifteen
years) all ecclesiastical benefices were to be surrendered (p. 21),
and all other temporal goods were to be disposed of ('Primum
ac generale examen', cap. IIII); finally, from the scholastic point
of view, logic, natural and moral philosophy, and metaphysics
should all follow Aristotle's line of thought; and, more generally, dishonest and pagan classics were to be abandoned where
they could not be expurgated (p. 167).

But it was not easy for Beni to escape from familial and finan-

---

² Note the primitive nature of the warder's language which requires some
annotations. *Teletta* was a thin cotton material; *casacca*: 'vestimento che cuopre
il busto, come il giubbone, se non che ha di più i quarti e le falde, ma assai corte'
(Tommaseo and Bellini); *ciamarra*='zamarra'='zimarra'; *mocheano* ='mocaiar-
do'='mocaiarro'='hair-cloth'(?); *gioppone*='giubbone' (?); *polisa* ='polizza'.

³ [Jesuits], *Constitutiones Societatis Jesu cum earum declarationibus* (Rome,
1583).

cial realities. On 10 November, when he had been in the novitiate only six months, he was constrained to write to his father (who clearly had not accepted the conditions of his son's novitiate). Francesco had asked for frequent letters; but Paolo had to explain that he could have no dealings with the outside world (ASVB 36). Most of Paolo's letter to Francesco centres on money. Evidently Francesco had complained that Paolo had not settled all his debts (especially those he owed to Federico—possibly his brother) before entering the novitiate. Paolo replies that he had not left any debts, and suspects Federico of wishing to involve him in 'intrichi'. In an abrupt and extreme formulation, he reminds his father of the vow of poverty which he had not by then made final; 'E siate pur certo, ch'io ho un desiderio straordinario di vedere una volta il fine di questi intrichi: poichè mi persuado anch'io d'esser venuto in questo mondo nudo, e povero come tutti gli altri huomini'. He goes on to excuse his present desire to retain (presumably against his father's wishes) 'l'uso di quel poco, che vi piacque di darmi', by which he meant his *cavalierato pio*.

Here Beni's poor relationship with his father and brothers was strained to breaking-point. Not only had he gone against his father's wishes in entering the Order, but he had more or less refused to give back to the family his knighthood and its income. (And, in any case, the Jesuit *Constitutiones* would not have allowed him to do that.) Despite his protestations to the contrary, Beni seems to be clinging here to material things, though he is trying intellectually to come to terms with the notion of poverty. However, even after the novitiate, things were not destined to improve for him on this score.

At this point a brief digression is necessary in order finally to clear up a problem of identity which we have already encountered. The problem arises from the presence in the Biblioteca Ambrosiana (Milan) of nine letters, dating from 2 July 1583 to 19 May 1584, from a certain Paulo Beni, Procuratore in Rome to Carlo Borromeo.[4] In these letters, the writer, once again under

[4] (1) 2 July 1583 (MA F. 164. Inf., fos. 9–10); (2) 6 August 1583 (MA F. 164. Inf., fo. 237); (3) 13 August 1583 (MA F. 164. Inf., fo. 282); (4) 10 September 1583 (MA F. 165. Inf., fo. 81); (5) 8 October 1583 (MA F. 165. Inf., fo. 386); (6) 28 January 1584 (MA F. 89. Inf., fos. 294–5); (7) 4 February 1584 (MA F. 89. Inf., fo. 298); (8) 11 February 1584 (MA F. 89. Inf., fo. 300); (9) 19 May 1584 (MA F. 89. Inf., fo. 301).

the direction of Cesare Speciano, shows that he was busy preparing and presenting (often in person) ecclesiastical legal
cases. Most of the letters are impersonal, but one stands out in
that it asks C. Borromeo to obtain a favour for the writer from
the Duke of Urbino:

la suplico si degni favorirmi in questo com'ella si degnò fare quando
passò per Pesaro, che credo farà opera pia et per me, et per altri che non
hanno havuto mai da me offesa alcuna anzi servitii relevantissimi, per
li quali hora mi perseguitano (MA F. 89. Inf., fo.298).

In some ways this could be read as a characteristic Benian
expression of persecution; and it is very tempting, for that
reason, to link it with Beni's anxious temperament and to his
Urbino connections. Yet it would be rash to draw the conclusion that, as soon as he finished his novitiate, he took up this
specialized post in Rome. For it is clear, for reasons which I
have already stated in this book,[5] that the 'Paulo Beni' who
wrote all the ecclesiastical legal letters is not our Paolo Beni. It is
not unlikely that Beni himself was aware of the existence of this
other 'Paulo Beni'; and that would explain why, from an early
stage in his career until his death, he signed himself 'Paolo Beni
d'Ugubbio' or 'Paulus Benius Eugubinus' (though not, of
course, in his personal letters).

Having completed his novitiate, and before the end of 1584,
Beni became a tutor in the humanities at the Roman Seminary
(ARSJ Rom. 53. 1, fo. 73[v]), where there were in all twenty-two
Jesuit priests and monks.[6] But he did not remain more than two
years in this position. It was very common at the time for Jesuits
to be transplanted from one Province to another. Under the
rubric *Mutati ad altre Province*, the Jesuit archives record that he
was removed somewhere in the Venetian Province in 1586
(ARSJ Rom. 53. 1, fo. 106[v]). In the years 1586–7 there were twelve
Jesuit centres in that Province, with three hundred Jesuits
spread throughout them.[7] Beni did not remain long in the
Venetian Province before returning to Rome, some time before
1587.

---

[5] See above pp. 22–3. The problem of identity does not arise elsewhere in
Beni's life and works.

[6] [Jesuits], *Annuae litterae Societatis Jesu anni MD.LXXXV* (Rome, 1587), 11.

[7] [Jesuits], *Litterae Societatis Jesu duorum annorum M.D.LXXXVI et
M.D.LXXXVII* (Rome, 1589), 110–28.

He once again left Rome in 1587 and did not return for six years. This is proved by the Dedicatory Letter (addressed to Cinzio Aldobrandini (1560–1610)) in the first decade of the commentary on the *Timaeus*. The letter is dated 10 February 1594 (although, as we shall see, Beni most probably returned to Rome late in 1593), and it begins: 'verum cum superioribus mensibus Romam ipse redissem, unde sexennio ante discesseram'. (For further proof of this dating, see also *OQ* 227 and *OQS* 3–4.) No trace of his whereabouts or activities for the next three years has been found.

It has always been thought that Beni taught theology at Perugia from 1590 to 1593 (see Casagrande, ed. cit., p. xiii, for the culmination of this long tradition which goes back to Mazzuchelli). However, this is not true. The Jesuit archives record that he was in Padua in 1590 (ARSJ Ven. 37, fo. 32^v), and in Milan (where he was not happy) in 1591 and 1592 (ARSJ Med. 20, fo. 351^v). Furthermore, there are records of lectures given by him in Milan in 1592. On the morning of 5 November 1592 he lectured 'De graecae linguae dignitate atque inprimis de Platonicae Orationis praestantia' (*OQ* 24–33); and in the afternoon of the same day he began a course of lectures on the *Rhetoric* (*OQ* 34–6). Both of these are the first evidences we have of his work on these topics, work which will form the nucleus of his massive commentaries on the *Timaeus* and the *Rhetoric*. On 1 March 1592 he began (still in Milan) a course of lectures on the *Ethics* (*OQ* 48–59). This later formed the basis for another immense commentary which remains unpublished, and which is now in the Archivio Segreto Vaticano.[8]

We cannot tell precisely when he went to Milan, but he was certainly there as early as 5 May 1590. This can be gathered from two complementary pieces of evidence. First, in his will dated 1 October 1621, he mentions an earlier will made during an illness in Milan about thirty years earlier (his memory is not very precise here) (ASGA II. D. 27, fo. 1^v). Secondly, as a Jesuit he had to obtain permission from the General of the Order, Claudio

---

[8] ASVB 89: 'Pauli Benii Eugubini in Aristotelis libros De moribus ad Nicomachum commentarii', unfoliated. It is on the lines of Beni's other Latin commentaries: it has a Greek text, and the Latin translations of Antonio Riccoboni and Bernardino Feliciano. An earlier *état* of the same commentary is to be found in ASVB 90.

Aquaviva (1543–1615), in order to make this will. A copy of the permission (ASVB 35), dated 5 May 1590, states that Beni, though still a Jesuit, had not by that date made any final vows regarding property and poverty (which is perhaps surprising when we recall his apparent willingness to do so as long ago as 1581). The General's permission states, therefore, that Beni was free to make a will: 'de bonis suis temporalibus quibuscunque pro sua Voluntate disponere, cum nullum ad ea societas nostra, vel aliquod illius Collegium, aut Domus iuxta constitutiones, et privilegia eadem ius habeat.' His desire to make a will at this time indicates that he at last had something to bequeath; and this could only have been the case if his father had died. As it turns out, his father had made a will on 3 July 1586, of which there is a copy in Gubbio (ASGN 554, fos. 141^r–45^r), and there is no reason to doubt that this was Francesco's last will and testament. This is an important document because it shows what bad odour Paolo was in at the time (1586), and it explains much of the future bitterness within the family. As was the custom, Francesco left money to ecclesiastical institutions and to servants, as well as food, lodging, and dowries for his wife and daughters. He made three of his sons (Federico, Giulio, and Giacomo) his 'heredes universales', who were to share the bulk of his property and money (fo. 144^v). In addition, Giacomo (the eldest) was to inherit the family home in Gubbio as well as the control of the family purse-strings (in other words, he was to cash allowances and annuities due to the other heirs) (fo. 143^r). Giulio was bequeathed his rightful place in the family home on condition that he could live in harmony with Giacomo, but otherwise he was to have the 'tres mansiones inferiores d. domus' (fo. 143^r), which would naturally revert to Giacomo on Giulio's death. Federico was to receive an annuity for each of his three sons, and a further allowance for the purpose of giving away in marriage any of his daughters (fos. 143^r and 144^r). Paolo fared the worst. He could retain his knighthood, but that was all:

Relinquit Reverendissimo D. Paulo eius filio legitimo et naturali congregationis sanctissimi hominis iesu in Urbe solum suam legitimam portionem sibi iure nature debitam in qua computari voluit officium equitis pii ab ipso pro eodem D. Paulo in Urbe emptum iubens ac mandans ipsum D. Paulum tacitum ac contentum se dicta portione vocari et nihil aliud petere posse quo iure etiam relinquit habitationem in supradicta domo si contingat ad patriam reverti aliquando recreationis gratia (fo. 143^{r-v}).

Here Paolo is virtually disinherited; and, worse, his father, who knew his difficult character, could foresee his resentment and his plots to stir up trouble with the brothers. In the event, Paolo did exactly as his father had foreseen. As a result of an agreement, made by all the brothers some time between 3 July 1586 (when Francesco made his will) and 5 May 1590 (when Paolo got permission to make his), Giacomo, Giulio, and Federico undertook to pay Paolo one third each of fifty *scudi* annually, as Paolo's will of 1621 states (ASGA II. D. 27, fo. 4^r).

We hear no more about this matter until 18 February 1593, when Giacomo wrote from Gubbio a strongly worded letter to Federico Borromeo in Milan (MA G. Inf., 160/60, fo. 118^r), in which he explains that Paolo had left Milan without permission, and had turned up in Gubbio to 'litigare con noi altri fratelli', having tried to enlist against them the support of the Duke of Urbino. According to Giacomo, Paolo was mendaciously putting it about that he had not received the agreed payments from the brothers; furthermore, in doing this (continues Giacomo), Paolo was breaking a promise made to another brother, Giulio, Proposto of Fano, to 'trattare amorevolmente con noi'. Instead, Giacomo claims that Paolo has acted in such a way that 'tutta questa città n'è restata malissimamente satisfatta, vedendolo trattare con noi come capitale nimico'. Giacomo does not say specifically what Paolo's demands were, but states that he was motivated by 'sdegno che ha che nostro padre gli habbia lassato solo la sua legitima'. And, despite a recall from his General, Paolo (in the harsh and acrimonious words of his brother) 'sene sta qua solo senza compagno attendendo sempre alle sue sottigliezze conforme alla mala natura con la quale ha sempre nel secolo tribulato tutti noi altri'.

Giacomo's language about his brother signals a long-standing hatred. His letter suggests that what angered him was Paolo's accusation of non-payment of the annuity. But the Jesuit archives reveal the full extent of Paolo's schemes here. It seems that he was trying, not merely to obtain agreed payments, but,

more seriously, to coerce Giacomo and Giulio to set up with
their own money Jesuit colleges in Gubbio (Giacomo) and in
Pesaro (Giulio, Proposto of nearby Fano). This is made clear by
the letter which Claudio Aquaviva (the General) sent to Paolo
two days later, on 20 February (ARSJ Rom. 14. 1, fo. 62ᵛ). Aquaviva repeats his earlier order that Paolo should go and stay in
'nostro collegio di Perugia' (hence, possibly, on this slim evidence, the tradition that Beni taught theology in Perugia from
1590 to 1593?), and he refuses to accede to Beni's request to be
sent to Rome. It seems that Beni had taken matters so far into
his own hands over these proposed colleges that he had already
entered into negotiations with the Bishop of Pesaro. In his letter, Aquaviva puts a stop to this, and dismissively pours cold
water on Beni's plans for a college in Gubbio: 'Quanto final-
mente al collegio di Ugubio, Nostro Signore, col tempo, mos-
trerà quello che si potrà fare in servizio di quelle anime alle
quali prego copiose grazie'—a consideration sublime enough
surely to instil a little humility into Beni's heart.

One's compassion for Beni is stretched to the limit by this
episode. It is true that he was unfairly treated in Francesco's
will, but then he *was* a Jesuit (albeit not a professed one), and he
had coldly lectured his father in 1581 on the joys of poverty and
isolation. What more could he have expected? Much more evidently. Despairing of ever receiving what he considered his
rightful inheritance, he set about concocting reasons why
Giulio and Giacomo should part with theirs. His actions
showed a mixture of severe jealousy on the one hand, and
material greed on the other. These alone were enough to secure
the displeasure of the Jesuit authorities. But Beni had also
broken Jesuit rules about family, property, and residence.

It is not surprising, therefore, that he was dismissed from the
Order on 23 September 1593, in a letter which states that he had
been ordained as a priest during his period as a Jesuit (we do
not know precisely when) but that he had made no definitive
vows. There is a longer explanation in the records (where a copy
of the letter is kept), but this has been diplomatically scratched
out (presumably to save the authorities from future embarrass-
ment), and in its place it is said that he was dismissed 'iustas ob
causas' (ARSJ Hist.Soc. 54, 13). We have seen how, through dis-
obedience and obstinacy over money, not to mention a certain

lack of tact, Beni had given his superiors sufficient cause for expelling him. The idea that he was expelled for wishing to publish an obscene commentary on the *Symposium* now seems most unlikely. But how does the commentary on the *Timaeus* (which Beni had written before leaving the Jesuits) fit in here? Could it be that, with their emphasis on St Thomas and Aristotle rather than on St Augustine and Plato, his superiors would not allow him to publish that commentary? Certainly, the *Approbatio* for the first decade of the commentary was not granted until 13 December 1593 (that is after he had left the Order). And the papal *Privilegii Summa* (giving sole printing and publishing rights to Beni for a period of ten years) was not granted until 28 January 1594. But, though his desire to publish the commentary may certainly have been a small contributory factor in his expulsion, it is hard to believe that it was at all decisive, for several reasons. First, as we shall see, there is little in the work (apart from its Platonism) which could give offence. Second, it is difficult to see why the Jesuit authorities should find it necessary to cross out the true explanation of his dismissal, if it were merely for his desire to publish a commentary which, in any case, came out in 1594 for all the world to see. Third, if the authorities were in effect so opposed to Plato, why did they allow Beni to lecture on him in Milan in 1592? And finally, why, since Beni always thought very highly of the commentary on the *Timaeus*, did he never mention it as the reason for his expulsion? He was proud of the work and would have been right to deprecate publicly any Jesuit ban on its publication. Instead he maintained an almost complete silence on this episode of his life. It remained secret and dark.

3

IN AND OUT OF PAPAL FAVOUR

As Beni fell, so the pope (Clement VIII) caught him. Almost immediately he invited the ex-Jesuit to return to Rome to lecture on Aristotelian natural philosophy in the Sapienza (Dedicatory Letter in *P.*), where Beni became a colleague of the rebellious Francesco Patrizi, as he will recall in his *Disputatio* of 1600 (fo. 8ᵛ). It has traditionally been stated by all Beni's biographers that he took up his new post in Rome in 1594, and left it in 1599 (see Casagrande, ed. cit., p. xiii, for the culmination of this tradition). This is possibly wrong on both counts. It is true that the earliest set of Beni's lectures which we have are entitled and dated 'Physicae disputationes habitae in Almo Urbis Gymnasio anno MDLXXXXIIII' (ASVB 70). These he probably adapted with little effort from his earlier work on the *Timaeus* and on allied subjects. Yet it is not unreasonable, despite the absence of proof, to suggest that Beni removed immediately to Rome late in 1593, as he had wanted to do some time before leaving the Order.

His return to Rome meant that he could meet Tasso again and, within weeks, witness the publication of the *Conquistata*, the idea for which Tasso had announced in February 1585 (Solerti, i. 510 and 596), and which he had worked on intermittently until it was published in early December 1593 (see Tasso, *Lettere*, ed. cit., v. 98 and 161–2). Beni later recalled this episode of his life in the commentary on the *Goffredo* (p. 23):

Et io che in Roma vidi benissimo l'occasione della Conquistata, et andai osservando, etiandio con vederne in penna buona parte, i suoi progressi, e lo stato dell'Autore ancor egro et infermo, sichè e per queste cagioni e per altre hebbi piena contezza di tal mutatione, darei di ciò pieno e largo ragguaglio, e farei chiaro come nè con mente in tutto sana, nè con intera elettione, cangiò il suo Poema.

This clearly suggests that there had been some contact between

Tasso and Beni over the previous years (1585–93), and it is possible—though this is mere guess-work—that Tasso had called
upon Beni (as a Jesuit) to help to turn the *Liberata* into a more
'religious' poem. Yet it is significant that Beni (for whom
religious considerations in the arts were often of primary
importance) did not accept the authority of the *Conquistata*, and
was to dismiss it throughout his commentary on the *Goffredo*.
For him the *Conquistata* was the product of a sick mind (his
judgement, based as it is on firsthand knowledge of the poet's
intimate circumstances, should count for a lot here); and the
Liberata remained for him the epitome of the Christian epic.

   Beni's ability to become involved in Tasso's career, as well as
to begin a new career himself, so soon after his apparent downfall, bears witness to his extraordinary resilience. He was lucky
to find his feet so quickly, and realized it. Yet he was also aware
of what he had lost. For the first time in years he was out in the
cold. In a lecture delivered on his return to Rome he speaks in
veiled terms of his transition (this is the only mention he ever
made of it), and he implies without good reason that it was the
offer of this new post in the Sapienza which drew him out of
the Jesuit Order. The addressee is Cinzio Aldobrandini:

Sed quoniam Avunculo tuo Sanctissimo placuit, Cardinalis optime et
ornatissime, ut novum hunc laborem subirem, et in Almo hoc Urbis
Gymnasio Philosophiam publice profiter, equidem parebo libens. Etsi
enim quam vitae rationem delegeram atque adeo amplexus fueram, ea
mihi optima videretur, quasi vero aut tutum portum subiissem, aut
commodam stationem nactus essem, unde minus tempestatem ac nau-
fragium pertimescerem, fore tamen spero ut cum Clementi Summo
Pontifici [. . .] obediam, e cuius nutu pendere gloriosum, cui morem
gerere et obtemperare aequissimum et salutare, nova mihi effulgeat,
unde reliquum hoc vitae spatium praeclare adhuc foeliciterque decur-
ram (*OQ* 216–17).

This manipulation of facts for effect (in the autobiographical
opening to an important public lecture) is understandable if we
remember how precarious Beni's position must have seemed to
him. For the next five years or so, while he remained in Rome,
he produced a series of works, the majority of which aim (sometimes desperately) to serve and impress the pope. He worked
hard during these years as a lecturer on subjects not unrelated
to his previous writings and teaching. Some idea of the breadth

and demands of his new post can be gathered from three unpublished introductory lectures which date from this period. In 1596 he began a course of lectures on the Aristotelian *De generatione et corruptione*. On 5 November 1597 he began a course on the *De anima*. And on 4 November 1599 he began a course on the *Meteorologica*.[1]

Little biographical information—apart from the testimony of these works—has come down to us, except two financial facts: in 1596 (24 August and 23 December) Beni acknowledged receipt of payments (according to the agreement) from Giacomo (ASVB 36); and, on 2 May 1598, he was told in a letter from the Jesuit authorities that he need not trouble himself about a debt which he owed to the Roman College, and which he had claimed he could not pay (ARSJ Rom. 14. II, p. 335). It is as if the Jesuit experience had not saved Beni from the evil of greed, but had rather served to justify him in his practice of it. Materially, he had a lot of catching up to do after the barren years. From now until his death his material wealth progressed from little to plenty: his experience had sadly taught him to let no chance of gain pass by. All the works written between 1594 and 1599 have short-term gain (of wealth, but also of renown) as their aim. This does not, however, apply to two works, written before his break with the Jesuits, which it is convenient to examine next.

II

The first of these,[2] a dialogue set in Muret's house, with Beni present, on whether it is right for the orator to stir up emotions, was published in 1594 (before the publication of the commentary on the *Timaeus*) and was reissued with some modifications in 1624, as the first of five *Oratoriae disputationes* (a companion work to the commentary on the *Rhetoric*). It will be better discussed in that context;[3] and it is sufficient to note here that it was the fruit of his acquaintance with Muret around 1577 and of his teaching in Milan around 1592. As we shall see, Beni's

---

[1] The three Aristotelian lectures, dated as I have indicated, are in ASVB 113.

[2] *Disputatio: In qua quaeritur, an sive actori, sive reo, et in universum oratori ingenuo; liceat in iudiciis et concionibus affectus concitare: ac iudicum animos flectere et permiscere* (Rome, 1594).

[3] See below, Chapter 15, Section VI.

interest in rhetoric remained constant throughout his long career, and it is fitting that his first serious scholarly work should concern it.

The second of these works is the commentary on the *Timaeus*. The first of the three decades of this commentary was published in 1594.[4] Beni had written all three decades by 1594, and wished to publish them all at the same time; he would probably have done so, were it not for the fact that he was ordered (as he put it) to Rome. As it was, he had to give up preparing the work for publication halfway through the second decade (see Dedicatory Letter in *P.*), and it was not until 1624 that the first two books of the second decade saw the light.[5] The eighteen copious books which make up the remainder of the commentary, and which Beni worked on intermittently for the rest of his life, are to be found (some with the *Nulla Osta* and ready for printing) in the Archivio Segreto Vaticano.[6] It will be convenient to consider the whole project at this stage in Beni's career, since, as we have seen, the conception of the work lies in the years before 1594.

The situation of Plato in the Renaissance is now admitted to be more complicated than before: the old equation, Aristotle equals the Middle Ages and Plato the Renaissance, is seen to be inaccurate and misleading.[7] Geographical, academic, and personal factors make the relative positions of Aristotle and Plato

---

[4] *In Platonis Timaeum sive in naturalem omnem atque divinam Platonis et Aristotelis philosophiam decades tres* (but in fact only the first decade) (Rome, 1594). All references to this work quote decade (in large Roman numerals), book (in small Roman numerals), and page number.

[5] *Platonis et Aristotelis theologia* (Padua, 1624). This contains the first two books of the second decade. References are given as for the first decade.

[6] For the eight remaining books of the second decade see: ASVB 97: Book III (pp. 1–127) and Book IV (pp. 129–344); ASVB 98: Book V (pp. 344–581) and Book VI (pp. 1–200); ASVB 99: Book VII (260 pp.); ASVB 100: Book VIII (pp. 1–367) and Book IX (pp. 368–950); ASVB 101: Book X (460 pp.). In addition the Archivio has earlier unfoliated versions and notes for the following books of the second decade: Book IV (ASVB 102); V (ASVB 103); VII (ASVB 104); VIII (ASVB 105); IX (ASVB 106); X (ASVB 107). For the third decade—which is not in such a finished state as the second—see: ASVB 108: Book I (complete); ASVB 109: Books II–X (complete); with some fragments at the end of the commentary of Book II.

[7] For the background to Plato and the *Timaeus* I have used: A. E. Taylor, *Platonism and Its Influence* (London, [1925]); B. Nardi, 'Platonismo', in *Enciclopedia cattolica* (1952), 1614–123; P. O. Kristeller, *Renaissance Thought: The Classic, Scholastic and Humanist Strains* (New York, 1961), 24–47 ('The Aristotelian Tradition') and 48–69 ('Renaissance Platonism'); C. S. Lewis, *The Discarded Image* (Cambridge, 1964).

unstable in this period; and no simple formula can take adequate account of these contingencies and nuances. However, it is clear that, of all the Platonic texts, the *Timaeus* had been most constantly present to Western scholars: during the Middle Ages it (alone of Plato's dialogues) was kept alive through the partial translations by Cicero and, more important, Chalcidius, who also provided a commentary. Chalcidius interpreted the work in a Christian light, and saw enshrined in it a monotheistic cosmogony comparable and at times identical with that of the Bible. The Greek Church Fathers had repeatedly held Plato to be closer to Christianity than Aristotle; and, later, it was St Augustine who did most to reconcile Plato and Christianity. The resultant Platonic–Augustinian line of thought about religious matters was a potent influence on Anglican and Protestant reformers. (This last fact might be relevant to Beni's choice of the *Timaeus* for commentary, as well as to his Jesuit Counter-Reformation approach.) In the thirteenth century the close links between Plato and Christianity, which were centuries old, were threatened and weakened by Aquinas' successful attempts to reconcile Aristotle (not Plato) with Christianity. Plato's reputation and influence lived on, however, and, around the time of Petrarch, began to grow (with the gradual discovery of a far larger selection of the dialogues) until, in the fifteenth and sixteenth centuries, Plato was seen, not only as a theologian, but also as a political thinker, a logician, and, most importantly, as a philosopher of love. In Ficino we find a mixture (or rather a contamination) of these various strands; but gradually they go their separate ways and, principally through the activities of the academies, Plato's philosophy of love (or what was understood of it) finds its outlet in Italian lyric poetry and other literary genres, while his theology stands once again alone (except that now it can be viewed in the more informed context of Plato's other works).

When Beni wrote his commentary, therefore, a wide variety of approaches and a seemingly overwhelming bulk of materials were at his disposal. Yet, despite all the enthusiasm for Plato and the considerable activity of Platonists in the Renaissance, it is remarkable that he never enjoyed any scholastic institutional support: Aristotle still dominated university courses; and attempts to make Plato his academic equal regularly failed (see Kristeller, *Renaissance Thought*, p. 60).

This largely explains why the present commentary was not related to Beni's teaching programme in the way his Aristotelian commentaries will be. It also explains why Clement VIII should have asked him specifically to lecture on Aristotelian natural philosophy. Indeed, in the course of the commentary Beni laments the lack of institutional basis for Platonic studies in Italy (I. i. 36). The work is thus the result of private research for the most part, and bears the signs, in its various parts (published and unpublished), of being the fruit of hard, long, patient, and dedicated labour. Beni's Dedicatory Letter to Cinzio Aldobrandini (there is also a dedication to Clement VIII) emphasizes that he had been working on the commentary for many years; and it is possible that he began work on it in the 1580s when he was training as a Jesuit. Indeed, the work can be seen as part of his Jesuit activities (Jesuit preoccupations occasionally rise to the surface). It is as if Beni, a Jesuit in the Counter-Reformation, is anxious to legitimize the study of Plato (and Aristotle) in a religious context. But, on a larger view, the work is to be seen primarily as an effort to understand what might be called the Christian Plato; and it is to be linked with Beni's other works of the same (or earlier) period. Of these we can mention his translation of, and commentary upon, the *Euthyphro*, one of Beni's earliest works, which he originally intended as the beginning of a complete translation of all Plato's dialogues (a project he abandoned as he became involved in the work for the commentary on the *Timaeus*).[8] Another work of this period, closely related to the *Timaeus*, is Beni's translation from the Greek of the first two books of Proclus' commentary on the *Timaeus*. This was done (almost certainly) after Beni wrote his own commentary (for he does not mention his translation in his commentary in the numerous places where one would expect him to do so, for example, I. viii. 543 and 549); and the translation of Proclus' work was completed just before Beni left the Jesuits (in his MS translation of the second book we find the

[8] MS in ASVB 116: 'In Platonis Euthyphronem, sive in dialogum de sanctitate, copiosa commentaria: in quibus etiam ad platonicos dialogos reliquos sic introducitur et instruitur lector'. For Beni's much later judgement on this early work I have summarized from ASVB 132 (a list of his own works).

date 6 August 1593).[9] Beni's commentary on the *Timaeus* sums
up his activity and interest in this area of Platonism; and
nothing is clearer than that he always attached the greatest
importance to the work.

The care with which he prepared his enormous commentary
is evident from his MSS, where the work of revision is so
thorough that even corrections are corrected. His MS of the first
decade (VA Vat.lat. 7065) allows us to see how the commentary
evolved. Evidently his first plan was to compose three books as
an introduction to Aristotelian and Platonic philosophy, but
towards the end of Book Three he altered his plan, and used the
first three books instead as an introduction to the commentary
on the *Timaeus*. Thereafter he was on course, and throughout
the thirty books (divided equally amongst three decades) he
provided a slow-moving, wide-ranging, and meticulous commentary on Plato, the *Timaeus*, Aristotle, and the relationship of
all three to Christianity. Some books (like the first three) take
the form of general discussions of philosophic doctrine unrelated to the text of the *Timaeus*, while others continue the word-
by-word commentary, giving the Latin translations by Ficino,
Serranus, and by Beni himself (whose versions are accurate and
eminently clear). Nothing Beni will later accomplish will bear
greater witness to his solid erudition. Each point is surrounded
by a tangle of supporting references. No previous opinion
escapes his notice. No possible argument for or against his own
view is overlooked. Any one who picks his way through this
jungle of erudition is likely to feel, with Mazzacurati (who,
however, could not have seen the half of it since he had no
knowledge of the Archivio Segreto Vaticano's holdings), that

gli interessi del Beni, in questa vigilia, si rivelano sempre piuttosto
eclettici, dilettanteschi, chiusi tra la piccola tradizione antiquaria del
morente umanesimo e una generica ambizione di conciliare tra di loro
arti e tendenze filosofiche diverse, di pacificare i sistemi della filosofia
classica e le esigenze della teologia, in una visione dei problemi
sempre elusiva e pericolosamente approssimativa (art. cit., pp. 494–5;
exactly repeated by Casagrande, ed. cit., p. xiii).

[9] MS in ASVB 111: 'Procli Diadochi commentariorum in Platonis Timaeum,
liber secundus'. Another MS version, including also Book One, is in ASVB 110.
For Beni's later comments on this early work (which I have summarized) see
ASVB 132.

Such a judgement is unfair to Beni and to the guiding principles in his commentary.

What then are his principal objectives? In the first place, of course, there is an effort to understand what Plato wrote: to elucidate key concepts (for instance, what Plato meant by *universum*, which Beni takes to be the central subject of the *Timaeus*), to compare the *Timaeus* with Plato's other works, and to resolve problems of a technical nature. In this, Christianity is usually not brought into the picture. Secondly, and Beni felt that this had often been attempted but never achieved, the commentary compares, in a sporadic way, Plato with Aristotle; and for the reason that Plato (*Plato noster* is how Beni usually refers to him) seems to be the nearest (of all the Ancients) to Christianity, Beni tends to be on his, and the Platonists' side. Here the *Adversarii* are mainly Peripatetic (though it will not be long before Beni is forced, by his professional commitments in Rome and Padua, publicly to become an Aristotelian). Finally, and most importantly, there is Beni's explicitly Christian aim. His treatment of Plato and Aristotle is never for long carried on without reference to Christianity, and his aim is to establish the validity of Plato's theology. This does not mean that Beni tries to reconcile conflicting philosophies and tendencies: Mazzacurati is wrong to attribute to him a 'generica ambizione' in this respect. For, throughout, Beni's avowed intention is to discriminate rather than to seek consensus at all costs (I. v. 313). And he always maintains the principle that 'quae Christianam veritatem oppugnant, nusquam ferenda sunt' (I. vi. 372). His position here is highlighted by a comparison with Ficino, whose indiscriminate eclectic syncretist approach Beni rejects in the strongest terms: 'non Christianum [*Ficinum*] esse sentias sed Ethnicorum, atque Ethnici more philosophari' (II. ii. 119; see also II. ii. 143–4).[10] Accordingly, Beni separates the Biblical from the Platonic, Moses from Plato (on the subjects of the flood, the creation, eternity, and so on) and, contradicting earlier writers, notably Ficino, he gives a cautious historical view of the relationship between Plato and the Bible (see, for example, I. vii. 424 and 432–3; I. viii. 514–21; II. i. 88–9). Indeed, on the question

---

[10] Interestingly, C. S. Lewis expresses an identical view about Ficino in *English Literature in the Sixteenth Century* (Oxford, 1954), 11.

of Plato's sources, Beni takes what is now the modern view, and sensibly refuses to accept that Plato read and used the Bible (i. x. 669). Thus he appears for the most part as the critic and unraveller of the muddled and unhistorical thinking of earlier times.

Beni's commentary is also of interest to us since it contains many of the seeds of his future development as a critic. His Jesuit Christian angle of vision in the commentary helps to explain why, in his later treatment of history and poetry, usefulness in the moral sense is always at the forefront: it is remarkable that, before he had begun serious work on these subjects, and long before he had published works on them, he enounced in this early work definitions of them which will not be altered in later works wholly dedicated to them. Beni had already decided that history was useful for the teaching of prudence (though, of course, that was a common view) (i. vii. 422); and, more remarkably, he had already found his threefold moral definition of poetry's function (whereby the epic, the tragic, and the comic are specifically directed to the teaching of exclusive social classes of men) (i. vi. 383–4); and finally, he gives the same definition of rhetoric as in his commentary on the *Rhetoric* (i. iv. 245–6).[11] Here it is clear that the residual Christianity in Beni's later works, written in the more secular atmosphere of Padua, had its roots in his Jesuit years. Moreover, his broad conception of history, poetry, and rhetoric clearly underwent little change after his removal to Padua (in 1600) where he was more or less obliged to adhere to Aristotelian texts and where he certainly devoted long hours to the further study of those subjects. It was the details, the arguments, and the scholarly apparatus which he later added in order to flesh out these broad conceptions.

III

While the commentary on the *Timaeus* was produced over a long period, the four works which followed it were written quickly and for occasional purposes.

---

[11] For his later views on history, poetry and rhetoric, see below, pp. 209–10 (history), pp. 179–87 (esp. 179) (poetry) and p. 228 (rhetoric).

The first of these is the Ash Wednesday sermon which Beni delivered to the pope and his cardinals in the church of St Sabina on the Aventine Hill in Rome in 1594.[12] In giving this sermon Beni was participating in a traditional ceremony which dated back to the eleventh century (at least), and in which the pope and cardinals (covered with ashes) processed barefoot up the Aventine Hill to the church where the sermon was given. The text for the day was invariably Genesis 3: 19 ('In sudore vultus tui visceris pane, donec revertaris in terram de qua sumptus es: quia pulvis es et in pulverem reverteris'). Beni treats this with a wide range of impressive oratorical devices: crescendos, repetitions, emphatic and ornamental procedures, and whatever else he could use. The climax of the sermon is yet another rhetorical device, whereby Beni portrays the corpses of former cardinals lying in Roman graves and waiting for Judgement Day. As they wait, they sternly remind the present congregation (through Beni) not to waste their precious time on earth or to shirk their religious duties. The speech which Beni puts into their mouths provides a stirring and dramatic close to his sermon. It effectively softens his presumption in criticizing the pope and his cardinals; but, at the same time, it is near enough to obloquy (and that from a minor ecclesiastic) to satisfy the pope's and the cardinals' traditional desire for punishment on this special day in the Christian Calendar. This is one of the few examples we have of Beni's pulpit oratory;[13] and it is as different as can be from the Latin style of his scholastic commentaries, which constitute the bulk of his literary output.

IV

A little more than two years later, towards the end of 1596, Beni published his *De Ecclesiasticis Baronii Cardinalis Annalibus disputatio*.[14] In the Dedicatory Letter to Clement VIII (dated Rome, 23

[12] *Oratio habita in sacro Clementis IIX. Pont. Max. et Amplissimorum S. R. E. Cardinalium consessu. Feria IV. Cinerum. In B. Sabinae Templo* (Rome, 1594). This was reprinted in *OQS* 1–4.
[13] There are other sermons—or rather speeches for religious occasions—but these were mostly written for others to deliver. See *OQS*.
[14] Rome, 1596 (hereafter *DBA*). This work was reprinted in C. Baronio, *Epistolae et opuscula*, ed. by R. Albericius, 2 vols. (Rome, 1759), ii. 1–45, with some general explanatory notes. Albericius also supplies a brief and highly favourable (but not altogether accurate) account of Beni's life and work (pp. 3–4, n. *b*).

October 1596) Beni explains that he wrote the present work at the suggestion of G. V. Pinelli all in a few days, circulated it in MS, corrected it, and published it. Presenting himself as on the threshold of old age (little did he know that his life's work had barely begun), he announces that this work is something of a departure from his previous work on Aristotelian and Platonic theology (pp. 5 and 8). Nevertheless, he is willing to drag himself away from such studies to satisfy his friend Pinelli. Pinelli (1535–1601), whom we have already met briefly as Tasso's host in 1575, was an important figure.[15] He wrote nothing (except many letters); but he encouraged and supported others, exerting a quiet influence on the literature and culture of the period. Though born in Naples of a Genoese family, he moved in 1558 to Padua, where he kept an open house, and built up a scientific museum and an important library which was later (in 1609) acquired for the Ambrosiana. According to his first biographer, Paolo Gualdo (op. cit., p. 45), Pinelli was particularly attached to the Jesuits (though he was not part of the Order); and Beni may have become acquainted with him while in the Order. However, it is more likely that they knew each other in Padua in the 1570s.

Be that as it may, Pinelli had asked Beni to write an appreciation of Baronio's *Annales*.[16] These, as is well known, were a reply to the *Magdeburg Centuries*, which represented the culmination of Lutheranism. The *Magdeburg Centuries* were primarily the work of Matthias Flaccius Illyricus (1520–75) who, with nine others, began around 1557 a thirteen-volume history of the Church up to 1400, and this was published (as the *Magdeburg Centuries*) between 1559 and 1574. Many historical documents were quoted in the work to show that the papacy was the instrument of Satan and that, under its power, the real teach-

[15] For Tasso's visit to Padua, see above, Chapter 1, Section III. There is room for a modern study of Pinelli. In the mean time many indications can be gathered from: P. Gualdo, *Vita Ioannis Vincentii Pinelli patricii genuensis* (s.l., 1607); C. Frati, *Dizionario bio-bibliografico dei bibliotecari e bibliofili italiani dal sec.XIV al XIX raccolto e pubblicato da A. Sorbelli* (Florence, 1933), 460–1; M. Parenti, *Aggiunte al Dizionario . . . di Carlo Frati*, 3 vols. (Florence, 1952–60), iii (1960), 82–5.

[16] For the background to Baronio's work I have used, apart from the standard theological works, A. Pincherle, 'Baronio, Cesare', *Dizionario biografico degli Italiani*, vi (1964), 470–8; C. K. Pullapilly, *Caesar Baronius: Counter-Reformation Historian* (Notre-Dame and London, 1975).

ings of the Christ of the New Testament had become overlaid and obscured. With these arguments, the case was made, on historical grounds, for Protestant separation from Rome.

Baronio (1538–1607) spent many years preparing his reply. In his lifetime he produced twelve volumes, the first of which came out in 1588 and the last (which covers the years 1100 to 1198) in 1607. His death cut the projected work off before completion, and left others unavailingly to attempt to complete it. From the first Baronio's work was hailed throughout the Catholic world as the definitive justification of the Catholic Church. It was immensely detailed and well researched, and still remains valuable for its sources; but it is now seen to be inevitably biased and, as a recent critic has said, excessively subtle and casuistical in its use of scholastic procedures (Pincherle, art. cit., p. 476). Such defects, however, would not have seemed like defects to Beni and to most of his contemporaries: such modes of argument were the very thing to confound the Devil, or any other adversary, as much of Beni's own work amply proves. When Beni wrote his *Disputatio*, Baronio had just published his seventh volume (1596) (*DBA* 27).

The first part of Beni's work—where he succinctly accounts for the rise of heresy—is the most interesting. According to his theory, heretics had always used pagan writers in order to demolish the Scriptures, but had originally been defeated by Christians who, in their turn, adduced pagan authorities for Christian purposes (pp. 10–14). The Church Fathers made use of Aristotle and Plato, taking from them only what was useful to Christianity (p. 14). Christians used Aristotle to combat the heretics, and thus scholastic philosophy (such as Aquinas practised) was born (pp. 15–16). However, when discord broke out in the scholastic camp, the Schoolmen neglected the study of Greek and Hebrew and so lost the very weapons of knowledge and enquiry with which the heretics could be overcome (pp. 16–17). It only remained for the heretics to cultivate Greek and Hebrew and to use them to deny the basis of the Roman ecclesiastical tradition (p. 17).

In this state of affairs (says Beni), it was necessary, first, to clarify the message of Scripture and, secondly, to give a clear, honest account of ecclesiastical history (pp. 17–18). The first was accomplished by the Council of Trent, very much (he says) to Clement VIII's credit; and the second was only then being accomplished by Baronio, again under the decisive influence of Clement VIII (pp. 18–21). (Here Beni's need to flatter the pope, whose role he exaggerates, got the better of him.)

The remainder of Beni's work attempts briefly to show that Baronio has justified the Church of Rome and all its trappings (pp. 23 ff.). Clearly, Beni was writing under pressure, and he tends to send Pinelli back to Baronio's own words. His praise is vague; and he goes no further than hyperbolic and ornately turned comments (see, for example, p. 41, where he explains his method and approach).

His appreciation of Baronio's work is admittedly superficial. Deeper discussion of the merits and demerits of it, discussion which Beni says he might one day undertake (p. 43), would have suited him better. As it is, his adulatory style is apt to sound a false note and to appear insincere, especially in respect of Clement VIII (to whom he owed a great deal, it is true). No doubt this is a work by which Beni hoped to achieve some sort of (ecclesiastical) promotion: he had been plunged to the depths only three years earlier, and was eager to climb out as soon as possible. Furthermore, he was not the only man who praised Baronio and his work in the hope of receiving some mention in future volumes of the *Annales* (see Pullapilly, op. cit., p. 59). And it is significant, in considering the question of Beni's sincerity here, that his favourable judgement of Baronio is to some extent reversed in the later *De historia* of 1611.[17]

In 1596 his interest in Baronio and his work does not appear to be profound. His reading of the work is indeed a sort of self-justification. For what he most admires in the *Annales* is Baronio's inclusion of pagan material which is used, not to besmirch Christianity, but to glorify it (*DBA* 42). This justified Beni's own discreet use of Aristotle and Plato in his theological studies. Equally, Beni's theory of the rise of heresy, whether or not it is accurate (and it is surely too simple to be truly accurate), can also be read as a justification of his own preoccupation in previous years with pagan Greek authors.

---

[17] See below, p. 214 and Chapter 14 n. 10.

V

In his next work he involved himself for the first time in papal politics. On 27 October 1597 the long and peaceful reign of Alfonso II d'Este, Duke of Ferrara (b. 1533) came to an end with his death.[18] Alfonso had produced no successor despite his three marriages, and so nominated his cousin, Cesare d'Este, the son of his father's illegitimate brother, as his successor. This proved unacceptable to Clement VIII, who, on 2 November 1597, after some mild disagreement with his cardinals, declared an end to the Este rule in Ferrara (which the papacy had been granting for more than three hundred years). With this, Cesare was threatened with excommunication and was summoned to Rome. Hoping in the end to prove his right to succeed, he prevaricated. The pope wavered for a time, and seemed inclined to consider Cesare's case; but his cardinals, and above all Baronio,[19] encouraged him to stick to his guns. A papal army was prepared (still in November) and Cardinal Pietro Aldobrandini sent to command it. Meanwhile, Cesare refused to yield, and was finally excommunicated on 23 December.

On that very day Beni began his 'Due discorsi sopra l'Impresa di Ferrara, et altre occorrenze per tutto l'Anno Santo del Giubileo'.[20] The work has three aims.

The first is religious. Beni writes as an *ecclesiastico* who, perhaps presumptuously (he says), wishes to further the Catholic cause (pp. 6 and 85–6). Like the cardinals, he tries to persuade the pope that war is the best course for the purpose of ousting Cesare and, furthermore, the course which God desires. The war is a just one (proclaims Beni), and likely to succeed. It will be a curtain-raiser to the imminent Jubilee Year. And, willingly

[18] For the background I have used A. Frizzi, *Memorie per la storia di Ferrara*, 2nd edn., 5 vols. (Ferrara, 1847–50), iv (1848), 466–7 and v (1850), 1–12.

[19] E. Cochrane, *Historians and Historiography in the Italian Renaissance* (Chicago and London, 1981), 459.

[20] MS in PU 911. It is not attributed to Beni in the catalogue (for it is signed only with his initials (in the title)). The 'presente giorno della scommunica' (by which it is possible to date the composition of this work) is mentioned on p. 3. There is a slightly later copy in VA Vat.lat. 6557 (parte seconda), fos. 203^r–33^v. This is attributed, wrongly, to the Venetian historian Paolo Paruta in the catalogue, probably because it is in the same (copyist's) hand as another work, clearly by Paruta, which precedes it.

assuming the role of papal secretary and adviser, Beni drafts a
Giubileo which he urges the pope to circulate amongst his flock
(pp. 80 ff.).

Second, and closely related to the first, is Beni's political
aim in the work. Much of the first *discorso* centres on the
possible reaction of Venice to the proposed annexation.
Against doubts that Venice might come to Cesare's aid, Beni
argues that Venice would welcome, and benefit from, papal
rule in Ferrara. However, and here we glimpse the main purpose of the *discorsi*, the Venetians would have to be convinced of this by a suitably gifted papal ambassador. Once
again Beni drafts a letter or speech which could be presented
as a package to the Venetians, with diplomatic explanations
(pp. 38–45). This gives a clue to Beni's personal ambitions. A
former Jesuit with a depth of ecclesiastical experience, a
favourite with the pope, and a strong-willed and determined
fighter, Beni might well have considered himself fit for such a
mission. Yet his lack of tact and humility (which must have
been evident to the pope) cannot have recommended him;
and there is no evidence that anything came of his tacit offer
of service.

The third aim of the work is practical. Beni considers possible
tactics (how the papal army should sow the seeds of discord in
the Ferrarese ranks, and cream off the best of their soldiers with
offers of high wages), and considers the problem of financing
the war.

In the event his ink was wasted. A few days later (on 27
December) Cesare capitulated. The Treaty of Faenza was
drawn up and signed on 12 January 1598. Whereupon Cesare
removed to Modena. Yet the pope seems to have been grateful
for Beni's work: he increased his salary and awarded him two
pensions on the strength of it (ASGA II. E. 9, Sect. 145; Dedicatory Letter in *P.*). There is a clarity and directness in this
work which was absent from the *Disputatio* on Baronio. Beni
shows a good grasp of the political situation and carefully
weighs arguments and counter-arguments, an activity which
well suits him. Furthermore, his Italian (different in this from
the Latin of the *Disputatio* on Baronio) is unadorned, practical,
specific: it does a job of arguing a case and it does it effectively.

VI

The same qualities are present in his next work, again addressed to the pope and again the solution to a papal problem. The *Due discorsi sopra l'inondation del Tevere*[21] were written at the beginning of 1599, following the immense flood which had begun around 20 December 1598, and had risen to devastating proportions by Christmas Eve, when the flood waters reached the Vatican (*DSIT* 1–4). Beni's work might easily be dismissed as yet one more solution to the age-old problem: for as long as the Tiber had been flooding its banks, the Romans had been devising (but rarely implementing) such solutions. Yet in this work we have the key, not only to the temper of Beni's later major works, but also to the next crucial step in his biography.

He attempts to cover much in the *Discorsi*: not only the causes and remedies of the present flood, but also of all previous floods; and this in a scholarly and detailed (often mathematically calculated) way. Out of all this two important matters arise.

First, the present disaster is faced, paradoxically, by looking through the mirror of the past: in his discussion of causes and remedies Beni combines classical scholarship with practical realism. Thus, amongst the causes of the flood he lists rain (obvious, one would have thought, but supported by a quotation from Ovid (p. 21)), and then, turning to modern evidence, he blames the ruins, refuse, and excrement with which the Tiber is filled (pp. 23–4). As for the remedies, he compares the present with the past, and finds that the Ancients had the remedies but not the right circumstances in which to effect them. Thus, in the past the Romans needed to use the river for navigation; in 1599 that was no longer the case (p. 37). In ancient times the many private and public baths, each with a separate aqueduct, made the ground in Rome continually sodden; in 1599 there were (according to Beni) only two aqueducts serving the whole of the city (pp. 39–40). And though these circumstances lessened the chances of success for the Ancients, yet when Augustus and Trajan cleared the river-bed their measures

---

[21] Rome, 1599 (hereafter *DSIT*). For the background see G. Lugli and P. Frosini, 'Tevere', in *Enciclopedia italiana*, xxxiii (1937), 750–4 (esp. p. 751). For the sequel to this work, see the beginning of Chapter 6.

were effective for a time (pp. 63–4). Beni therefore returns to these, and proposes, with the authority and precedence of the Ancients and the mathematical calculations of the present, to clear, keep clear, and to widen the river-bed (as well as to divert a channel from it) (pp. 44, 46–7, 52–3, 65–6, and 77). What is significant here is the mixture of ancient and modern. The former derived from Beni's classical education and interest in the past; the latter from his desire to alter or improve the present. From Beni's point of view this mixture was balanced in favour of the ancient: the mathematics were partly the work of an unnamed friend who had accompanied him in his experiments on the banks of the Tiber; and his ultimate practical solution (to clear the river-bed) was based on a rather flimsy and over-optimistic calculation (viz. that at one place on the banks, where the river had not flooded but had risen very high, the volume of excess water which caused the flood could have been contained in the rest of the river, had it not been for the debris on the river-bed) (p. 66). This amateurish quality is to be contrasted with the later and far more technically assured work of F. M. Bonini, *Il Tevere incatenato: overo l'arte di frenar l'acque correnti*, which did not rely much on ancient authorities.[22] It is in this mixture of old and new, authority and reason, that we perceive for the first time Beni's particular brand of modernism, so different from Tassoni's and Galileo's. As we shall see in his treatment of literary and linguistic issues, he is not the pure Modern (in the *Querelle des anciens et des modernes*) that the critics have so often described.[23]

The second important element in Beni's work is religious. This is no surprise in a work written by an ecclesiastic for the pope; and to view the flood as a *flagello* sent by God was in no way exceptional (see Bonini, pp. 64–5). But Beni went further, and saw the flood as God's punishment for the excessive greed and concern with material gain in the Roman people (all of which is interpreted by Beni as the direct result of the pope's recent absence from the city) (pp. 27–9). Beni bitterly denounces the lack of Christmas spirit which preceded the flood in Rome; and, with considerable temerity, he sets out to

[22] Rome, 1663.
[23] See, for example, B. T. Sozzi, 'Lingua, Questione della', in *Dizionario critico della letteratura italiana*, ii. 436.

show how the poor of Rome were ill treated. But, suddenly, his words are cut short in the text, and an editorial note intervenes: 'Mancano alcuni versi che per esser mal leggibili nell'essemplare non si son potuti copiare' (p. 29). This is a clear piece of censorship (for Beni's hand is eminently legible, as are all the copies of his works which he supervised): no doubt he had gone too far in his audacious criticism of the pope. Throughout the past six years his confidence had steadily increased: he was favoured by the pope; his work was appreciated; he was beginning to turn his religious experience to good account. But, never the master of tact and discretion, he carelessly ruined his chances of further advancement in Rome. It is probable—as a future instalment of his work on the flooding of the Tiber will make clear—that Clement VIII did not even acknowledge Beni's *Discorsi*; and it is certain that none of the measures suggested by him were put into practice. In fact, very little was done in future years to prevent floods in Rome; and it was not until 1870 that the Italian government finally walled up the Tiber and thus solved the problem.

Beni was never to regain the pope's favour, and his lack of it was soon to cost him dearly, in Padua.

VII

While Beni was trying to establish a reputation for himself as a papal adviser, Antonio Riccoboni died and left vacant the chair of humanities in Padua. The post was first offered to the Belgian humanist, Justus Lipsius, who declined it. It was then offered to Beni, presumably on the basis of his published work on the *Timaeus*, at a salary of six hundred florins (soon to be increased to one thousand) on 3 November 1599 (Tomasini, *Gymnasium patavinum*, p. 342). Beni accepted, no doubt gladly, for several reasons. His poor relationship with the pope, the renown of the Paduan chair and of its previous incumbents (Portenari, p. 235), the chance to return to Padua where he had been happy, and finally the lure of the *studia humanitatis*: all these must have made him eager to accept this new appointment. He did not remove immediately: as we have seen, he began a lecture course in Rome on the day after his appointment was announced in Padua. He must then have left Rome early in

1600, and certainly before 12 March.[24] On leaving Rome he must have given up all hopes of a successful ecclesiastical career. He was to begin a new life—the relatively secular life of a teacher of eloquence at the Paduan Studio. Almost all his major works were yet to be produced.

---

[24] In his will of 1621 (ASGA ii. D. 27, fo. 1ᵛ) he mentions an earlier will made in 1600 when he removed to Padua.

4

PADUAN INITIATIONS

I

On his arrival in Padua Beni quickly and almost at the same time settled into two new roles, that of teacher and that of academician. Examination of these two roles will help to set the scene for his future career.

He gave his inaugural lecture on 16 March 1600.[1] All his loyalties appear to have shifted here. A year earlier, in the Preface ('Sommario e scopo di tutta l'opra') to the *Discorsi* on the Tiber, he had described Rome as the centre of the universe; now it was Padua's turn for that title (*DHS* fo. 12^{r-v}). Similarly, philosophy and theology have now given way in his affections to the humanities. Is this shift to be interpreted as insincere opportunism? Doubtless, Beni said in each place what was expected of him, and said it in a characteristically emphatic way. Yet he had always maintained a regard for Padua; and he had been forced to leave it by the advent of the plague of 1575–6. Equally, he had hoped before leaving Padua in the mid-1570s to follow a literary career (one connected with the *studia humanitatis*). But his religious interlude (what a failure it must now have seemed) had separated him from those aspirations. He was now picking up the pieces left behind twenty-five years before. Not that he had utterly wasted those years: they had yielded a valuable if unpleasant crop of experience. Yet he had been unhappily lost throughout the intervening years; he was now safe and suitably rewarded (financially). Those years now seem like years of preparation and consolidation for the work to come.

His prime task in Padua was to teach the humanities (poetry, rhetoric, and history) according to the precepts of Aristotle and, to a lesser extent, Plato and Cicero. In his inaugural lecture he introduces his new pupils to these disciplines. Since they will

---

[1] *De humanitatis studiis oratio* (Padua, 1600) (hereafter *DHS*). This was reprinted in *OQS* 4–13.

all three be discussed in separate chapters of this study they need not be mentioned in detail here, except to show how, in his introduction, Beni is careful both to distinguish them one from another, and to distinguish them all (as a corporate discipline) from other disciplines, especially theology and philosophy. He argues that, while these last two are broad and difficult subjects, they are none the less circumscribed, even predictable, in the range of their subject-matter; the humanities, on the contrary, aim to cover a limitless area of knowledge. He does not—for this is a simple introductory—expatiate on the common factors amongst history, rhetoric, and poetry; nor does he draw—as he will later draw—a distinction between *poetica* (theory) and *poesis* (poetry in practice).

This inaugural lecture has none of the technical pedantic distinctions, arguments, and counter-arguments which will fill his future courses on the humanities. Instead, there is an enthusiastic faith in the value of these disciplines, and, above all, a faith in the inseparability of rhetoric and wisdom (fos. 5ᵛ and 8ᵛ). This fervour finds its way into Beni's style, which here (as in the *Disputatio* of Baronio of 1596 and the Ash Wednesday sermon) aims to be elegant and florid: it is a style which Beni reserved for openings, for *captationes benevolentiae*; and it is quite different from the practical workaday Latin style usually to be found in his lectures and writings.

In this lecture Beni is, as one would expect, reminiscent of his immediate predecessor, Antonio Riccoboni, who had delivered his inaugural lecture in the same chair on 4 November 1571.[2] Their two lectures have much in common: discussion of the immensity of the subject, of the close bond between rhetoric and wisdom, of the value of the subject. But where Riccoboni seemed half-hearted and perhaps weary, Beni is pugnacious and alive. Both have been described as representatives of a dying humanistic tradition;[3] yet it is very hard to see any evidence of tiredness in Beni. If anything, his humanism is

---

[2] Published, first, in *Orationes decem* (Padua, 1573) as 'Oratio 2' (fos. 19ʳ–33ʳ). In later editions this *Oratio* was entitled 'De studiis liberalium artium'. See *Orationum volumen primum* (Padua, 1592).

[3] See G. Mazzacurati, *La crisi della retorica umanistica nel Cinquecento (Antonio Riccoboni)* (Naples, 1961). The writer's theory is that humanism (where form matched content, eloquence matched wisdom) broke down in Bembo (pp. 46–7); and this marked the beginning of a separation in rhetoric between

stronger, more assured than that of Riccoboni. This fire is accompanied (here as elsewhere) by a new awareness of the distinctive value of the *studia humanitatis*: for Beni it is not that they are valuable (as Riccoboni had argued) to other disciplines, such as law and medicine, so much as that they contain their own separate academic value.[4]

It is tempting to see here the first signs of the modern academic temperament: out of the ashes of a dying humanism was born a new humanism, more rigorous and self-contained than its earlier incarnation. (This would in part account for the often remarkable gap between theory and practice in Beni's future work.) But more research is required here into Beni's academic predecessors before such a generalization can be properly supported. It may be that what seems new in Beni had been in some measure present in at least some of his predecessors.

However that may be, there can be no doubt that Beni put much thought into his teaching in Padua. Apart from his scholarly publications (many of them originally lectures), his unpublished 'Modo di riformare lo Studio di Padova'[5] bears ample witness both to his thoughtful approach to academic matters and to his affection for Padua. It is a general rather than a personal survey, and was prompted by what Beni saw as the chaotic state of the university. It contains a review of university discipline, teaching matters (lectures, lengths of terms), student accommodation, fees, and the organization of the faculties; and it proposes (amongst other things) the setting up of a University Congregation. It forms an interesting attempt to regulate university life, to make it more disciplined and less haphazard. It shows in Beni the desire, if not the ability, to organize education on a large scale; and again one might see here a new humanism. For while the early humanist educators had concen-

---

form and content (p. 81), and the disappearance of wisdom (*sapienza*) from rhetoric in the seventeenth century (p. 93 and *passim*). Riccoboni and Beni are neatly slotted into this scheme, quite mistakenly as far (at least) as Beni is concerned (e.g. p. 131).

[4] Compare with Mazzacurati's comment in his article on Beni in the *Dizionario biografico degli Italiani*: 'Il contenuto non presenta alcuna novità né di temi polemici né di riferimenti rispetto alle ormai tradizionali prolusioni sullo stesso argomento' (art. cit., p. 496).

[5] ASVB 123 contains several drafts and fair copies of this work. The first, quarto, version seems to represent the final and best draft, and contains corrections not to be found in the others. I hope to do an edition of this.

trated for the most part on the teaching and forming of the individual, Beni, with his Jesuit training and his background of mass teaching, saw education in terms of large numbers (classes, faculties, universities). His treatise was not published. Like so many of Beni's polemical works (especially the linguistic ones), it goes too far in its impatient and often tactless quest for perfection. While its arguments are sound, it fails to accommodate itself to present realities.

Finally, it is incidentally interesting as a reflection of Beni's own teaching methods. He argues that it is better to write lectures than to improvise them (a choice which is still often debated, more amongst students than lecturers!); and secondly, that it is better to rely on classical authorities than on modern lecturers and their ideas. This goes some way towards explaining Beni's own methods whereby he published much of what he delivered as lectures, and whereby he relied for the most part on classical authorities. His ideas cannot have been congenial to Galileo and the medical scientists who were making such advances in experimentation in Padua at that time. In this work we see a Beni out of step with the forward-looking Paduans. Casagrande—who has not had the benefit of seeing this treatise (for it was presumed lost when he wrote)—associated it (because of its title) with the Paduan effort to reform the

programma accademico dello Studio, il cui *cursus studiorum*, fondato sull'imitazione dei testi canonici della tradizione classica, era sentito ormai come un peso e visto come un danno alla scienza e alla cultura contemporanea in genere (Casagrande, ed. cit., p. xiv).

Nothing could be further removed from Beni's plans in his treatise for reform: he is decidedly old-fashioned in this generally forward-moving place. While his humanism is novel in its vigour and energy and regulated methods, it nevertheless strongly rejects the modern anti-authoritarianism of some other (unnamed) university teachers (the very ones whom Casagrande would associate with the Beni of this treatise).

II

Closely related to Beni's *persona* as teacher in Padua was his *persona* as academician. Three days before he delivered his inaugural lecture (which I have found it convenient to examine first) he was admitted to the Accademia dei Ricovrati (Atti, fo. 17^{r-v}).[6] It had been set up on 25 November 1599 (Atti, fo. 1^r) in an effort to revive the extinct Animosi. It met in the home of Federico Cornaro and was primarily composed of learned men from the Studio (Atti, fo. 1^v). It had twenty-five founder members, amongst whom were Sforza Oddi, Francesco Pigna, Cesare Cremonino, Ottavio Livello (Beni's future friend and companion), Galileo Galilei, and other prominent Paduan scholars. It does not seem to have commanded the attractive array of luminaries associated with the Animosi; but, as time went on, it drew some of the most impressive men of the age: Giovanni Battista Guarini joined on 30 March 1601 (Atti, fo. 49^r); Vicenzo Contarini on 5 July 1604 (Atti, fo. 95^r); Lorenzo Pignoria on 16 December 1604; Cardinal Silvestro Aldobrandini (Clement VIII's nephew) became Protettore on 23 December 1601 (Atti, fo. 57^r); G. B. Marino was admitted on 6 March 1602, and two of his sonnets were read to the Academy between 15 and 21 April of that year (Atti, fo. 68^{r-v}).

To have been welcomed so readily into this group was no small honour for Beni. Not only that, but he soon became an official Censore (on 20 April 1600) along with Giovanni Belloni and Cesare Cremonino (Atti, fo. 35^r); and he was again elected to that office on 7 October and 2 December 1601 (Atti, fos. 35^v and 55^v). According to the Statutes (which form part of the 'Atti'), the Censori were the most important officials, responsible for all major policy decisions (Atti, fos. 4^v and 5^r).

The Academy met with considerable frequency (on four occasions in May 1600, for instance). At first it spent much time working out rules and voting procedures, as well as conducting elections. Of these, the most relevant and interesting to us was the decision (taken on 9 June 1600) to elect the Paduan Francesco Bolzetta as the official publisher: 'che niuno degli Academici possa d'altre stampe prevalersi se non con licenza

---

[6] On this academy see Gennari, pp. lvii–lxvii, and Maylender, iv. 440–5. The best source of information is still, however, the 'Atti', already quoted (Chapter 1 n. 12): for both Gennari and Maylender (who follows Gennari very closely) perpetuate some factual errors and contain some surprising omissions (they fail, for example, to record that the famous G. B. Marino became a member) for which see below.

dell'Academia, sì per riputatione nostra, come ancho per maggior nostro avantaggio' (Atti, fo. 32^v). Along with this went the election of Censori Sopra Le Stampe.

What else did they do? The Atti provide some fascinating insights here. Meetings were divided into two parts: first, paper and discussion; second, music. Nothing specific is recorded in the Atti of the music. As for the first, papers were read, and discussions followed, until 16 December 1601, when the Principe of the Academy introduced a new format: moral, political, or literary 'doubts' or questions were to be debated briefly by the academicians, each in turn (Atti, fo. 56^{r-v}). This is almost the recipe for Tassoni's later and very popular work (*Pensieri diversi*); and it is clearly reminiscent of Beni's own methods in his writings. This is not to say, however, that this form of debate in the Ricovrati directly influenced Beni or Tassoni: rather, it underlines the way in which the minds of many men of their period worked; and it testifies to the widespread popularity of that type of polemical question-and-answer debate.

We do not know when Beni left the Ricovrati. He is not mentioned in the Atti after December 1601; and it is perhaps indicative of his unpopularity in the Academy that it was Simone Stamini who read his paper on Tasso to the Academy on 8 April 1604 (Atti, fos. 92^v–93^r). In any case, the Ricovrati did not meet from 14 June 1609 to 10 April 1619 (after which it met only for a short time). And then it closed down again until 1633 (Atti, fos. 109^v–112^v).

5

WHO'S AFRAID OF PAOLO BENI?

I

His two new roles came together in his next work, *Disputatio in qua ostenditur praestare comoediam atque tragoediam metrorum vinculis solvere*,[1] published soon after July 1600 (the Dedicatory Letter is dated 14 July 1600). This is a work which involved him in an ever more complex tangle of controversy, as we shall see. The arguments of the work were destined to be expanded in the later commentary on the *Poetics* (1613), and will be better discussed in a later chapter. However, a brief account is necessary here in order to explain the subsequent polemical outpourings to which the work gave rise. A well-focused and strongly argued treatise, whose commonsensical thesis is clearly and persuasively presented, the *Disputatio* was (probably) read to the Ricovrati (*DIQO* fo. 19ᵛ), where, as we shall see, and as Beni no doubt intended, it effectively caused a sensation.

The question of whether drama should be in verse or prose had had a long history in Italy even before the 'discovery' of the *Poetics*.[2] But, after about 1548, and the beginning of Aristotle's influence on poetic theory, the idea that imitation (and not verse) was essential to poetry became widespread, and numerous attempts were made to define non-metrical poetry.[3] These attempts were answered in 1586 by Francesco Patrizi, who, directing his attack against Tasso's (as well as others') definition of poetry as imitation, proved to his own satisfaction that Aristotle (though not the Aristotle of the *Poetics*) and other ancient

---

[1] Padua, 1600 (hereafter *DIQO*). This work was reprinted in *Trattati di poetica e retorica del Cinquecento*, ed. by B. Weinberg, 4 vols. (1970–4), iv (1974), 345–95.

[2] For a glimpse into this pre-Aristotelian history see P. M. Brown, *Prose or Verse in the Comedy: A Florentine Treatment of a Sixteenth-Century Controversy* (Hull, 1973), p. 28 n. 1.

[3] See below, pp. 173 and 194–5.

authorities all made metre essential to poetry.[4] Patrizi's 'ferma conchiusione' was that 'poesia non possa, nè farsi, nè esser senza verso' (Della poetica, p. 118). He reaches his conclusion about poetry in general and its need for metre, not so much through common sense, experience, or logic, as through ancient authorities. Beni specifically relates his work to Patrizi's, seeing it as a reply to Patrizi and his followers (DIQO fo. 8ᵛ). Amongst the many who held the same view as Patrizi could be mentioned Faustino Summo. Summo taught logic at the Studio, was a respected member of the Infiammati and the Ricovrati, and was wont to splash around in literary pools, often creating or contributing to an uncomfortable turbulence.[5] He had something to say on most of the literary controversies of the day, and the question of verse in drama understandably drew his attention. His views—that drama in prose cannot be called poetry, and that verse should be retained in drama as a delightful entertainment—were published in a discorso in 1600, probably some months before Beni's Disputatio.[6] Summo goes through the opposite arguments, and answers them. He does not mention Patrizi, but supports his own arguments (unlike Patrizi) with many practical illustrations from sixteenth-century playwrights and critics. Summo's specific arguments and illustrations are not those which Beni will counter, though both writers inevitably cover the same theoretical ground. However, Beni's intention was not to attack Summo's views, but to go back and attack Patrizi's.

So much for the background to Beni's Disputatio. What now of its content? This can be roughly divided into arguments from authority and arguments from reason. It is significant that Beni separates the two (as he will do in the commentary on the Poetics), the more so since he puts authority second to reason (fo. 1ʳ), and argues that Patrizi placed too much stress on authority (fo. 15ʳ). In this work Beni appears proudly anti-authoritarian: as far as he is concerned, authorities could be adduced to

[4] Della poetica la deca disputata: nella quale, e per istoria, e per ragioni, e per autorità de' grandi antichi, si mostra la falsità delle più credute vere opinioni, che di poetica, a dì nostri vanno intorno (Ferrara, 1586), Book Five ('Se poesia si possa fare in prosa'), pp. 93–122.
[5] On him see Vedova, ii. 325–8.
[6] See Discorsi poetici (Padua, 1600), Discorso 9 ('Se le tragedie, e le comedie possono con egual lode spiegarsi sì in prosa come in verso'), fos. 61ʳ–69ᵛ.

port either side (fo. 16^v). Yet there is one authority which he has
to face squarely and which he cannot ignore: Aristotle. Beni can
find no words strong enough to praise the Stagirite (and this is
just as well since the bulk of his future work will of necessity
entail the exposition of his works). Like Patrizi, Beni finds Aristotle contradictory on the relationship between verse and
poetry (*DIQO*, fo. 18^r), and, in a long section which foresha-
dows the commentary on the *Poetics*, Beni tortuously makes
Aristotle square with his own thesis (fos. 17^r–26^r). In this way,
the *Disputatio* reads like a chapter of the later commentary, and
Beni's anti-authoritarianism in the work is thus very heavily
diluted and seems more apparent than real.

Yet it is not so much in his treatment of Aristotle (which is by
no means unimpressive) as in his own empirically based arguments that Beni's treatise is valuable and important. These
arguments can be briefly and schematically stated. Poetry is
essentially the imitation of human actions: verse has nothing to
do with such imitation (fo. 1^v). (It should be noted that this
reasonable premiss is admittedly derived by Beni from the
Poetics, from authority, in other words, and so the distinction
between authority and reason soon breaks down, as one of his
future opponents will observe.)[7] Art and poetry must (according to Beni) follow nature, and are, therefore, dependent on
either truth or verisimilitude for their credibililty (fos. 1^v and
3^v). Poetry must be credible in order to be morally effective: its
task is to describe and prescribe moral examples of behaviour
(fo. 3^v). Verse in drama (continues Beni) reduces or eliminates
this effectiveness in three ways: (*a*) the prolonged use of iambics, especially by low comic characters, destroys verisimilitude
(fo. 14^r); (*b*) verse is harder to understand than prose, and does
not therefore reach so readily the intelligence of the audience;
(*c*) the use of verse satisfies the claims of *voluptas* (which is bad)
rather than *utilitas* (which is good). For Beni this is intolerable:
the delight of a drama should derive from its plot rather than
from its metre (fo. 9^r). Metre is allowable in other genres (epic
and lyric) because, there, verisimilitude and comprehension are
not threatened: neither aims to create the illusion of extempore

---

[7] See Summo, *Discorso in difesa del metro nelle poesie, e ne i poemi, et in particolare nelle tragedie, & comedie* (Padua, 1601), fo. 16^v.

speech, and both are read privately by individual readers who can ponder the meaning of such literary works at their leisure (fo. 11ʳ).

Such are his arguments. They were clinched (for him) by the fact that drama (especially Paduan comedy) had suffered a decline. Towards the end of the *Disputatio* he is visited at night by two allegorical figures, one representing tragedy and the other comedy. Comedy piteously laments her recent ill-treatment at the hands of Paduan dramatists, who had prostituted her and forced her to offer intemperate pleasure to the masses instead of decent honest usefulness (fos. 26ᵛ–27ᵛ).

In all this one can see, in conclusion, the coming together for the first time of two strands in Beni's literary criticism. First, there is his Aristotelianism: he swears here, for the first time, a new loyalty to Aristotle, the poetic theorist; and this no doubt reflected the requirements of his new post in Padua. But secondly, mixed with his Aristotelianism, are two linked elements which had earlier joined forces in the commentary on the *Timaeus*: his Jesuit training and his Platonism. These largely dictate his almost exclusively moral preoccupation in poetic matters; and such a preoccupation will recur in all his literary (not to mention rhetorical and historical) criticism. Together, these various elements determine his conception of poetry as a moral tool which works on rhetorical principles (not the rhetorical principles of ornamentation and *elocutio*, but those instead of persuasion for moral ends).

It is difficult, given these potent influences and their indelible effect on Beni's criticism, to see any truth in those many Italian critics (Toffanin, Croce, Belloni, Jannaco, and Mazzacurati among them) who have described Beni as a Baroque literary theorist who, through a distorted reading of the *Poetics*, contrived to place delight above usefulness, complication and obscurity above simplicity.[8] In fact, rather than squaring with the Baroque tendencies of Padua, tendencies which can be traced back to the middle of the previous century,[9] Beni reacted

[8] For further discussion of this prevailing thesis, see below, pp. 165–8, 170, 174–8, and 188–205.

[9] See E. C. M. Roaf, 'Bartolomeo Cavalcanti, 1503–62: A Critical and Biographical Study', D.Phil. thesis, Oxford University, July 1959, p. 362. See also below, Chapter 13, for a comparison of Beni with earlier commentators of the *Poetics*.

strongly against them. Hence the Paduan outcry against the *Disputatio* which was soon to make itself heard.

II

The next stage in the controversy looks like a *non sequitur*, and indeed it is. But it reveals, first, how vulnerable and touchy Beni was at this time and, secondly, how involved literary polemics could become in this period.

This is how it started. In June 1600, shortly before Beni published his *Disputatio*, a young man from Vicenza, Giovanni Pietro Malacreta, published a set of *dubbi* (entitled *Considerazioni intorno al Pastorfido*) on Guarini's famous pastoral drama (written between 1580 and 1585 and published in 1590).[10] Malacreta examines the work so far produced on the *Pastor fido*, which might seem to be enough, but finds that there are many questions which still remain unasked and unanswered. Refusing to stir up the old questions (questions which centred mostly on the legitimacy of the mixed tragicomic genre, on the moral value of the pastoral drama, on the absurd discrepancy between the long involved *Pastor fido* and the traditional eclogue, and so on),[11] Malacreta asks a set of new ones.

He deals first with the external parts of the play (title, scene, prologue, and *antefatto*) and then with the Aristotelian qualitative and quantitative parts. He finds the *pastorale* of the title unsuitable, for the characters do not guard sheep or even talk of such an activity (p. 31); and the title *Pastor fido* is incongruous because it is not as a shepherd, but as a lover, that the *pastor*

[10] Malacreta's work was reprinted in G. B. Guarini, *Opere*, 4 vols. (Verona, 1737–8), iv (1738), 1–122. In what follows I refer to this eighteenth-century edition.
[11] The principal works in the debate, up to and including Beni's, are reprinted in vols. ii–iv of the four-volume ed. of Guarini's works (see n. 10). In particular, Beni's *Risposta* (hereafter *Risp.*) is to be found in iv. 123–278. In what follows I shall quote from this eighteenth-century reprint. A useful and quite detailed summary of the documents in the *Pastor fido* debate is contained in B. Weinberg, *A History of Literary Criticism in the Italian Renaissance*, 2 vols. (Chicago, 1961), ii. 1074–105. (All future references to this work by Weinberg will give his surname, volume number, and page reference.) A less detailed, but sound and still valuable summary is to be found in V. Rossi, *Battista Guarini ed il Pastor fido* (Turin, 1886). N. J. Perella's *The Critical Fortune of Battista Guarini's Il Pastor fido* (Florence, 1973) also gives a summary of the documents, but is unreliable.

(Mirtillo) is said to be *fido* (p. 34). The scene, though called
Arcadia, is not the Arcadia historically described by Pausanias
or reconstructed by Sannazaro, but instead a figment of Guarini's imagination (pp. 34–9). The prologue is said by Malacreta
to have no function (p. 42). The speaker of the prologue (Alfeo)
is said to be a poorly conceived character who erroneously attributes the art of poetry to the Arcadians (pp. 42–9). Next, Malacreta criticizes various aspects of the *antefatto*: Aminta's (the
priest's) lack of chastity (pp. 50–1), the preponderance and
over-importance of the six oracles in the play (p. 55), the unrea-
sonableness and complication of Arcadia's divine law, and the
improbability of Mirtillo's miraculous escape during the floods
(pp. 60–4).

Next Malacreta considers the qualitative and quantitative
parts of the play. He finds that the plot (*favola*) drags on for too
long, that it lacks verisimilitude, and that the numerous episodes are not well integrated (pp. 67–90). As for the *costumi*,
Malacreta finds that not one of the characters behaves consistently and that their morality is suspect (pp. 91–8). Similarly,
what the characters say (the *sentenza*) is badly adapted to their
situations: Livio, Montano, and Titiro all speak like Platonic
philosophers rather than lowly shepherds (and comparisons are
drawn with Tirsi's more appropriate speech in the *Aminta*)
(p. 99). On *locuzione* Malacreta spends little time, partly because
(according to Aristotle) it is the least important part, and partly
because there are no comparable plays which provide a standard by which to judge it (though strangely this consideration
does not prevent him from making comparisons with the
Aminta) (p. 116). Generally, however, the style of the *Pastor fido*
is judged by Malacreta to be more suited to madrigals than to
drama; and though isolated purple patches are effective, they
are not suited to their context (pp. 116–17). The remaining qualitative parts (*apparato* and *melopeia*) are virtually ignored
(p. 119). Of the four quantitative parts (prologue, episode,
exode, and chorus), Malacreta only considers the chorus. He
finds it impractical (should it remain on stage throughout?) and
improbable (pp. 120–1).

He ends by expressing the hope that someone might think fit
to disperse his doubts, and, apologizing for his youthful fervour, he quietly makes his exit from the polemical arena.

III

Who should be waiting to enter the same arena but Paolo Beni? In August of the same year (that is, very shortly after the publication of his *Disputatio*) Beni brought out (reluctantly, he says) his *Risposta alle considerationi o dubbi dell'eccellentissimo Signor Malacreta*.[12] The letter to the reader leaves us in no doubt that his purpose was in no way to defend Guarini (Beni does not seem to have had any particularly strong feelings about Guarini and his work, contrary to the opinion of recent critics (for example, Mazzacurati, art. cit., p. 496 and Doglio, p. 274)). Instead, his purpose in writing the work was merely to parry a possible attack which he had heard that Malacreta was preparing against his recently published *Disputatio*. Beni was puzzled and annoyed by the news of this imminent attack: puzzled first that it should come from Vicenza, a town he had studiously praised in the *Disputatio* of 1600, and secondly that Malacreta had not made use of the arguments in favour of prose drama which Beni had propounded in the *Disputatio*. He was annoyed at the prospect—at his age (he was forty-seven) and with his experience—of having to involve himself in an Italian literary polemic, his first (little did he know it) of many (*Risp.* 126). However, the only way to ward off such an attack is to 'metter in difficoltà il nemico prima di venirne assalito' (*Risp.* 128), and this he proceeded to do, following Malacreta's text point by point.

He begins by stating that Malacreta was wrong to criticize the adjective *pastorale* in the title: for the scene and the language are thoroughly pastoral. He denies that shepherds have to restrict their interests to sheep and allows (following Theocritus, Virgil, and others) that they can also fall in love, cultivate knowledge of the stars, and so on (pp. 129–37). He maintains that *fido* and *pastor* go well together as long as *pastor* is taken to mean 'a pastoral lover' rather than 'a keeper of sheep' (p. 137). Beni then succinctly propounds a series of eleven doubts which he has entertained about the title, and which ought not to have escaped Malacreta's notice; but he does not develop any of these doubts (pp. 138–41).

[12] p. 125 in the Dedicatory Letter, dated 31 August 1600, to G. B. Bernardi, Podestà of Padua.

Unlike Malacreta, Beni finds Guarini's Arcadian scene in line
with that of Pausanias and Sannazaro, and argues that Guarini
did not capriciously invent it (pp. 141–5). Before listing his own
doubts about the scene, Beni refutes Malacreta's argument that
the prologue serves no purpose: it offers some idea of the place,
scenery, characters, and actions; it honours the couple at whose
marriage celebrations it was first performed; and it allows the
audience to settle into the play (pp. 147–56). Beni defends the
character of the river Alfeo (pp. 172–8 and 188). His doubts
about the scene and prologue are similar to Malacreta's: he too
finds it improbable that the river Alfeo should start out in Arcadia and arrive in Piedmont, ludicrous that an audience should
be led to believe that Arcadia could be transported to them, and
so on (pp. 189–95).

Next Beni turns to Malacreta's doubts about the *antefatto*. He
defends the lack of chastity in the early Arcadian priest,
Aminta, as verisimilar: for, since societies always move from
the imperfect to the perfect, so it is natural that Aminta's moral
sense should be elementary (pp. 201–8). He defends the irratio-
nality and apparent injustice of the divine punishments (offering incidentally an eloquent sermon on the weakness of human
vision in such matters), and he defends the use of the oracle in
the play, maintaining that it is quintessentially dramatic (in
that it gives rise to sudden changes of fortune) (pp. 211–19). He
finds Malacreta's pernickety dissection of the Arcadian law to
be inappropriate in criticism of a poem, and warns Malacreta
that he should prove not its injustice but its inverisimilitude
(pp. 237–58 and 261). And he denies that the *Pastor fido* has a
machina-engineered denouement (pp. 262–4). Beni's own doubts
about the *antefatto* are minor and little different in quality from
Malacreta's (pp. 272–4).

Such is his reply to the first part of Malacreta's work. He has
remained (he maintains) an impartial 'amator della verità' and
has answered Malacreta's sixty doubts, adding many more of
his own (p. 244). Already Beni had written more than Malacreta, and he was by now clearly working under considerable
pressure of time and disinclination. It is understandable, therefore, that he did not go on with his *Risposta*. He broke off, leaving the work unfinished (he had not discussed the qualitative
and quantitative parts), but threatening to take up his pen

once more and further expose Malacreta's incompetence should the latter audaciously attempt any criticism of Beni's latest work (pp. 276–7). Beni ends on a note of pugnacious intimidation and blackmail (pp. 277–8).

Beni's contribution here tells us more about him than about the *Pastor fido*. He betrays a fear of being shouted down by a young upstart and of cutting a poor figure in Padua. And, as if by accident and against his will, he enters the *Pastor fido* debate merely to ward off a possible attack. It is clear that Beni had no particular point of view in regard to Guarini and the *Pastor fido*. His lack of commitment about Guarini is balanced by his strong feelings about Malacreta. Throughout the present work, Beni's doubts are started but never fully run to ground: they are vaguely directed against Malacreta's critical incompetence rather than at Guarini's artistic (or other) success or failure. His reply is thus badly focused. His ideas (some of which are promising, others of which are to us now pedantically absurd and petty) remain embryonic. Beni does not properly address himself to the critical problem of the mixed genre, though he touches upon it; he does not develop the thesis that Italian verse forms were unsuitable in drama; and his valuable distinction between the poet and the historian appears in this work to have more theoretical than practical value. Indeed, some of his arguments are so out of step with the views he expressed elsewhere (especially in the *Disputatio* of 1600 and the commentary on the *Poetics*) that it has to be asked how far such arguments were concocted solely for the polemical purpose of putting down the young Malacreta. Beni's need to contradict his opponent forced him to express views on poetic matters which either are not properly thought out (and we should remember that this was his first work of practical literary criticism) or go against his own convictions and better judgement as expressed elsewhere.

IV

Beni's polemical tactics were evidently successful in restraining Malacreta's critical hand. But he was powerless to silence two further replies to the *Disputatio*, both published in 1601.

The first came from Lucio Scarano,[13] and is dated (at the end of the text) 25 August 1600 (p. 118). This indicates that it was composed within weeks of Beni's original *Disputatio*. Indeed, it is a poorly constructed and lengthy Latin dialogue which purports to have taken place in its publisher's house. There can be no doubt that it was conceived as a reply to Beni although no explicit reference is made in it either to Beni or to his work. Instead, one of the interlocutors (Limpius) adopts a diluted version of Beni's position, and insidiously paraphrases from the *Disputatio*. Thus, where Beni had written

Et sane quis verisimile illud iudicet, ut ganeo aut servus, stolidus fingatur interdum, ebrius, stultus, et tamen horas integras bonos elaboratosque versos subito et ex tempore fundat? (fo. 2ʳ).

Scarano writes:

Non enim verisimile videri potest, ebrium aliquem, aut mancipium, aut ganeonem, per diem integras horas, versus elaboratos ex tempore, tam apto sonantes effundere (p. 12).

Limpius is also equipped with Beni's argumentative manner, and it is pointed out to him (and to Beni indirectly) that the truth is most often simple and does not require to be hedged about by complicated arguments (pp. 11 and 67). Accordingly, Beni's arguments are not refuted by counter-arguments so much as by counter-statements, as well as by the puzzling fact that Limpius, having maintained Beni's views as far as page 99, suddenly agrees with the opposite view (viz. that drama should be written in verse).

Scarano's point of view is radically different from Beni's. Where Beni was interested in what was morally good for an audience irrespective of what it enjoyed, Scarano is interested in what is dramatically and theatrically pleasurable to an audience. Both are interested in what is possible on stage, but, for Beni, 'what is possible' tends to be 'what is morally good and therefore possible'. Thus, having adduced at length the authority of Aristotle and others to prove that verse and imi-

[13] *Lucii Scarani, philosophi medici academici veneti Scenophylax dialogus, in quo tragaediis, et comaediis antiquus carminum usus restituitur, recentiorum quorundam iniuria interceptus. Et de vi, ac natura carminis agitur* (Venice, 1601). Little is known about Scarano, but see Cinelli Calvoli, iv. 217, and C. M. Riccio, *Memorie storiche degli scrittori nati nel regno di Napoli* (Naples, 1844), 322.

tation are both essential to poetry (for how otherwise could history, rhetoric, and even Scarano's present work be distinguished from poetry—a point Beni will later face in the commentary on the *Poetics*), Scarano shows (against Beni) that it is both verisimilar and natural to write drama in verse (pp. 24–43, 85–93, and 99). On this point he provocatively asserts that verisimilitude and decorum are not threatened even when a modern character speaks in Virgilian Latin on stage (pp. 53–4). (This is a challenge which Beni will answer in a practical way, as we shall see.) And, for Scarano, there is no difference in verisimilitude between drama and the epic: if epic characters can speak in verse (because the poet is speaking deliberately through them) the same applies to characters in drama (whose speeches are prepared for them by the dramatist). This misses Beni's valid point that all dramatic representation is founded upon the illusion that the characters speak extempore.

This weakness in Scarano's case suggests that verisimilitude was not at the top of his list of priorities. It is mentioned merely because Beni had mentioned it. Scarano's case for the use of verse in drama is not based on the fact that verse is more verisimilar and useful, but, more significantly, on the fact that verse is more delightful (p. 63). He does, however, balance this by stating that the usefulness of drama lies in its being a mirror of life, full of useful examples (p. 72). But this idea appears only fleetingly and has no bearing on his overall view.

Scarano's work is not convincing and is often muddled. Yet it clearly had repercussions in Padua, for it was in many ways a defence of Paduan theatrical practice, which Beni had specifically criticized. This can be gauged from a note (dated 20 May 1601) in the 'Atti' of the Ricovrati, where Scarano's work is praised (Atti, fo. 51^v). And it is later recorded in the 'Atti' that Scarano was elected a member of the Ricovrati on 2 December of the same year (fo. 55^v).

V

Though there is no proof that Scarano read his work to the Ricovrati (though they were clearly aware of it), the second reply to Beni's *Disputatio* came firmly from one of that Academy's most venerable members, Faustino Summo, whom we have already encountered as a supporter of verse in drama. His reply to Beni[14] (dated 20 July 1601) is dedicated to the Accademici Olimpici of Vicenza. Once again, Beni had shown his curious ability to set people against him.

This is not to say that Summo's reply is vicious. It is friendly and honest; and is presented as a reply to a reply (for Summo felt that Beni had originally intended to criticize one of his *Discorsi*) (*Discorso in difesa del metro*, fo. 22^r). In the present work he does not name Beni, except on the title-page; and he clearly refers throughout to Beni's *Disputatio*, without naming it. He summarizes all Beni's arguments, in Italian, and much more faithfully than Scarano had done. And he replies to each one, using the same arguments as he had deployed in his earlier work (the *Discorsi poetici*). Throughout the present work he stresses that both verse and imitation are inseparable elements of poetry (fo. 22^r). But, though the premiss is the same as Scarano's, the method is more satisfactory, for it follows Beni's arguments more closely and produces in reply a coherent view of poetry.

Unlike Scarano, Summo does not take Beni's lead and pretend that poetry should be or appear natural. For him beautiful means 'strange', a quality metre has the power to confer: 'perchè quanto più s'allontana dal comun uso & dall'ordinario tanto ha più del pelegrino e diletta. Il che fa il verso, & non la prosa' (fos. 13^r). Beni's arguments about verisimilitude (and, by implication, moral benefit) are thus dismissed and replaced by an unashamedly hedonist concept of drama and poetry:

E qualhor dicono non esser verisimile, che genti vili, populari, & indotti, parlino con tanto artificio con quanto sono introdotte a parlare da poeti ne i lor poemi, dovemo rispondere che questa è licenza poetica, concessa alla lor arte a fin di dilettare, senza il qual diletto, di cui buona parte & principale è il metro, [. . .] non è poeta il poeta, come io stimo (fo. 13^v).

And such delight (argues Summo) comes, not from the plot (as Beni had said) but from various tricks of style and language:

---

[14] *Discorso in difesa del metro, op. cit.* (n. 7).

Il poeta ha per suo proprio fine il dilettare, che pende del mirabile, e 'l mirabile della dittion pellegrina, la quale consiste nella varietà delle lingue, nelle metaphore, nell'ornato, nell'allungare, nello abbreviare, nel trasporre & nel tramutare delle parole & delle sillabe (fo. 16^v; see also fos. 17^v–18^r).

It is true that Summo says that delight sharpens our attention and increases the usefulness of drama, but he makes so little of this idea (in comparison with Beni), and is so unspecific about the type of usefulness involved, that his point appears perfunctory (fo. 14$^{r–v}$).

It has been necessary to quote Summo at some length in order to compare him with Beni. Summo's aesthetic is clearly 'Baroque' (if that term can usefully be employed here) while Beni's appears stiffly sober. The debate, therefore, about verse in drama is useful as a prelude to Beni's commentary on the *Poetics*; and it has allowed us a glimpse of Beni's true relationship to the Baroque (which will assume some importance in our consideration of the commentary on the *Poetics*). In this present dispute Summo seems up to date in Padua while Beni seems behind the times. This is highlighted by Summo's criticism of Beni's use of Latin, and his justification of his own use of Italian: 'oltre che par più dover nostro la nostra [lingua] vivente e domestica essercitare & abbellire che la già meza morta & poco men che strana volere resucitare & arricchire' (fo. 3^r). Paradoxically, Beni is a Modern, but a Modern who wishes to go backwards rather than forwards; and, in Beni's case, it is backwards into the never-never land of proportion, common sense, and reason. It is always so with him.[15]

VI

Beni replied immediately and almost by reflex to these two critics in an unpublished treatise.[16] Though he grouped his two replies together, he felt differently about each of them. He had

[15] Another (brief) critical letter on Beni's *Disputatio* of 1600, written around this time, by Antonio Scaino, describes Beni's views on metre in drama as 'questa sua singolar opinione' (MA R. 102. Sup., fos. 358^r–59^v (fo. 358^r)). This is further evidence that Beni was out of step.

[16] ASVB 125: 'Apologetico del Beni agli eccellentissimi dottori Faustin Summo e Lucio Scarano'. Unfoliated.

(he says) never wished to quarrel with Summo; and here he does not reply in full; his reply is tame. But it is of great interest to us because it shows for the first time Beni's interest in the *questione della lingua*, and suggests that some of his ideas on the linguistic question were formed as early as 1601, or thereabouts.

In the first place, Beni agrees with Summo that these sorts of polemics are best written in Italian since 'da' nostri dispute tali vengon lette più volentieri nella nostra Italiana favella che nella Latina': for such disputes were read for pleasure and recreation (rather as, in modern times, the television debate, about whatever subject, frivolous or serious, has become a form of entertainment). Secondly, Beni argues that the use of Italian should not be extended to the exegesis of Aristotle 'tanto più che la Italiana favella [. . .] è assai povera, et a petto della greca può dirsi sterile et infeconda'. Hence his continued use of Latin in his scholarly publications. Finally, and most importantly in view of future developments, Beni tentatively criticizes Summo's command of Italian in terms which he will use about the *Crusca* and its authorities after 1612:

E certo Signor Summo altro ci vuole per abbellir'et arricchir la lingua, che cominciar per un Quantunque e seguir'alla [Padov *crossed out!*] Lombarda. Sì che lasciamo pur questo pretesto d'abbellir'et arricchir la lingua a i Tassi, a i Marini, et a qualch'altro tale, che a voi non conviene.

This linguistic consciousness is new in Beni's writings. Perhaps it is the result of his new position as professor of humanities, where he felt that language and style came under his department. The early occurrence of such criticism suggests that Beni's apparently sudden reaction to the *Crusca* was motivated, not solely by polemical belligerence, but also by deep and long-held convictions.

The second part of Beni's treatise is roughly ten times longer than the first, and attacks Scarano and his work from all possible (and some seemingly impossible) angles, thus removing the debate from its previously narrow arena. Scarano (whom Beni says he has never met) is castigated for his offences against Christianity, his ignorance of Latin, his inability to handle the dialogue form, as well as his failure to think clearly ('al presente

non è più tempo di chimerizzare o dar fieno a oche: conve-
nendo filosofar sul saldo e provar con ragioni le sue dottrine').
Finally, and this is the most distasteful of his criticisms (many
of the others are valid), Beni alleges that Scarano had
attempted to obtain the chair of humanities in Padua, and was
piqued by Beni's election. As usual with Beni, his idea of an
attack is that of an onslaught from all possible angles, whether
or not they are relevant to the question at issue. It is no doubt
fortunate, not least for Beni (whose venom eventually got the
better of him here), that his reply to Scarano was never published.

Taken together, Beni's *Disputatio* and the polemics which followed it can be seen as a training exercise for him: training in
the writing of polemical works (which will be of use in the
Crusca debate), training in the exposition of the *Poetics* (which
will lead to the great commentary), and training (albeit in a
small way) in the criticism of Italian language and style.

VII

As a postscript to the debate, I must mention an unpublished
drama (Beni later described it as 'simile a Poema Drammatico')
which was probably composed during his early years in the
Paduan chair: the 'Actio constantiana'.[17] This is a curiously
hybrid work: a modern Paduan finds himself mysteriously in the
Rome of Constantine the Great and of one of his sons, Caesar
Constans; and he is silently present at the latter's formal corona-
tion as Emperor of the West. The drama has five acts, with musi-
cal interludes at the opening and close of each. What is most
remarkable in the play is the attempt to render with verisimilitude the different speeches of the modern Paduan (Italian) and of
the Romans (dignified oratorical Latin), though never do both
types of speech occur in the same scene. This—it can hardly be
called successful—attempt to resolve the problem of verisimilitude in drama can be seen as an answer to Scarano's polemical
point that Virgilian Latin from the mouths of foreigners is
readily believed by theatrical audiences (*Scenophylax*, pp. 53–4).

---

[17] ASVB 118. There are three drafts, of which the second (as it appears in the
folder) is the most authoritative. None are foliated. I hope to do an edition of this.

The result is little more than a stolid exercise in stately *conciones*, and a plot whose drama is conceived entirely in terms of aurally and visually appealing happenings on stage, which Beni produces intermittently in the play in 'order to break the monotony of the Latin speeches. One of his (numerous) stage directions makes clear his conception:

Hor passando all'Atto Quarto, non è dubbio ch'ei converrà d'accrescere con alcuna bella novità, il diletto et applauso de' circostanti, massime per non tediarli con Latine Concioni. Dunque nel bel principio di quest'Atto, tosto che cessi la Musica e il madrigale, entreranno nella Curia Ambasciatori di Persia e di Media.[18]

The two aims of this work—to entertain (which in practice Beni had to follow) and to solve the problem of foreign speech in drama—do not cohere, and the result is decidedly but interestingly odd. The work was never performed; and music (which was to play a large part in the whole) was never written for it, as a MS note in Beni's hand indicates on the cover of one of the drafts. The interest of this work lies for us in its attempt to put into practice Beni's theoretical views. Clearly, he was not best equipped to practise what he preached, in this matter, as in others.

[18] Beni's stress on the delightfulness of the sights and sounds here seems to go against his own strictures (especially those in the commentary on the *Poetics*). See also his comment on his 'Actio constantiana' in ASVB 132: 'Denique is qui in hac Actione ea servaverit [. . .] sentiet fore ut huiusmodi spectaculum tum aures oculosque mirifice capiat, tum animos ac mentem delectet vehementer'.

6

A BACKWARD GLANCE TOWARDS ROME

It might be thought that, with his teaching and his duties in the Ricovrati, not to mention his polemical writings, Beni would have found himself sufficiently occupied in these first years in Padua. But all that was evidently not enough to expel Rome from his thoughts; and we find that, in two works, one minor and one major, he returned his attention to ecclesiastical Roman matters.

The first is a letter and a *discorso*, dated 9 February 1601, and addressed to the pope, on the flooding of the Tiber.[1] Since Beni had first written on the subject, someone (it is not known who) had proposed to wall up the river (fos. 2^r–3^r). Beni rejects this view and cogently repeats his earlier views in a clear effort to catch the pope's attention. Nothing seems to have come of this sequel, however; and the existence of this further document on the flooding of the Tiber merely serves to highlight the pope's refusal in the first place to acknowledge Beni's earlier work.

The other work in which Beni looks back to Rome was published at the very end of 1603: *Qua tandem dirimi possit controversia quae in praesens de efficaci Dei auxilio et libero arbitrio inter nonnullos Catholicos agitatur.*[2] As its title suggests, it is a highly specialized theological treatise which must have involved a good deal of labour and thought about one of the most complex of contemporary theological issues.

Controversy over the relationship between grace and free will has preoccupied the Catholic Church from the time of Augustine and Pelagius (early in the fifth century). But the fiercest and perhaps most important debate on the subject occurred towards

---

[1] There are two MS copies: (1) VA Vat.lat. 6557 (parte prima), fos. 1–6; (2) MA R. 102. Sup., fos. 432–7. They are identical except that (2) is longer by a few lines than (1).

[2] Padua, L. Pasquati, 1603. The *Imprimatur* was granted on 2 November 1603.

the close of the sixteenth century.[3] The Council of Trent had blandly affirmed the reality of both free will and grace but had not attempted to define their interaction. A quarter of a century later, in 1588, Luis de Molina (1535–1600), a Spanish Jesuit, sought to settle the question once and for all in a work entitled *Concordia liberi arbitrii cum gratiae donis, divina praescientia, providentia, praedestinatione, et reprobatione, ad nonnullos primae partis D. Thomae articulos.*[4]

Molina's theology was opposed to the pessimism of the Protestants, who had denied the existence of free will. Molina taught that sufficient grace, which God gives freely to all men, only becomes efficacious by the free consent of man; and that the act of Justification is the result of simultaneous co-operation between God and man. Efficacious and sufficient graces are not therefore intrinsically or ontologically different from each other, but depend for their complexion on free human consent or dissent. Such human freedom of choice does not, however, impinge on God's infallible ability to predetermine events. For, although man is free to decide this way or that, God (according to Molina's theory) has foreknowledge of hypothetical future contingents, of things as they would be if certain conditions were realized. By this knowledge (*scientia media*) of *futurabilia* God can see in advance which graces will be sufficient and which efficacious, and can secure the arrival in heaven of the elect and the damnation of the reprobate without prejudice to free will. The Achilles' heel of such a theory is that it implies that God can predetermine man's fate; but pure Molinism avoids this by stressing that God has foreknowledge of each man's future merits from eternity (*praedestinatio ad gloriam post praevisa merita*) and merely complies with the fulfilment of each individual's fate. A later development of Molinist theology

---

[3] For the theological background I have relied on the following works, from which further bibliographical information may be obtained: P. Parente, 'Grazia', in *Enciclopedia cattolica*, 1019–28; M. Flick, 'Congruismo', ibid., iv. 355–7; C. Baisi, 'Congregatio de Auxiliis divinae gratiae', ibid., iv. 339–40; id., 'Molinismo', ibid., viii. 1223–4; L. Bournet, 'Auxiliis (Congrégation de)', in *Dictionnaire d'histoire et de géographie ecclésiastiques*, ed. by A. Baudrillart, A. de Meyer and Ét. Cauwenbergh (1912–), v (1931), 960–70; G. H. Joyce, SJ, *The Catholic Doctrine of Grace*, 2nd edn. (London, 1930); N. P. Williams, *The Grace of God* (London, 1930).

[4] Lisbon, 1588.

(often called Congruism and principally represented by the Jesuit, Francisco de Suarez (1548–1617)) stressed that God can choose man's fate, and so engineer matters that the requisite number of merits are obtained for the salvation of any individual (*praedestinatio ad gloriam ante praevisa merita*). In this doctrine—which was imposed on all the Jesuit schools in 1613 by the General of the Order, Claudio Aquaviva—it is difficult to see how the problem of determinism is avoided. It is this later development which Beni seems most to resent in his work.

Instead of providing definitive 'and universally acceptable answers to age-old questions, Molina's work brought to a head the controversy, which had begun in Spain in 1582, between the Jesuits and the Dominicans over the relative status of grace and free will. On the publication of Molina's work the Dominicans revolted; and Molina's theology was fiercely controverted by the Dominican, Domingo Bañez (1528–1604), an indefatigable and scholarly exponent of Thomist doctrine. Bañez thought that Molinism, with its stress upon free will, smacked of heresy. He argued, with close reference to Aquinas, that man is completely dependent on God and that God exercises a physical predeterminism over man's fate: his efficacious grace works infallibly and cannot be rejected.

The debate grew so hot that in 1596 Clement VIII decided to set up a Special Congregation in Rome to hear the arguments on both sides in the attempt to decide whether the Molinist doctrine was heretical. From November 1597 to November 1598 a secret commission examined Molina's work on eleven occasions and finally censured sixty-one propositions. The pope then set up a Congregation of Cardinals who sat from 1599 to 1600, but failed to reach any conclusion. In 1600 a fresh Congregation was nominated: after twenty sittings it censured twenty-one propositions on 12 October 1600. (Molina died in Madrid on the same day.) Subsequently, sixty-nine further meetings were held, most of them very long and arduous (they sat for nine hours on 6 August 1602 for instance), up to the time of Clement VIII's death on 3 March 1605. Leo XI reigned briefly (1–27 April 1605) and was followed by Paul V who was reluctant to condemn either side. Under him the Congregation sat until 1607 but ended inconclusively; the pope postponed a formal

condemnation *sine die*, and later declared that Thomism and
Molinism were equally legitimate interpretations.

Beni's *Qua tandem* . . . occupied a central chronological position in the controversy *de auxiliis*. His presence in Rome from
late 1593 to early 1600, and his close relationship with Clement
VIII (who then favoured him), must have allowed Beni to fami-
liarize himself with the arguments and personalities in the
debate. He was able, therefore, to follow the controversy at its
height; and he no doubt developed many of his views, and did
most of his research on the subject, during his Roman period. It
is possible that he did not dare to publish his ideas until he was
safely in Padua out of the theological mêlée. But it is also possible that he did not feel the publication of his work to be necessary until the controversy had reached a bitter and apparently
insoluble impasse, as it evidently had by 1603. This latter possibility is strengthened by the presence in the Archivio Segreto
Vaticano[5] of an early draft of the work, dated specifically 1603,
and with the more provocative title of 'Qua tandem dirimi ac tuto
definiri possit controversia, quae de efficaci Dei auxilio inter religiosas Dominicanorum Jesuitarumque familias agitatur'.

As this title suggests, Beni's work was intended to settle defi-
nitively the question of the relationship between grace and free
will; and it was offered to Clement VIII as a full-scale solution to
the problem. Beni finds that he cannot agree with either the
Jesuits or the Dominicans. With the best will in the world (he
writes) he has tried to patch up an agreement between the two
Orders, but all to no avail (pp. 258–9).

He begins characteristically by shaking the foundations upon
which the whole controversy was built on both sides. All con-
tenders subscribe to the scholastic division of grace into sufficient and efficacious: sufficient grace is never successful, for
man neither consents to it nor is ever saved by it and it is
offered at an unpropitious moment; efficacious grace, on the
other hand, works infallibly and is offered at a propitious
moment.[6] Such a division—which Beni sees as a relatively
recent scholastic invention—undermines Scriptural, patristic,

---

[5] Archivio Beni, 117.
[6] This distinction, which is as Beni describes it, is summarized by Joyce,
pp. 138–9: 'Actual graces are distinguished by theologians into *Efficacious* and

and Tridentine teaching about grace and free will. For, if efficacious grace works infallibly, then human freedom is denied
and the heresies of Luther and Calvin are committed (pp. 11
and 22). Conversely, if sufficient grace is never actually 'sufficient' to save (pp. 48–9) and is offered at an inopportune
moment (pp. 28–9), then divine grace is denied and unjust
cruelty is imputed to a traditionally merciful and benign God
(pp. 30–2, 39–40, 60, 167–71, etc.).

Beni finds no support for such a distinction of grace into efficacious and sufficient in the Bible, the Church Fathers, Ecclesiastical Councils, or experience. He searches these sources
thoroughly and weighs up all the evidence, firmly rejecting it
and constantly repeating that the Scriptures should not be read
too literally (see, for example, pp. 133–4).

Instead of grace which is divided into sufficient and efficacious, Beni culls from all the authorities the following concept
of grace which can be briefly summarized. First, though grace is
one (p. 329), it comes in three stages (p. 298). In the first stage
gratia excitans (sometimes called *praeveniens* or *operans*) is
offered to all men at birth (pp. 147 and 153). There is nothing
man can do to prepare for this and Beni, arguing against the
Jesuit, Suarez, whom he accuses of semi-Pelagianism, stresses
that God continually calls and recalls sinners to him (pp. 299
and 304). In the second, and later, stage *gratia adiuvans* (sometimes called *subsequens* or *cooperans*) is offered to the man who
has freely accepted *gratia excitans* and who has disposed himself
by faith to receive this second instalment, without which it is
impossible to be saved (pp. 153 and 262–4). In the third stage, to
which Beni does not pay much attention, *gratia perseverantiae* is
offered as a final push along the road to salvation (pp. 143–6 and
290–1). Secondly, grace in Beni's view is by nature indifferent

---

Sufficient graces. By a sufficient grace is meant a grace which confers on the recipi-
ent the capacity to form a particular good action, but which nevertheless remains
without effect, because he refuses to avail himself of it. An efficacious grace, on
the other hand, is a grace which not merely gives the capacity, but which through
the consent of the will, effects the good act in view of which God bestowed it. [...]
It will be noticed that efficacious graces have a right to be called "sufficient": for
were they not sufficient they could not achieve their result. But custom has fixed
the sense of the words: and by a sufficient grace we always mean one which *de
facto* is not efficacious'. Beni attempted to break such a custom.

(p. 17). Different qualities, or strengths, of it are not offered by God to different men, but all men are offered one and the same grace. What makes that grace efficacious in some and not in others is governed, not by God, but by man's rejection or acceptance of it (pp. 35 and 117–19). Man and man alone can affect his reception of grace according to the obstacles—or sins—he puts in its way:

Ut enim qui angustam fenestram aut amplam aperit, minorem maior-emve luminis vim et copiam aperiendo suscipit: lumen aut illumina-tionem non efficit: sic qui magis minusve per voluntatis concursum conatumve cooperatur, nec gratiam nec iustificationem efficere dicen-dus est, sed ad eam plus minusve recipiendam se disponere et compar-are (p. 265).

And Beni supports this view by reference to the Biblical 'Perdi-tio tua ex te: ex me autem tantummodo salus' which the Council of Trent had also quoted (p. 118). Thirdly, grace is always offered at a ripe time to all men (p. 40). There is no evidence that God picks and chooses amongst men: he is above all else fair (p. 61). In the fourth place, grace is free: it is not based (at first, at any rate) on merit (pp. 262 and 307 ff.) and is described in Augustinian terms as God's debt to mankind (p. 297). Finally, man is at liberty either to refuse or to accept grace but, at the same time, he is obliged freely to assent to it if he is to be saved: there is no such thing as passive salvation (pp. 91 and 226).

Such a view allows both grace and free will their full value in the act of Justification and neatly avoids both the Pelagian (free will overstressed) and the Calvinistic (free will denied) heresies (pp. 261–2). But Beni finds it necessary in the midst of the subtle controversy *de auxiliis* to go further in defining the precise rela-tionship between grace and free will, especially in terms of pre-destination. For it was no longer possible to uphold the validity of both quantities (grace and free will), as the Council of Trent had done, without being specific about their interaction in the act of Justification. Both grace and free will are necessary; but free will is only (in Beni's view) a *conditio sine qua non* while grace is the ultimate cause of salvation (pp. 35, 65, and 383). Man's free will is God-given; and man is always dependent on him, powerless without him (p. 167 and 225). At the same time

man is a free agent, not a passive puppet in the hand of God.[7]
Divine grace does not impinge on human freedom for it does
not determine human will to a specific end, but generally dis-
poses it to salvation; makes it generally receptive, but not
receptive to any one particular thing (pp. 185–6). God fore-
knows events but he does not predetermine them (pp. 190–1,
456 and *passim*), just as Christ knew what Judas was to do but
was powerless to alter it: for his knowledge was not the cause of
it (pp. 458–9). Beni therefore rejects the Molinist theory of God's
scientia media by which he is said to foreknow what would
happen if certain circumstances were fulfilled, and by which he
can choose this or that sinner or saint according to future con-
ditional circumstances. Beni argues that God has no need of
such knowledge, for he knows from the beginning of time what
so and so will do (pp. 68–9). God first sees what will happen
and then he determines that it should happen 'quia Deus ante-
quam eos vocaret, explorasset num illi electuri an recusaturi
essent Christum ipsum sequi' (p. 69: see also pp. 130–1, 142,
464–5, etc.). God foresees who will accept and who will reject
his gift of grace, but he never predetermines man's will before
he has obtained such foreknowledge (*ante praevisa merita*)
(pp. 135–6).

God is said therefore not to determine man's reaction to *gratia
adiuvans*, but to co-determine it (pp. 241–2). There is no priority
on either man's or God's part in the final act of Justification: the
two agents work together simultaneously (pp. 268–9 and
349–75), and the help that man receives from God is likened to
the help a patient, willing to be cured but too weak to take the
cure, might receive from his doctor (p. 268).

The foregoing sketch of the message of Beni's long work does
not convey the thoroughness and complexity of his treatment of
the subject. All the current arguments (very seldom related to
particular personalities in the debate) are painstakingly
reviewed and destroyed, often several times over during the
course of the poorly organized work. Beni's manner is generally
intolerant of any dissension from Tridentine doctrine (to which
he looks back as to a golden age in theology); but he is rarely

---

[7] pp. 206–7. It is interesting to see here how Beni introduces as authorities
Aristotle and Plato, and likens the Plato of the *Timaeus* to Moses.

inept or fatuous in his intolerance. His solutions are not presented as highly personal ones: they appear traditional and orthodox, though they tend more in the direction of the (Molinist) Jesuit side than the Dominican; and the differences of opinion between Beni and Molina are possibly more apparent than real (though Beni is clearly opposed to later Jesuit developments of Molinism).

Beni sets himself up as an arbiter, confident that he can offer Clement VIII the right answers to the thorny question of grace and free will, just as he had been confident in 1597 that he knew how (and why) the pope should act in the recapture of Ferrara, and how he should avoid future flooding of the Tiber after 1598. In these works Beni shows his belief, not only that there is a (rational) solution to every problem, but also that he is privy to such a solution and that it is his duty to broadcast it. His confidence, even arrogance, about the answers to the burning theological issues of his day (upon which three successive popes and their cardinals could not bring themselves to decide) was enough in itself to make Beni's forthright work—his first and last foray into theological controversy, written by an ex-Jesuit safely installed in Padua—difficult to receive and accept in Rome. And his attempt (logical and convincing as it is) to deny the fundamental and universally accepted distinction between sufficient and efficacious graces must have seemed to the popes and their cardinals unhelpful, inconvenient, and perhaps too radical. Beni's work does not seem to have had any impact on the controversy *de auxiliis*, and was finally placed on the Index on 16 December 1605.[8] On 15 May 1604 Clement VIII (Beni's onetime ally and saviour) had ordered the immediate confiscation of all copies of the work and had summoned Beni to Rome and severely reprimanded him (VA Vat.lat. 8225, parte seconda, fos. 318^v and 319^r).

It is difficult to tell now exactly why the work was banned. The Inquisitional documents—which Spampanato has studied[9]—suggest that the cardinals did not want to aggravate further the debate which had badly split the Jesuits and the

[8] *Raccolta de libri prohibiti* (Milan, 1624).

[9] V. Spampanato, *Sulla soglia del Seicento* (Milan–Rome–Naples, 1926), pp. 197–8. An earlier version of Spampanato's work is to be found in *Giornale critico della filosofia italiana*, 5 (1924), 118–21. I have used the later version.

Dominicans since 1582. Furthermore, it seems that Beni published more than was originally submitted to the Inquisition,
and other portions which were submitted and duly corrected
were subsequently published without the agreed corrections
(Spampanato, p. 198). It is also possible that Beni's work was
put on the Index because it failed to please Pope Leo XI (who,
though he reigned only in April 1605, still may have resented
the attack upon the Dominican Order, to which he had
belonged) and Pope Paul V (who was open in his tolerance of
both sides, who did everything possible to quell the controversy, and who would not have welcomed Beni's attempt to
undermine the whole basis of the previous debate).

Whatever the truth of this, the work brought no immediate
reward to its author. It ended for good his relationship with
Clement VIII which had already been weakened in 1599. But it
also earned him the nickname of *Quatandem*, which was still
remembered on 24 January 1614, when the Arciconsolo della
Crusca wrote a letter against Beni's *Cavalcanti* to Curzio
Picchena in Florence.[10] Finally, since the publisher of Beni's
Qua tandem . . . was the Paduan Lorenzo Pasquati and not the
official Ricovrati publisher (Bolzetta, who had already published theological works by Panigarola), it is fair to ask whether
Beni had not perhaps somehow incurred also the wrath over
this work of his Ricovrati colleagues.

[10] VA Urb.lat. 1206, fos. 22^r–24^v (fo. 22^v). This is a copy. The original was published in the appendix to [D. Moreni], *Illustrazione storico-critica di una rarissima
medaglia rappresentante Bindo Altoviti opera di Michelangelo Buonarroti* (Florence,
1824), pp. 149–73 (with copious notes, of a very biased pro-Florentine kind).
The reference to Beni's nickname is on pp. 155–6.

Part Two

THE YEARS OF FULFILMENT

7

SECURITY

I

The discomfort Beni experienced over his theological treatise must have determined him to turn his back once and for all on Rome, and to dedicate himself wholeheartedly to his work in Padua (the theory and practice of the *studia humanitatis*) with which the remainder of his life's activity was concerned. Although most of his work was the result of his teaching in Padua, it is desirable and possible to separate Beni's biography and his written work throughout the rest of this study. He was now settled in Padua: place and chronology were no longer as important as they had been in his earlier works. With amazing energy he composed a large number of works over the next twenty years or so. These often overlap in subject-matter; they were not necessarily published as soon as they were written, indeed they were published amid tangles of other publications (notably in two groups: 1612–16 and 1622–5). To treat these texts (and others) chronologically (even if we chose only the major ones) would give a false impression of Beni's activities and of the ideas and issues involved in these works. Furthermore, since what remains to be considered are Beni's major works, it is appropriate that they should receive here a broader treatment than would be possible or comfortable in a chronological survey. Before examining these works (in Part Three), I shall first complete the narrative of his life in the next three chapters. In these I shall mention his writings and publications only in so far as they affected him personally.

II

In 1604 Beni was working on criticism of the epic. On 8 April, as we have seen, Simone Stamini read a paper composed by Beni on Tasso, Homer, and Virgil to the Accademia dei Ricovrati

(Atti, fos. 92^v–93^r). This was to form the nucleus of his *Comparatione* (1607 and 1612), in which the 'academic' framework is retained, two *discorsi* (in the second edition) being assigned to five different speakers, including Nomista (an anagram of Simone Stamini), who delivered the first two *discorsi*.[1] Also linked to this work was Beni's teaching at the Studio. For, as he says in a letter to Francesco Bartholino, dated 20 December 1604, he had been persuaded to lecture on the *Aeneid*, and to compare it with Homer's works (see 'Epistolae et praefationes' in *OQS* 37–9). All this work formed the basis also for the commentary on the *Goffredo* and for the Latin Commentary on the first six books of the *Aeneid* (which was not published until 1622).

It is as if now, after his recent failure in his work for the pope, Beni threw himself unreservedly into Paduan commitments. In addition to giving formal lectures, he offered at this time to do private readings of the Greek authors at home in the afternoon with his pupils (*OQS* 69). His teaching programme was so heavy that he complained that it left him no time for writing (see 'Epistolae et praefationes' in *OQS* 10). Some of this pressure was relieved by the appointment in 1606 of the Venetian Vincenzo Contarini as his second in command in the Studio (Tomasini, *Gymnasium patavinum*, p. 344). Beni was no doubt pleased to have Contarini, who, writing on 17 November of the same year to Paolo Gualdo in Rome, said he had been persuaded to remain in Padua 'colla concorrenza dell'Eccellentissimo Beni'.[2] According to some authorities, however, Contarini proved to be a far more popular lecturer than Beni, and would steal the latter's audience (see, for example, Papadopoli, i. 350–1). Other authorities, on the contrary, have noted Beni's success and popularity as a lecturer (notably Crasso and Renazzi).[3] Whatever the truth of these two polarized views, it is fair to conjecture—from the evidence of his publications—that Beni's lectures were almost unrelievedly serious, prolix (how long they must have been!), and tortuous, overloaded as they were with chop-logic and hypothetical doubts. The Latin prose

---

[1] For further details, see above, pp. 9–13 and 64.

[2] *Lettere d'uomini illustri, che fiorirono nel principio del secolo decimosettimo, non più stampate* (Venice, 1744), 476.

[3] Crasso, ii. 80; F. M. Renazzi, *Storia dell'Università degli studi di Roma*, 4 vols. (Rome, 1803–6), iii (1805), 35.

of Beni's lectures (as we see it in his publications) was primarily functional: and its function was to convey as much information as possible in as plain a style as possible. There was no relief; there was little colour; there was only a dogged search after truth (and often truth of a petty kind). Add to this Beni's high regard for thoroughness, his dour and austere appearance ('in vita fu quasi sempre sano per essere molto sobrio e regolato nel vivere sebene fu oltre modo magro e macilente' (ASGA II. E. 9, Sect. 1. 45; see also Tomasini, *Illustrium virorum elogia*, p. 350)), and finally his proselytizing attitude in his lectures, and you have a worthy but forbidding concoction.

Yet he seems to have been happy in Padua. Giacomo, who by this time was Podestà of Urbino, wrote urging him to return to his *patria* and to the service of the Duke of Urbino. Beni replied on 3 August 1607, saying that he felt secure in Padua and did not wish to return to Gubbio, the more so since 'chi si trova dopo lunghe tempeste giunto, Dio gratia, in salvo, anzi [. . .] in porto sicurissimo e tranquillo, non de' agevolmente tornar'a solcar l'onde, massime con picciolo e mal provisto legno' (ASVB 36). He stresses that he is well paid ('mi trovo intorno a mille ducati d'entrata'), honoured, and healthy in Padua. There is a cold stubbornness in this letter. What deeply motivated Beni here was the financial inequality between him and Giacomo. For Giulio, another of the brothers, died around this time (1607) (ASGA II. D. 31), and, being unmarried, left all his possessions to Giacomo and the three sons of the by now deceased Federico (as we learn in some detail from Paolo's will of 1621). Paolo was thus again left out. Predictably, he complained; and he managed to alter the previous agreement (whereby the three brothers, or their heirs, had given him annually a third each of fifty *scudi*) so that now Giacomo agreed to pay him one half, and the three sons of Federico agreed to make up the other half, of the fifty annual *scudi*) (see his will of 1621 (ASGA II. D. 27, fo. 4ᵛ)). Despite this new agreement, Giacomo did not honour his payments, and so his relationship with Paolo could not improve. In recalling Paolo to his native Gubbio perhaps Giacomo hoped for a reconciliation; but in reply Paolo only emphasized his security in Padua, with a confidence which will turn out to be far from justified.

Also in 1607 the first edition of the *Comparatione* appeared.

With its seven *discorsi*, it shows signs of arbitrary and haphazard termination: the seventh *discorso* breaks off in the middle
of a comparison of Homer with Ariosto. Beni was too eager to
publish this work. Again, too, he employed Lorenzo Pasquati
rather than the official Ricovrati publisher, Bolzetta. This suggests that there was still a rift between Beni and the Academy
(especially since the first *discorso* of the *Comparatione* had originally been read to the Ricovrati). Beni also began a Latin version of the *Comparatione*, but completed only two *disputationes*
of it before deciding that it was best to finish and publish in full
the Italian version.[4]

He had hoped to complete the *Comparatione* for a second
edition during the Christmas vacation of 1609–10, but he fell
ill in December with a mysterious leg pain and had to stay in
bed for fifty days.[5] This led him to abandon the *Comparatione*
for a time and to begin work, for the first time, on the theory
of history. The result was the *De historia libri quatuor*, published as early as 1611.[6] By this time he also had almost ready
for publication, in some form or other, his commentaries on
the *Poetics* and on the *Rhetoric*, and he intended to publish
these after Easter 1610 (see *Lettere . . . a . . . Bonciario*, p. 13).
Yet the first was not published until 1613, and the second not
until 1624–5.

By 1611 Beni was evidently completely at home in Padua: his
reputation was steadily increasing; and he had several learned
publications ready to appear and increase his fame and fortune.
So at home did he feel in Padua that he made plans to end his
days there, and, together with some others, he founded a
sepulchre in the Paduan church of St Clare (no longer standing),
with the following inscription: 'Pauli Benii/Eugubini/Et Exter-
orum Patavini/Gimnasii Doctorum/Quos iuverit hoc saxo/
Condi/Annos Salutis/MDC XI' (quoted by Crasso, ii. 81). At the
same time he began to make modest financial investments
(*livelli*) of varying amounts of money (from 100 to 1,200 *ducati*:

---

[4] The Latin version is listed and commented on by Beni in ASVB 132 and is to
be found, in a finished state, in ASVB 119. There is also an earlier draft of the
Latin *Comparatio* in ASVB 120.

[5] Letter to M. A. Bonciario, dated 19 February 1610, printed in *Lettere di
uomini illustri scritte a M. Antonio Bonciario perugino* (Venice, 1839), pp. 11–14
(p. 11). See, for a full and useful account of Bonciario, Mazzuchelli, ii/3. 1571–7.

[6] For a fuller discussion of this treatise, see below, Chapter 14.

his annual income was 1,000 *ducati*) at $5\frac{1}{2}$ per cent interest. The first of these investments was made on 31 January 1612, and five more were made before 1 October 1621, the date of the will from which this information derives (ASGA II. D. 27, fos. 5^v–6^v).

8

THE CRUSCA INTERLUDE

Just when security and success were, for the first time in his life, as assured as they could be, all his plans were shattered in 1612 by his decision to criticize (albeit obliquely, as we shall see) the *Vocabolario degli Accademici della Crusca*, published early in 1612. The first part of Beni's *Anticrusca* was dedicated to Vicentio Grimani on 28 October 1612, and published in what must have been a small edition (few copies now survive).[1] The *Anticrusca* was the first of a series of (mainly) Italian works which were composed by Beni and printed in his house (*nella Beniana*). His interest in printing, however, went beyond the desire to get his own works published, very strong though that was; for he composed at some point during his Paduan years his 'Modo di riformare e ridurre a perfettion l'arte della stampa' which remains unpublished.[2]

According to the *Cavalcanti* (p. 154), the first part of the *Anticrusca* was written in ten days, and was not considered by Beni to be as important as his Latin commentaries. Later historians and critics have perhaps exaggerated the importance Beni attached to his campaign against the *Crusca*, and have allowed it to overshadow much of his other work. For instance, Maylender has written that Beni founded in his house in 1612 the Accademia dell'Anticrusca (see Maylender, ii. 138). But there is no evidence for this, and it wrongly assumes that the *Anticrusca* became Beni's whole life at this time. That this was not the case is proved by the fact that, a few weeks after writing the dedication for the *Anticrusca*, on 26 November, Beni wrote the dedication for the second edition of the *Comparatione*, consisting now of ten *discorsi*. Between 28 October 1612 (dedi-

---

[1] *L'Anticrusca: overo il paragone dell'italiana lingua* (Padua, 1612). The 2nd edn. (1613) is identical to the 1st (hereafter *AI*).

[2] ASVB 130. There are two versions. Beni intended to publish this with his 'Modo di riformare lo Studio di Padova' (to which I have already referred) as one work in the *Opera omnia*. See BB 243 for his publication plans.

cation of *Anticrusca*) and 15 July 1613 (dedication of *Poetics* commentary) Beni's almost completed commentary on the *Goffredo* was stolen from his study (*G.* 395; see also Dedicatory Letter in *P.*). This involved him in a good deal of feverish work: for he was impatient to rewrite and publish the commentary as soon as possible in case a piratical edition should appear. Hence the decision to publish in 1616 the commentary of only the first ten cantos of the *Liberata*. He did, as we shall see, go on after that to complete the commentary, but this has not yet come to light, and is presumed lost.[3] But while he hastened to finish the commentary, he became more and more deeply involved in the anti-Cruscan campaign.

In 1613 (during which year the *Anticrusca* was so in demand that it ran into a second edition) various dissenting voices rose up against Beni. Typical was the prefatory letter to a new edition of Ongaro's *Alceo*, dated 4 March 1613, in which Arsiccio, Accademico Ricreduto (Ottavio Magnanini (1574–1652)), strongly refutes Beni's thesis, and points out that the fourteenth-century authors who so disgust him are those he has read and assimilated into his own language.[4] More wounding was Orlando Pescetti's *Risposta all'Anticrusca*, dedicated to Cosimo II, Grand Duke of Tuscany, on 25 May 1613. According to Beni's unpublished 'Difesa del Cavalcanti' (written before 24 January 1614),[5] Beni had not intended to respond to Pescetti, but was provoked into reply by a number of books and pamphlets against him which were distributed clandestinely throughout Paduan bookshops, and elsewhere, and even sent anonymously to Beni himself,

sì come apparisce etiandio nel Santo Uffitio di Padova dove detti libelli famosi, di ordine degl'Illustrissimi Rettori sono stati levati dalle librarie, e dalla cella d'un frate Heremitano Fiorentino, il qual le dava sottomano a' librai, e sottocoperta li mandava in varie Città ('Difesa del Cavalcanti', fo. 26ᵛ).

---

[3] Beni gives the full title of the finished commentary in BB 243. For the history of its completion and projected publication, see below, pp. 113–17.

[4] A. Ongaro, *L'Alceo: favola pescatoria* (Ferrara, 1614), 'L'Arsiccio a' Lettori', fos. 6ᵛ–8ᵛ (fo. 8ʳ⁻ᵛ on Beni and his views).

[5] A copy of this brief anonymous document, which is almost certainly Beni's work, is to be found in VA Urb.lat. 1026, fos. 26ʳ–27ᵛ. I quote in what follows from this copy, not having found the original.

Only two of these pamphlets have been found. Both were the work of the Florentine Alessandro Allegri (1560–1629), about whom very little is known.[6] His *Fantastica visione di Parri da Pozzolatico, poderaio moderno in Piandigiullari*[7] is a mock-rustic *canzone* in which the Florentine peasant Parri narrates how he went to sleep on a haystack, and was visited by a piteous woman (Florence), who swoons in misery and confides to him the cause of her distress (Beni's *Anticrusca*):

> [. . .] va intorno un quadernuccio
> Che lacera il Boccaccio,
> Pugne Dante il Petrarca, e gli altri affligge
> Padri di mia favella.

The second of Allegri's pamphlets is the highly ridiculous and linguistically affected *Lettere di Ser Poi pedante nella corte de Donati a M. Pietro Bembo, M. Giovanni Boccacii* [sic], *& M. Francesco Petrarca*.[8] In this, as in the *Fantastica visione*, Beni (never so named) is clearly the target of ridicule; but there is nothing personally offensive, except the obvious fact that Beni's serious and earnest work is treated with mock-levity and burlesque by one who was in many ways a literary descendant of Francesco Berni.

While intrigue of this sort was threatening Beni's reputation, he tried to continue with his scholarly work. The commentary on the *Poetics* was published in 1613, and, in the Dedicatory Letter, he explains (amongst other things) that he has already completed his commentary on the first six books of the *Aeneid*, his commentary on the *Rhetoric*, and a volume of fifty orations. The *Orationes quinquaginta* were published shortly afterwards in Padua, but the other two works, no doubt delayed by the increased intensity of the *Crusca* polemics, were not published until the 1620s.

---

[6] See the article on him by A. Asor-Rosa in the *Dizionario biografico degli Italiani*, ii (1960), 477–8, where the works which I discuss are listed but not, unfortunately, related to their linguistic context (Beni and his criticism of the *Crusca* dictionary).

[7] Lucca, 1613, no printer or publisher mentioned. Reprinted, with some slight modifications, in *Saggio di rime di diversi buoni autori che fiorirono dal XIV fino al XVIII secolo* (Florence, 1825), 209–15. Beni himself alluded to the *Fantastica visione* in *Cav.* 116–17.

[8] Bologna, 1613.

There is no evidence that Beni actually enjoyed this unhappy polemic. But once he had entered the fray, with the *Anticrusca*, he was forced, by personality as well as polemical convention, to go on. He reveals his poor health and depressive personality, surely aggravated by recent developments, in a letter, dated 30 July 1613, to Giovanni Battista Fazi:[9]

Io [. . .] me la passo con sanità mediocre, spendendo il tempo in queste mie cosette, convenendomi ballare poichè mi trovo in ballo: ma certo mi trovo stanco e pien di nausea (fo. 53ʳ).

He was probably working at this time on the *Cavalcanti*, a reply, ostensibly from Bartolomeo Cavalcanti, to Pescetti, of which the dedication and the colophon are dated 1 December 1613. It was Beni's unrealistic intention in his (linguistically) anti-Florentine campaign to dedicate the *Cavalcanti* (ostensibly the work of a Florentine) to the Grand Duke of Tuscany, and thereby gain official Florentine support for his views. Predictably his intentions fell flat, and the Duke rejected the dedication and prohibited the book's publication. At first, as we have seen, Beni replied with his anonymous 'Difesa del Cavalcanti', before 24 January 1614; and, in turn, the Arciconsolo and the Accademici della Crusca replied on 24 January.[10] They completely divorce themselves in their reply from Pescetti's work (Beni had accused them of complicity in it), and they plead ignorance of all the pamphlets against Beni. For their part, they did not consider the *Anticrusca* worthy of a Florentine reply (fo. 22ʳ). They maintain, however, that his case against the Academy and against Salviati in the *Cavalcanti* (not yet published of course) was invalid, and that the choice of Bartolomeo Cavalcanti as a 'dispregiator della propria lingua, e de' più illustri scrittori della sua Patria' was scandalously inappropriate and mistaken (fo. 24ʳ⁻ᵛ).

[9] Pesaro, Biblioteca Oliveriana (hereafter PO), MS 429, Fasc. xiv, fos. 53ʳ–56ᵛ. Fazi was at this time Residente in Venice for the Duke of Urbino. There are MS notes on his life and work in PO 384, Fasc. xxi, fo. 61ʳ.

[10] VA Urb.lat. 1026, fos. 22ʳ–24ᵛ (a copy). It is addressed to Curzio Picchena (c.1550–1629), who became one of the Grand Duke's most trusted and able ministers. Picchena protected Galileo in Florence, and corresponded with Justus Lipsius who, in his own publications made use of Picchena's notes on Tacitus (which were published in three editions: 1603, 1607, and 1609). See on Picchena, *Nouvelle biographie générale*, xl (1862), column 56.

But Beni's pleading cut no ice in Florence. The *Cavalcanti* remained (understandably) unacceptable to the Grand Duke. Towards the end of October 1614 Beni went to Venice to plead yet more. With him he took his good friend Ottavio Livello, who taught law (useful qualification for a friend of Beni) at the Studio from 1596 to some time after 1623, was a member of the Ricovrati (Atti, fos. 2^r, 35^r, 50^v, 59^r, and 74^r), and a Commissario and beneficiary in Beni's will (ASGA ii. d. 27, fo. 8^v).[11] At the time of Beni's trip (31 October 1614) Lorenzo Pignoria in Padua wrote of it to Paolo Gualdo in Rome: 'Il Beni è andato a Venezia col Signor Livello (soccorso di Pisa, diranno gli Accademici della Crusca) per vedere quid juris dopo 'l quid facti del suo libro' (*Lettere d'uomini illustri* (1744), p. 166). By 5 November Beni had returned from his trip to Venice, and on that day he wrote to Nicolò Contarini (1553–1631), future Doge of Venice.[12] Beni was still anxious and unsure about the outcome of his case and, in his letter, he entreats Contarini to defend his innocence (presumably this refers to his writing the *Cavalcanti*). Beni confirms, however, that Florence has by now reconsidered the *Cavalcanti*, and has admitted officially that Beni had indeed been provoked by *cartelli* as well as by Pescetti's book ('che pur'è bruttissimo') into making some personal defence of himself. Finally, he hopefully looks to Florence for 'qualche giusta et honorata risolutione'.

His hopes turned out to be groundless. In a letter to Paolo Gualdo, dated 14 November 1614, Pignoria announced the outcome of Beni's petition, in gleeful terms: 'Il Signor Beni ha riavuto da Fiorenza il suo libro ch'esso mandò a donare al Gran Duca, e la bellezza saria a vedere la lettera remissiva, che m'imagino sia bella, e voglio tentare in ogni maniera di vederla' (quoted by Mazzuchelli, ii/2. 846 n. 50). It is easy to imagine from this that Beni must have been the butt of such gossip and ridicule for some time. (The Grand Duke's letter has not come to light.)

The *Cavalcanti* was nevertheless published in 1614. It had taught Beni a hard lesson, not altogether unlike the lesson he

[11] On him see Cinelli Calvoli, iii. 197, and Vedova, i. 515.
[12] The letter is to be found in Venice, Museo Civico Correr, MS 1375, pp. 655–7. On Contarini see, G. Cozzi, *Il doge Nicolò Contarini* (Venice–Rome, 1958).

should have learned from his Jesuit career, but one which, after this episode, he showed no desire to repeat. For, although he went on to compose parts two, three, and four of the *Anticrusca* (1615–17), yet he did not wish to publish them for some years and they did not appear in print until 1982.[13] And although the commentary on the *Goffredo* (which is much concerned with the linguistic debate) did not come out until 1616, it was however completed and being dispatched to the printer while Beni was working on the *Cavalcanti* (during the second half of 1613) (see *Cav.* 115). In the overall pattern of his life and works, the anti-Cruscan campaign now appears as a minor interlude, one that distracted him from his more serious pursuits, and which caused him no small amount of vexation.[14]

[13] Ed. by G. Casagrande, ed. cit. (hereafter *A.*). For the dating of the work, see ibid., pp. lxi–lxii.
[14] For a full treatment of the ideas and issues involved in the linguistic works, see below, Chapter 11.

9

THE FINAL YEARS

The commentary on the *Goffredo* came out before 15 July 1616 (ASVB 36). The Duke of Urbino immediately wrote to Beni to congratulate him, reminding him of his own intimate acquaintance with Tasso, and praising Beni for having done so well for himself, for his family, and for Gubbio.[1] This tribute must have been gratifying after all the obloquy he had lately received over the anti-Cruscan works. The Duke's letter was evidently written on his behalf by Abbate Giulio Brunetti (1559–post-1632), the Duke's Residente in Venice, who had had Carlo Borromeo as a patron and Federico Borromeo as a co-pupil.[2] Beni replied to Brunetti, whom he had known for many years, and thanked him for his praise:

Gli scrittori amano d'esser letti, e tanto più se ne godono, per non dir se ne gonfiano; quanto più il Lettore è d'ingegno e valore, et insieme si mostra benigno e cortese (PO 429, Fasc. xiv, fos. 54^r–55^v (fo. 54^r)).

It would seem that at last Beni was gaining some appreciation for his work. Yet he did not publish anything for the next six years. It is as if his confidence, which curiously had not faltered in the past, had been shaken by the recent controversies. We know, however, that he completed the *Anticrusca* during these years, that he worked on the unpublished treatise 'Della veneta libertà' after the publication of the *Goffredo* (1616), from which he quotes in his 'Della veneta libertà' (PU 412, p. 6, for example), that he lectured on the *Rhetoric* on 5 November 1619 (ASVB 71), and that he was writing his commentary (as eventually published) on that work around 1621 and 1622 (*R.* ii. 121).

Between 10 August and 16 December 1620 he wrote thirteen letters, addressed to Andrea Dandolo in Venice, on the subject

---

[1] PO 781, fo. 22^{r-v} (a copy). Another (partial) copy is in VA Vat.lat. 10975, fo. 17^r. The letter was published by Solerti, ii/2. 394.

[2] See, on Brunetti, L. Rossi, 'Brunetti, Giulio', in *Dizionario biografico degli Italiani*, xiv (1972), 580.

of the Italian language. He later decided to collect these, and to publish them in the seventh volume of his projected *Opera omnia*, under the title 'Avvisi per ben comporre in prosa et in rima' which, in the final draft, he redated 20 January 1622 and addressed to a Paduan *Signore*. They were never published.[3] They substantially repeat his linguistic views expressed elsewhere, though in a more direct and concise fashion (for they are letters), and with more emphasis than in the earlier works on the problems of writing Italian. As a companion piece to the 'Avvisi' he intended to publish 'Un trattato della memoria locale e modo d'acquistarla' (also in ASVB 129). This work offers a lucid account of how physical *luoghi* can be used to remember the logical steps of an argument. Beni gives a concrete example of his own use of the interior of the church of Santa Giustina in Padua to remember a series of hypothetical arguments against Aristotle's definition of rhetoric. Each argument is assigned a place from left to right, and is converted mentally into an image which can represent the whole *concetto* (rather than individual *parole*). Beni shows the classical ancestry of this process; but it must not be forgotten that his method bears some resemblance to the Ignatian meditation, which he would have learned as a Jesuit.[4] Such Jesuit meditations influenced to some extent poets such as G. M. Hopkins, George Herbert, and John Donne in their discovery of vivid imagery; in Beni such meditation influenced his ability to remember the drift of an argument.

[3] They are in ASVB 129. Beni's plan was to publish these in the seventh volume of his *Opera omnia*, with his other Italian works, as the cover of the present MS shows.

[4] The classical art of memory originated in Greece, passed to Rome, and was eventually codified in the *Ad Herennium* (III. xvi–xxiv). Beni is in line with the anonymous author of this rhetorical treatise when he advocates memory for things and notions (*concetti*) in preference to memory for words (*parole*). Artificial memory played an important cultural role from classical times to the seventeenth century, when Leibniz was still working in the memory tradition. Notable contributions to the art were made by Aquinas and Albertus Magnus in the thirteenth century and by Giordano Bruno in the sixteenth, while many minor reformulations (including Beni's) were produced in Italy during the Renaissance and Baroque periods. Some idea of the extent of this mostly unpublished *ars memorativa* literature can be gained from the indices of P. O. Kristeller's *Iter italicum* (under 'Memory, artificial', vol. 1 and 'Memory treatises', vol. 2). Further work is needed on the subject. Frances A. Yates's pioneering *The Art of Memory* (London, 1966) remains a fundamental starting-point. On the Jesuit practice of meditation and its influence on poetic technique, see G. Storey, *A Preface to Hopkins* (London and New York, 1981), p. 34.

Beni was probably also polishing his other works during these silent years, possibly with a view to publishing them in his *Opera omnia* (1622–5), though there is no evidence to suggest that he conceived that project before 1621.

Alongside this literary activity, and closely bound up with it, went Beni's personal relationships. Especially important here is his correspondence with his nephew in Gubbio, Francesco Beni, of which twenty letters from Paolo (dating from 15 July 1616 to 21 February 1625) survive in the Archivio Segreto Vaticano.[5] Francesco was the son of Giacomo (Paolo's eldest brother) and Trinzia di Vincenzio Baldinacci. He married Caterina del Conte Muzio Beni and thus reunited two branches of the Beni family, eventually inheriting the titles and riches from the principal branch (we do not know exactly when) (see ABSFG 17. G. 7, pp. 46–8). From his small commonplace-book, which is also in the Archivio Segreto Vaticano,[6] Francesco emerges as a sincere family man, with a shrewd sense of finance, but not highly educated. A man who wished to improve his mind (he made elementary lists of historical events, principal cities, the lives of famous Romans, very basic Latin idioms), but with his feet firmly on the ground. He treated Paolo, as far as we can tell, with the respect due to an uncle and a scholar; and he was in turn treated by Beni with a mixture of avuncular concern and financial harassment. In his first letter (15 July 1616) Beni offers Francesco, on the eve of his marriage, advice on the need for good health before taking a wife. He also begs for money:

Mi sarei rallegrato che mi haveste mandato almeno un mezzo migliario di scudi affinch'io possa resistere a tante spese: massime che il Commento sopra il Tasso, come è Volume di circa 160 fogli, mi ha finito di render'esshausto, importando la sua spesa vicino a quattrocento scudi.

The link here between the need to publish and the need for money will become stronger in Beni's dealings with his family; and his apparent greed is thus to some extent explained. But it is difficult to see that Beni was all that poor. He had investments

[5] These are all to be found in ASVB 36. None are foliated. In what follows I shall therefore quote from and allude to them without however giving further references.

[6] Archivio Beni, 7: 'Hic est liber Francisci Benii suorum amicorumque ad usum'.

which would have covered the expense of publication; and he had not found it arduous to be generous in his dealings with his Paduan landlord, Flaminio Butironi, who, in a tenancy agreement, dated 7 December 1615, had praised Beni for his generosity: 'voglio sempre riconoscere la sua amorevolezza con esser tenuto tanto alle spese del restauro e miglioramento fatto fin'hora' (ASVB 35). Beni seems to have tried to exert over Francesco some moral pressure to give him money. In this his motive was once again to achieve financial parity with Giacomo and his heirs. While he could get nowhere with his brother, he assailed his nephew in the hope of receiving his due at last.

On 10 March 1617, after hearing of Francesco's plans for celebrations at his forthcoming wedding, Beni is suitably avuncular but also, one fears, alarmed at the prospect of so much money, which could be in his hands in Padua, being wasted on frivolities:

Ne però stimo che vi sia necessario entrar in larghe spese, come mi accennate, per tal occasione [. . .]. Oltrachè i banchetti e bagordi non fanno punto a proposito per chi ha bisogno di confermarsi e conservarsi in sanità. Per lasciar ch'egli è pur troppo vero quel proverbio tanto commune; che cioè i pazzi fanno le feste, e i savii le godono. E però meglio è tenersi dalla parte de' savii, o piuttosto haver per partito migliore il restarne digiuno, tralasciando il farle e goderle insieme: seben qualche moderata allegrezza e domestica non può ne dee riprendersi: e tanto mi prometto della prudenza vostra.

On 31 July 1618, having by now married, Francesco records in his commonplace-book that 'poco avanti le dodici hore nacque Modesta, mia prima figliola' (ASVB 35). Beni wrote on 16 August, lamenting the fact that it was not a boy, but with a grudging word of congratulation: 'poichè dall'imperfetto si passa ordinariamente al perfetto, habbiamo da rallegrarci'. This can hardly have suited Francesco's mood.

But Beni was now ageing rapidly, and was struggling to keep up with the pressure of all his work, as he explained in a letter, dated 20 November 1618, to Camillo Giordani *seniore* (1588–1636), Residente in Venice for the Duke of Urbino and minor poet.[7]

[7] The letter is to be found in PO 1594, Fasc. II, 1. On Giordani I have found most useful MS notes in PO 458. II. Mis. 101, and in PO 1063 (under the letter 'G').

On 22 October 1620 he tells Francesco, in his usual plaintive tones, of the poor harvest in Padua (which had made everything scarce), and of the straitened circumstances in which he was forced to live in Padua. Soon Francesco and Caterina were eagerly awaiting the birth of a second child; and on 19 February 1621 Beni wrote hoping for a boy. By 5 March he was able to congratulate Francesco on the birth of a son: 'potrà come giglio giacersi tra due rose'.

Beni was by now old and frail. On 30 April 1621 he told Francesco that he wanted one of the sons of his deceased brother, Federico, to go and live with him in Padua. Clearly he wanted service from these nephews (who were, he admitted in his will of 1621, poor, and had not paid him his share of their inheritance), just as he wanted money from Francesco (who was rich). In his old age Beni thought that at last he could get out of his relatives what he thought was owed him; and it is sad to see him using this motive as the basis for what could have been fruitful relationships.

This unhappy situation is brought out in his will dated 1 October 1621 (ASGA II. D. 27). In it he leaves all his money (except for a few annuities) to the three sons of Federico;[8] he is at pains to exclude Giacomo and Francesco: if Federico's sons should predecease him then the money should go to the poor of Gubbio (fo. 1^v). He gives full information about his financial relationship with the brothers and reveals that Giacomo had not paid anything since about 1604 and that he now owed Beni between four hundred and five hundred Gubbian *scudi* (fo. 4^r). Though Federico's sons owe him the same amount, he is prepared to waive that (fo. 4^v). But Giacomo's debt seems to have exerted a compulsive effect on Paolo: he stipulates that, if Giacomo has not paid up before Paolo's death then the Convento dei Frati di Santa Maria in Gubbio should claim the money Giacomo owed him; and if they do not claim it within a year of his death then it should go to the hospital in Gubbio (fos. 4^v–5^r).

Beni's other bequests reveal the extent of his possessions. To his housekeeper, Donna Prudenza dei Bianchi, loyal, old, but

---

[8] Another will was drawn up on 23 June 1623, in which the only difference is that, instead of three sons, only two (Giovanni Battista and Felice) are mentioned. Presumably the third son had died in the interim. The will is the last item in ASVB 36, and is a copy, made later in the century, by Luca Beni.

now ailing, who (he says) had borne patiently with all his infir-
mities, he leaves some investments (fos. 5^v–6^v), all his furniture
('i quali [mobili] vagliono molte centinaie di scudi') (fo. 7^v), his
two carriages, a pair of horses, and his wines. As housekeeper,
Donna Prudenza is enjoined to ensure that all his servants go
into mourning and that they attend his funeral (fos. 7^v–8^r).

To his three Commissarii (Francesco de Leoni, Leonello Papa-
fava, two former pupils, and his friend and colleague Ottavio
Livello) he leaves his various pictures (all of them religious subjects, except one—of Petrarch and Laura) and, significantly,
copies of his own published works (the commentaries on the
Goffredo and the *Poetics*, the *De historia*, and the *Orationes*). The
choice of these works indicates what Beni thought were his
most significant works; and it is interesting that he did not
include any of his specifically linguistic works. (He might well
have wished to include his commentary on the *Rhetoric*, had it
been published in 1621.) One unpublished work about which
he expresses particular concern in his will is the commentary on
the *Timaeus*, for the publication of which he gives Ottavio
Livello explicit instructions. (The quest to publish this commentary can be traced back to 1593.)

In some ways Beni's most important possession was his well-
stocked library which he bequeaths in his will to the 'Frati
Zoccolanti di San Francesco vicino all'Hospidale' in Padua.
Characteristically he lays down many conditions: for instance,
that the library should be kept intact and housed separately,
that the order of the volumes should not be altered, that no book
should be removed from the library, and that it should be kept
under lock and key. With the library he also leaves the shelves,
globes, clocks, maps, mathematical instruments, pictures, and
ornaments which are housed in it (fo. 7^r). It was probably for the
purpose of making this bequest that, before making this will,
Beni compiled a catalogue of his library, 'Beniana bibliotheca',
to which I have already referred. This is a *catalogue raisonné*,
arranged according to faculty and language (Latin and Italian),
of all Beni's books, including most of his own writings, published and unpublished. The aim of the 'Beniana bibliotheca'
was no doubt to give the Zoccolanti some guidance in the use,
and usefulness, of his library. It would therefore be wrong to
read this work as a general review of all human knowledge, or

of all the faculties, as I think some critics have done;[9] instead, it is limited in its scope by the books in Beni's library, and it is intended to meet a specific rather than a general need.

As part of his 'Beniana bibliotheca' (p. 244) Beni also drew up a list of his own writings, arranged in seven classes. This was to form the prelude to his *Opera omnia*. Briefly, his aim at this time (1621) was to have sections (or volumes) for the following: (1) history; (2) poetry and poetics; (3) rhetoric; (4) *vita et mores*: politics and ethics;[10] (5) Platonic and Aristotelian natural philosophy: in effect, the commentary on the *Timaeus*; (6) miscellaneous Latin works: the commentary on the *Somnium Scipionis*,[11] the *Disputatio* on Baronio, the Latin version of the *Comparatione*, the commentary on Proclus, the 'Actio Constantiana', the translation of and commentary on the *Euthyphro*, unpublished 'Disputationes' and 'Digressiones',[12] and the 'Beniana bibliotheca'; (7) all the Italian works (this list is to be found in ASVB 132). In all this, it is significant how small a part the Italian works were intended to assume. The work for which Beni has become famous (or infamous)—the *Anticrusca*—seems insignificant beside the quantity and weight of his learned Latin commentaries.

By 15 April 1622 financial anxieties had once again beset him. His *Opera omnia*, which were being published by the Venetian

---

[9] See, for instance, R. G. Faithfull, 'Teorie filologiche nell'Italia del primo Seicento con particolare riferimento alla filologia volgare', *Studi di filologia italiana*, 20 (1962), 147–313 ('doveva essere una guida bibliografica generale del sapere', p. 184), and Casagrande, ed. cit., p. lvii. On Beni's library see also F. Foffano, 'Il catalogo della biblioteca di Paolo Beni', *Giornale storico e letterario della Liguria*, 2 (1901), 327–36. Foffano quotes extensively from the Italian section.

[10] Following Aristotle's conception of political science and ethics as the two halves of one subject (human affairs or man's happiness on earth), Beni intended to publish his commentaries on both the *Ethics* (which I have already mentioned) and the *Politics* together in one volume. The commentary on the *Politics* is in ASVB 91: it has a Greek text and the Latin translation of Leonardo Bruni, followed by a Latin commentary (full for the first book, summary for the rest) by Beni. Was all this ever published? A comment in BB 100 suggests that it was: 'Nos etiam in Aristotelis Ethicam, Politicam, Oeconomicam scripsimus Commentaria et Notationes. Ven. in fol. 1623', but nothing has been found of this edition. For the bibliographical problem of the *Opera omnia*, see 'A Note on Paolo Beni's *Opera omnia*' in my Bibliography, Section A.

[11] Unpublished in ASVB 115: 'Pauli Benii Eugubini in Somnium Scipionis commentarii', in two incomplete versions.

[12] These were items which he did not include in *OQ* or *OQS*, and are in ASVB 69, 70, and 71, mostly on natural philosophy.

Giovanni Guerigli, were proving to be a very costly exercise, and Beni was exceedingly anxious to rake together as much extra money as possible. He confided his worries to Camillo Giordani, by now (15 April) in Pesaro:

L'opera va inanzi: ma se non havrò soccorso temo di restar tra via: perchè il Gueriglia mira troppo alto, mentre si tenta d'addossarli tutti i venti tomi. Nè ha temuto di rispondermi che quattromilla [sic] ducati ancora sarebbono un'insalata a tanta spesa. Ma Dominus providebit (PO 1594, Fasc. II. 2).

The Providence Beni had in mind was, needless to say, Giacomo! In the same letter Beni also informed Giordani that Giacomo had by then been ordered by law to pay the capital sum which he owed. But evidently Beni was not willing to leave it at that for he wished now to hold out for the costs, which (he said) almost equalled the capital (ibid.). It is as if two obsessions in Beni unite here: his obsession with getting money out of Giacomo, and his obsession with the publication of all his hundreds of writings. He conveniently (but not altogether truthfully) links them together in his letter to Giordani, and he makes the second dependent upon the first; yet, in fact, he had been claiming the money from Giacomo for longer than he had been publishing his *Opera omnia*.

On 17 May 1622 a Portuguese Synod nominated and elected him as one of eight 'inter summos Theologos illius temporis' (VA Vat.Lat. 8225, parte seconda, fo. 320^r). This was important recognition, presumably for his work on grace and free will and possibly also for his commentary on the *Timaeus*. There is no evidence that Beni knew of it.

Even if this good news had reached him it would have done little to solve what he saw—rightly or wrongly—as imminent financial downfall. On 20 May we find him adopting an even tougher approach than hitherto towards Francesco, exerting increased moral and religious pressure on that long-suffering nephew, in the hope of shaming him into paying the costs which had accrued throughout the long and bitter course of his case against Giacomo (Francesco's father). His letter is unpleasant in tone and throws into focus much of his earlier correspondence with Francesco:

Con questa occasione non lascierò di dirvi ch'io non risposi ad alcune vostre ai mesi passati, sì per l'occupationi ch'io mi trovo, massime in questa età grave, sì perchè mi pareva che la vostra conscientia potesse rispondervi a bastanza; sapendo voi con quanta modestia io vi havessi sempre et a Venetia et a Ugubbio fatto instanza delle mie paghe, massime per occasioni honorate et urgenti, alle quali havreste piutosto dovuto contribuire alcuna cosa del vostro che ritenermi del mio: tanto più che il fabricar'e comprar possessioni, e lo spender'in simili altri affari, dee posporsi a quello che è d'obligo. E però havendomi voi fatto ventar tanto, et astrettomi a spender quasi il Capitale nelle spese [*of the case against Giacomo*], con cagionare che mi sono state fatte in ciò etiandio ruberia di grossa somma, havete dato efficace cagione a tutti i miei danni: dei quali la conscienza [*sic*] vostra medesima sarà sufficiente testimonio appresso colui che non giudica con giuditio humano, ma divino: il quale sarà giuditio di tutti i guiditii.

It is not known whether Francesco succumbed to this. He may have thought that Beni had no moral right to money which he seemed glad to sacrifice on entering the Jesuit novitiate. It is known, however, that, some time before February 1623, Felice Beni, his nephew and one of Federico's sons, came to live with him in Padua and to help him in a secretarial capacity (ASVB 36). Evidently Beni was active and in reasonable health at this time. On 13 February he wrote an *oratio* on someone else's behalf. He had sent off his *Orationes quinque et septuaginta* to the printers, and was busy collecting fresh material for another volume of *Orationes*, in which he intended to include the *oratio* just mentioned.[13]

On 18 August he wrote to congratulate the new pope (Urban VIII) on his election, reminding him of the success which Beni had predicted for him in his Ash Wednesday sermon of 1594 (the letter is in VA Barb.Lat. 6458 (LXXIV 4), fo. 39). Beni states explicitly in the letter that he was still teaching at the Studio; and, besides, his letter teems with energy and enthusiasm about his projected publications. The next day, he wrote again to Camillo Giordani: three volumes of the *Opera omnia* were now out 'e si vendono'.[14] Others (says Beni) were about to

[13] This work ('Oratio in amici gratiam exarata Patavii in laudem Francisci Erizi Generalis Terrestris Militiae Ducem Anno CDDC XXIII') is in ASVB 71, and is followed in the text by Beni's note of his plan to publish it. The projected further volume of *Orationes* was never completed and remains in a fragmentary state in ASVB 71.

[14] It is not at all clear what these three volumes contained. See my 'A Note on Paolo Beni's *Opera omnia*' in my Bibliography, Section A.

appear. In his letter Beni is full of plans concerning the dedi-
cations and lay-out of each volume: he asks Giordani's advice
about future dedicatees, and is clearly seeking financial advantages from his choice. Apart from this, he also hints mysteriously that his nephew Felice has left Padua on some business.
We shall return to Felice's 'business'.

It has traditionally been stated that Beni retired from the Studio (while retaining half his salary) in 1623 (see, for example,
Mazzacurati, art. cit., p. 498). But this was not the case. For
though he seems to have retired for a time (we know not for
how long), he returned to teaching on 3 November 1623, as the
presence in the Archivio Segreto Vaticano of an introduction to
Cicero's *Pro Archia* proves, dated 'Anni CDDCXXIII, III Non.
Novemb. cum Author ad intermissum docendi munus rediret'.
He also lectured at this time on Cicero's *L. Pisonem*: and the two
Ciceronian commentaries were published (with a commentary
on the *Pro Lege Manilia*) in 1625.[15]

By 15 December the complete commentary on the *Liberata*
was ready, and Beni wrote a Dedicatory Letter for it to Pope
Urban VIII, which he asked Felice di Conte Muzio Beni to present in person on his behalf to the pope. This Felice (not to be
confused with Beni's nephew of the same name, whom we have
already met) was a famous preacher, the author of works on
truth and faith, physics and metaphysics, an abbot, and,
towards the end of his short life, Procuratore Generale de'
Canonici Regolari di S. Salvatore.[16] At this stage Beni tended to
disown the 1616 commentary on the *Goffredo*: with perhaps a
muddled recollection of events, he maintained that it had been
stolen from him and published without his consent. He was
wrong in thinking this, for (as we have seen) he rewrote and
published it after it had been stolen around 1612–13. Now, ten
years later, he sought, by dedicating it to the pope, to lift the
completed work (as he says in the letter to Felice di Muzio Beni
which accompanies the dedication) out of vernacular baseness,

[15] These lectures of 1623 (clearly dated) are in ASVB 71. They contributed to
Beni's *In M. T. Ciceronis Orationem pro lege Manilia commentarii. [. . .] His omnibus
[. . .] subiicitur Oratio pro Archia poeta, pro M. Marcello, et in L. Pisonem* (Venice,
1625).
[16] He belonged to the main branch of the Beni family. I have extracted information about him from ASGA II. D. 31, p. 50; ASGA I. D. 3, fo. 151ʳ; ASGA I. D.
17, fo. 85ʳ; ASVB 25.

'acciochè per esser'Italiana non paresse bassa' (ASVB 36). This is another significant indication of the low esteem in which he held his Italian works, or (at least) in which he expected they might be held. In either case, he did not show much confidence in the vernacular.

At about this time Francesco requested that Beni transfer his *cavalierato pio* to one of his (Francesco's) sons. Beni agreed, on condition that Federico's sons should be compensated financially with the value of the knighthood (forty Gubbian *scudi* per year) (see his letter to Felice di Muzio Beni in ASVB 36). Subsequent letters (mostly to Francesco) show that the required documents were gathered together, and plans were made for the transfer; but it is not known when, if ever, it was made.

By January 1624 Beni had become very worried about the continued absence from Padua of Felice, who had gone to Rome on business for him. On 26 January Beni wrote of his apprehension to Felice di Muzio Beni (ASVB 36). By 16 February he knew the worst and, in a letter, he confides to Felice di Muzio what he has learned. It seems that, from the moment he had gone to live with Beni, his nephew had become involved with local prostitutes; and, whenever he went on business for Beni in Venice, he would take one with him. Finally, after Beni had been informed that some of his Roman assets might be disposed of against his will if he should die *extra curiam*, Felice volunteered to go to Rome to sort this matter out for him. But, selling the clothes which Beni had bought for him, he went instead to Rome with a prostitute disguised as a man, and there cashed Beni's assets and made off with the proceeds (ASVB 36). Beni did not become aware of all this until after Felice's departure for Rome; and it does not seem to have been difficult to dupe the old man. Why had this happened? Was Felice repaying Beni for harsh treatment? Had Beni been right in the first place to request service from his nephew (and the evidence suggests that he certainly made him work for his clothes and his keep)? What was wrong with Beni's judgement of character that he should have put so much trust in Felice? Why did Felice not respond to that trust? Clearly that relationship—which could have been satisfying on both sides—was an empty one: both parties sought nothing but their own advantage, and neither emerges with credit from it. In contrast, Beni's relationship with Francesco was kept alive (despite everything) mainly by Francesco's maintenance of respect for, and tolerance of, his difficult uncle. There can have been none of these qualities in his cousin. This was undoubtedly a harsh blow for Beni at this stage. He did not feel competent to deal with it, and left the problem of what to do next in the able and discreet hands of Felice di Muzio Beni. The matter was still preying on Beni's mind on 5 April (perhaps he felt responsible) when he again wrote to Francesco.

By 25 July he was very ill. The doctor had told him to expect death. Yet he was still hopeful that the pope would accept the dedication of the new commentary on the *Liberata*. By 16 August, however, his condition had improved, as he tells Francesco: 'me la passo, ma inparte infermo, ma benedictus Deus il qualle [sic] sa percotere e sanare'. It is hard to believe that he was now still teaching; and his other literary work had probably more or less ceased by now. His plans for the dedication of the commentary on the *Liberata* had also suffered a severe setback, for Felice di Muzio (only in his late thirties) had died; and so, to Beni's great sorrow, the project of publishing the commentary lapsed. On 7 October he received the *Imprimatur* of the remaining parts of the *Anticrusca*; but again he was probably too weak to act further on it, and so his plans came to nought.

Gradually his condition worsened, but he clung onto life.

By 24 January 1625 he was quite disabled, hardly able to read. He had given his library away, not to the Zoccolanti (as he had planned) but to the Padri Teatini of Padua. It is not known what had inspired this change of plan. Perhaps it was no more than a frail old man's whim. In a letter, dated 24 January, he explains all this to Francesco and asks him to ensure that all his unpublished works be published after his death; he suggests that this could be done with profit in Germany.

He was in a limbo between life and death, now looking forward to earthly success, now divesting himself of property and sacrificing at long last financial claims. Through this bleakness there shone a single bright light which brought a clarification, a falling off of illusions. For, by the luckiest of chances, Francesco showed Giacomo Beni's last letter (of 24 January). Giacomo was much moved by it and wrote to his brother, redeeming that blackened relationship. Beni dictated his reply on 30 January:

Qualunque si sia statta [sic] l'occasione per la quale vi siete datto a leggere quella lettera che ultimamente scrissi in risposta a vostro figliolo, debiam presumere che l'angelo della pace sia statto ragione, et auttore. Et di qui è, che la lettera appare pacifica e quieta (ASVB 36).

Beni repeats to Giacomo that the Teatini had carried off his books ('me volente et iubente'), and adds that his donation did not go uncontested in Padua. Again he gives no hint as to why he changed his mind. By this time (as he says) he was paralysed; and it is clear from the letter (quoted above) to Giacomo that he could no longer even supervise the spelling of his scribe.

Nothing could be done to relieve his suffering. He must wait.

Traditionally, his biographers have reported that he died on 12 February 1625 (see, for the culmination of this tradition, Casagrande, ed. cit., p. xvii). But he was more tenacious than that. For he wrote to Francesco on 21 February, saying that Giacomo too had by now agreed to help with the future publication of the unpublished works. (Clearly Giacomo achieved nothing with his brother's unpublished works, whether or not he tried.)

It is hard to believe that Beni lived on much longer. But Serassi (Beni's only biographer to question the traditional date) possessed a copy (unique, he thought) of the first part (five cantos) of the new commentary on the *Liberata*, with the dedication to Pope Urban VIII, dated 1 August 1625.[17] No one has heeded Serassi's testimony; and although the Dedicatory Letter which he (Serassi) prints as evidence is identical with the one Beni had drafted as early as 15 December 1623 (it is in ASVB 36), yet it would be unwise not to accept that Beni was at least still breathing on 1 August. Nor is it possible to explain the discrepancy between the traditional date of death (12 February 1625) and the dates of letters apparently written after that date by reference to the Venetian style of dating legal and other official documents:[18] for, even if the Venetian legal year began on 1 March, then by 1 August (Venetian or Common style) Beni would still have lived beyond his traditional date of death.

---

[17] Serassi, p. 552. Serassi's copy of the commentary is now in Bergamo's Biblioteca Civica 'A Mai' (see *La raccolta tassiana della Biblioteca Civica 'A Mai' di Bergamo* (Bergamo, 1960), 142).

[18] For an explanation of the Venetian style of dating, see *Catalogue of Books Printed in the Fifteenth Century now in the British Museum*, Part V (London, 1924), p. x.

Serassi thought that he must have died on 12 February 1626, but there is no good reason to believe that.

Beni was buried, not as a Dottore Leggente or in secular garb, but as a plain priest, as he had desired in his will (ASGA II. D. 27, fo. 1ʳ). We can assume that his wishes were obeyed. He was probably not much mourned. His family must have been relieved by his death; and he was no longer professionally indispensable in Padua. Furthermore, he had never been a popular man, as we have seen on more than one occasion. This was almost always the case in his personal relationships (especially within the family), though he does seem to have had at least one close friend in Ottavio'Livello. On the whole, however, he was either bullying on the one hand or flattering on the other in almost all his personal relationships: he seemed (like most of us) incapable of accepting other people as unique human beings, and saw them instead as the embodiment of wealth or rank or good or evil. On the professional level, a certain lack of tact led him again and again into difficulties (with the Jesuits, with the pope, with the Accademia della Crusca) and earned him an unpopular image in his day. His lack of charm as a man cannot but have lessened his reputation as a writer and teacher during his lifetime and for some time after his death. His personal unpopularity has influenced most subsequent judgements of him as a scholar and a writer; and this has led in turn to a general neglect of all his real talents. In Part Three I wish to examine his major works (those written after 1604) in isolation from his life, in order to discover how unfairly he has been labelled and, often, dismissed.

Part Three

THE MAJOR WORKS

10

THE WRITINGS ON TASSO

I

It was as a young man, around 1574 and 1575, that Beni made his first personal acquaintance with Tasso in the Paduan Accademia degli Animosi.[1] By that time flickering signs of discontent with the novelty of the *Gerusalemme liberata* (completed but not published) were apparent in Tasso himself, who, between 1573 and 1575, wrote feverishly to several Italian scholars for advice on the poem, and who, even then, pathetically displayed the deepest insecurity about his own worth as a poet.[2] Beni saw this. And, a decade or so later, he could witness the official flare-up of the controversy over the *Liberata* with Camillo Pellegrino's not altogether convincing defence of Tasso in *Il Carrafa*,[3] followed in 1585 by Lionardo Salviati's *Stacciata prima*,[4] the first of several rancorous attacks. The controversy generated many documents, all of which became grist to Beni's mill as the contents of his library prove (BB 261–2); but one can divine that some proved more valuable to him than others. Salviati's attacks left a lasting impression; Tasso's self-defence[5] and Orazio Lambardelli's *Discorso* of 1586,[6] in which sixteen principal

[1] See above, pp. 22–5.

[2] Solerti, i. 201–2; C. P. Brand, 'Stylistic Trends in the *Gerusalemme Conquistata*', in *Italian Studies Presented to E. R. Vincent*, ed. by C. P. Brand, K. Foster and U. Limentani (Cambridge, 1962), 145.

[3] 'Il Carrafa, o vero della epica poesia', in *Opere di Torquato Tasso colle controversie sulla Gerusalemme*, ed. by G. Rosini, xviii (Pisa, 1827). I quote throughout from this reprint.

[4] 'Degli Accademici della Crusca difesa dell'Orlando furioso dell'Ariosto contra'l Dialogo dell'epica poesia di Cammillo Pellegrino. Stacciata prima', in *Opere di Torquato Tasso colle controversie sulla Gerusalemme*, ed. cit., xviii. I quote throughout from this reprint.

[5] On Tasso's contribution to the formation of Beni's theories see A. Belloni, 'Il pensiero critico di Torquato Tasso nei posteriori trattatisti italiani dell'epica', in *Miscellanea di studi critici . . . in onore di Guido Mazzoni dai suoi discepoli*, ed. by A. della Torre and P. L. Rambaldi, 2 vols. (Florence, 1907), ii. 5–79.

[6] 'Discorso intorno a i contrasti, che si fanno sopra la Gerusalemme liberata di Torquato Tasso', in *Opere di Torquato Tasso*, vi (Florence 1724). I quote throughout from this reprint.

criticisms of the *Liberata* are neatly listed and refuted, foreshadow many of the arguments which Beni will use. Equally valuable to him were the two non-polemical commentaries by Scipio Gentili (1586) and Giulio Guastavini (1592).[7]

But to Beni perhaps the most effective blow was an indirect one: the omission of Tasso from the first edition of the *Vocabolario della Crusca* (1612). Beni retaliated immediately with the *Anticrusca* (1612), not in the name of Tasso's poetic language, but instead in the name of sixteenth-century Italian (mainly prose) language. That his commentary on the *Liberata* (*Il Goffredo*, 1616) forms a natural sequel to his anti-Cruscan campaign can be seen in a letter dated 5 July 1614 from Paolo Gualdo in Rome to Galileo. Gualdo gives a vivid idea of the freshly charged polemical atmosphere that surrounded the publication of Beni's new work, and of Beni's vehemence in not allowing the linguistic debate to close:

'Da Padova ho inteso che lo stampifero Bennio ha mo' sotto il torchio un aureo, vago, dotto e bel commento sopra dieci canti della Gerusalemme del Tasso, e, di più, presto farà vedere due centurie di lettere in forbita e tersa lingua italiana, scritte da lui per dar norma a voi altri signori toscani, e specialmente alli signori Cruscanti, del vero modo di parlare e dello scrivere elegante, poichè scorge che dal piccolo libricciolo intitolato *Anticrusca*, Le Signorie Loro non hanno ancora voluto *petere veniam* del loro troppo ardire [. . .]. S'è risoluto di stampare questo commento al Tasso prima che vi ponga l'ultima mano, perchè ha pur inteso che Sua Signoria Eccellentissima ha commentato l'istesso poema, onde ha dubitato d'essere prevenuto nell'edizione, e di vedersi così da lei tolta la gloria.

Galileo's reply, dated 16 August, is tersely ironic: 'Il commento del Signor Beni viene aspettato ansiosamente da tutti gli eruditi'.[8] It is clear from this exchange that Beni's message of protest was destined to fall on deaf ears, ears of *eruditi* closed to anything he might say in Tasso's favour. Beni knew Galileo as a colleague both in the Studio and in the Ricovrati; and it is likely

[7] For further bibliographical information on the controversy on the *Liberata*, see Weinberg, ii (bibliography).

[8] Both letters are quoted in Solerti, ii. 393–4. The Italian letters to which Gualdo refers were never published and have not been found.

that he was familiar also with the rationalist's then unpublished ideas about Tasso's poetry.[9]

This hostility, coupled with the conspicuous failure over a period of thirty years to make the *Liberata* officially acceptable, might have been enough to deter any other critic. But Beni thought he had a new voice; and though his arguments (taken separately) are not strikingly original, his serious effort to come to terms with the novelty of the *Liberata* constitutes a landmark in Italian literary criticism.

The commentary on the *Goffredo* (which covers the first ten cantos) is a continuation of the *Comparatione* (which had dealt in detail with the *inventione* and the *dispositione* of the *Liberata* in comparison with Homer and Virgil: see G. 9). The commentary thus represents the *summa* of Beni's Tasso criticism, and it will form the basis for the present chapter. However, though it repeats much of the material first presented in the *Comparatione*, the two works on Tasso do complement each other, and both will be taken into account in what follows. In the commentary Beni intended to adopt again the tripartite rhetorical structure (*inventio, dispositio,* and *elocutio*) which he had used in the *Comparatione*, and which Tasso had used in the *Discorsi dell'arte poetica* and later in the *Discorsi del poema eroico*; and Beni further intended in the commentary to devote most of his attention to *elocutio* (G. 9 and 244). But, despite this intention, the commentary—a compendium of all knowledge relating to the *Liberata*—contains much miscellaneous information. Its general method is to quote a group of stanzas, place them in their context from the point of view of plot, illustrate their significance and note any points of interest, trace all the literary imitations, and finally comment on the language. In the interests of clarity, it will be best now to examine Beni's criticism of Tasso under the three rhetorical heads, *inventio, dispositio,* and *elocutio*. Since, however, Beni's discussion of *elocutio* belongs more properly to the theme of the next chapter of this study, it will be but briefly summarized in the present chapter.

[9] On the possible relationship between Beni and Galileo, see P. Armour, 'Galileo and the Crisis in Italian Literature of the Early Seicento', in *Collected Essays on Italian Language and Literature Presented to Kathleen Speight*, ed. by G. Aquilecchia *et al.* (Manchester, 1971), 157–9.

II

For Beni, as for Salviati, *inventione* was synonymous with *imitatione* (*Stacciata prima*, p. 12). A poet was distinguished from an historian first by his use of imitation ('Poeta di cui è proprio l'imitar'e rappresentare ponendo in certa guisa i fatti avanti gl'occhi' (G. 749)) and secondly by his use of poetic ornaments, always seen by Beni in the commentary as a minor branch of literary imitation (G. 336 and 287).

Salviati had criticized Tasso for composing history rather than poetry, had called the *Liberata* 'l'historia del Bergamasco' (G. 419 and 336), and had accused Tasso of being a liar 'perchè nelle parole dell'autore non è imitazione: ned egli sa contraffare' (*Stacciata prima*, p. 225). That the *Liberata* should be thus criticized led Beni to develop with great thoroughness and worthy dullness the thesis that Tasso was the best imitator, and therefore the best poet, since Homer. Behind Salviati's description of Tasso as an historian rather than a poet there lay a complex and long-standing critical problem, to which Beni devoted much space in his commentary on the *Poetics* and in his *De historia*.[10] The *Comparatione* and the commentary on the *Goffredo* expound the same critical positions, relying heavily on the authority of Aristotle. Briefly, Beni's task was to distinguish poetry from history and to define precisely how far, in the quest for *meraviglia*, *admiratio*, and, ultimately, the reader's moral benefit, truth, falsehood, or verisimilitude are the legitimate subjects of poetry. In the *Comparatione* there are three stages in the discussion of this problem. In *Comparatione* VI the rival claims of historical and imaginary plots are put forward: the historical plot carries more weight, is more credible, and therefore of greater moral benefit to the reader; the imaginary plot on the other hand is more delightful (because it is novel) and more marvellous (*Comp.* VI. 228–31). But the sober and in no way Baroque Beni prefers historical to imaginary plots (*Comp.* VI. 231; see also *Comp.* II. 77). In the second stage of this discussion (*Comparatione* IX) Beni tries to distinguish history from the epic. He concludes that the difference is not that the poet tells lies and that the historian tells the truth: instead, the poet is free to

---

[10] For a more detailed treatment of these topics, see below, pp. 172–5, 181, 195–7, 207–8, and 217.

tell the truth not as truth but as verisimilitude. The point is justified by reference to Aristotle; and emphasis is placed on the
idea that the poet can tell the historical truth since Aristotle has
'liberato il Poeta dalla necessità del falso, collocandolo dentro a
confini del verisimile' (*Comp.* ix. 74). To those who have ceased
to see Beni as a Baroque distorter of Aristotle it will come as no
surprise to learn that Beni felt impelled to justify the factual
accuracy of poetry. Indeed it is perfectly natural that he should
have argued in this way, given Salviati's criticism of Tasso's
reliance upon history. For Beni, the epic can (and should) use
history; but such history should be altered and rendered ideal,
marvellous, and above all verisimilar (*Comp.* ix. 83–4). The third
stage is to describe those occasions on which the poet can legitimately abandon verisimilitude, notably when the resulting
impossibilities are widely believed to be true, or when they are
not germane to the poet's art (when, for example, the movement
of a horse's legs is incorrectly described), or when they can be
interpreted as allegories (*Comp.* ix. 81–2). But such lapses are to
be avoided, while, at the same time, *meraviglia* is to be maintained (*Comp.* x). According to Beni, Tasso achieved this
balance between verisimilitude and wonder better than all previous epic poets (*Comp.* x. 112).

It will be apparent that the weakness of this theory of the relationship between poetry and history is that, if the poet must
reduce his subject to verisimilar terms, why ever should he
bother to limit himself to history? This dilemma is evident in
Beni's commentary where we are shown that, as a poet, Tasso
altered history and told, not the historical truth, but an ideal
reduction of it (*G.* 66, 94, and 213). It was Tasso's duty, with the
aid of magic and *machina* (*G.* 847), to 'ingrandir'il fatto' (*G.* 213)
and to 'destar maraviglia' (*G.* 249); but equally it was his duty,
with the aid of imitation, to preserve verisimilitude (*G.* 409).
Thus, though in reality Goffredo was never the leader of the
Christian forces, Tasso made such a possibility verisimilar
(*G.* 112); he did likewise with the unlikely episode of Erminia
donning Clorinda's armour (*G.* 787); and he legitimately introduced Tancredi's love for Clorinda (*G.* 145).

And thus, armed with this convenient theory and with the
infinitely flexible quantity of the verisimilar, Beni might have
been able to explain away anything he found in the poem. But

on occasion he reveals a doubt about how poetry should be
read, as fact or fiction. For, in the commentary, there is on the
one hand a cavalier attitude to historical accuracy which often
appears as a tacit challenge to Galileo and to his oddly
inappropriate criticisms of the *Liberata*,[11] for instance where
Beni defends Tasso's expression *Ne l'isola di Francia*: 'Sichè Torquato chiama la Francia Isola con quella licenza che è propria
de' poeti, di non risecar'al vivo (per così dire) o co' termini
matematici misurar'ogni cosa' (*G.* 122). Or when he writes:
'Seben invero nel poema non debbon le cose tanto sottilmente
bilanciarsi e così minutamente mirarsi, ma ben a Mathematici
de' lasciarsi questo rigore' (*G.* 474). Yet despite such statements
Beni is often at pains to prove that Tasso *was* accurate, historically, mathematically, and geographically, when he proves, for
instance, that Tasso also knew how to measure the heavens: 'Il
semi diametro dell'ottava spera [. . .] avanza quello della Terra
45254 volte' (*G.* 69; see also *G.* 168–9, 175, 177, 1092, 1139, 1169,
etc.).

   The previous quotation takes us into the realm of natural
philosophy and to that, as to moral philosophy, Beni shows the
same ambivalent attitude as he showed towards history: he
allows the poet to render the popular version of philosophy
with the use of imitation, and he stresses that Tasso wrote in
the *Liberata* 'più poetica che filosoficamente' (*G.* 1139). Yet at the
same time he implicitly undermines such a theoretical confidence in the poet's freedom from the shackles of history and
philosophy by the very fact that he lavishes an inordinate
amount of space in the commentary on demonstrating Tasso's
qualifications as a philosopher. The commentary is studded
with philosophical and moral homilies. Tasso's poem becomes
a moral trampoline for the ex-Jesuit: Beni expatiates on philosophical commonplaces more than is strictly necessary even for
the full elucidation of the poem. The existence of these asides
proves that, unlike us, Beni read the *Liberata* as the work of a
Christian sententious sage, and not only as the work of a poet.
A list of such asides would include the government of the many
by the few (*G.* 110), skin colours (*G.* 130), love at first sight

---

[11] On Galileo's view of the *Liberata*, see A. Belloni, 'Il pensiero di Galileo
sopra la natura e i modi dell'arte', *Giornale storico della letteratura italiana*, 103
(1934), 86–7.

(G. 146–7), Capua (G. 152), the Roman attitude to scars on the chest and the back (G. 164–5), the relationship between *natura* and *arte* (G. 180 and 245), the advantages and disadvantages of foreseeing future ills (G. 216), the poisoning of rivers in warfare (G. 225–6), 'good' and 'bad' magic (G. 252–3), feminine beauty and its place in society (G. 283–4), Persian women (G. 309), the function and duties of messengers (G. 340), armies and war-mongers (G. 316–17 and 351), the whims of Fortune (G. 352 and 1071), contrition (G. 404–5), the benefits of chastity (G. 668), the 'right' use of lots (where proper choice and judgement cannot prevail (G. 680)), *turpe senilis amor* (G. 687), the origin and function of plagues (G. 889–90), the position of the sun in the universe (G. 1075), the feeding of the foetus through the umbilical cord (G. 1089). Beni's theoretical confidence in the poet's freedom to invent is thus belied by his practical preoccupation with the poet's moral philosophical and historical accuracy. His reading of the *Liberata* as a work of Christian wisdom furnishes important evidence of how Tasso was interpreted by some (at least) of his contemporaries. And the remarkable gap between Beni's reading and more recent readings only indicates how far changes in taste can affect the interpretation and understanding of a literary work.

III

Beni does not distinguish in his commentary between imitation of life (which we have examined) and imitation of other writers. He clearly sees the latter (literary imitation) as the main device of the poet; and it is as imitation of other writers that Beni chooses to discuss what we now call style and poetic devices.

The Crusca and Salviati had disparaged Tasso's literary imi-tation. And Galileo was to express his strong dissatisfaction with it:

Uno tra gli altri difetti è molto familiare al Tasso, nato da una grande strettezza di vena e povertà di concetti; ed è, che mancandogli ben spesso la materia, è constretto andar rappezzando insieme concetti spezzati e senza dependenza e connessione tra loro, onde la sua narra-zione ne riesce più presto una pittura intarsiata, che colorita a olio.[12]

---

[12] Galileo, *Scritti letterari*, ed. by A. Chiari, 2nd edn. (Florence, 1970), 493.

More sympathetic attention had been paid to this aspect of Tasso's art by Gentili and Guastavini. Beni wrote his commentary with their researches to hand and he respectfully acknowledges their help (G. 167, 180, and 853) while on occasion emending their findings (G. 128–9). Yet Beni's work in this area far supersedes that of his predecessors in bulk, thoroughness, and range. He supplies a wealth of new material, and leaves no imitation of the classics in the dark. His findings could furnish a solid basis for a modern study of Tasso's sources. Multineddu (following Rajna's pioneering work on the *Furioso*) used it for such a study in 1895; but his results were somewhat disappointing and less easy to consult than Beni's.[13] There is hardly a line of the *Liberata* (first ten cantos) for which Beni does not account in terms of literary imitation.

In the first place, the overall structure of the poem is shown to be a variation on the *Aeneid* and the *Iliad* (sometimes also on the *Odyssey*). Secondly, Tasso's characters are shown throughout to have their Ariostesque, Homeric, and Virgilian counterparts. They are shown to be idealized, perfected copies of their various models: Goffredo is Carlomagno, Agamemnon, and Aeneas (G. 223 and 134); Aladino is Agramante, Priam, and Turnus (G. 223); Tancredi is Rinaldo, Guidon Selvaggio, Ajax, and Diomedes (G. 134, 740, and 751); Argante is Ruggiero and Achilles (G. 740); Rinaldo is Achilles (G. 134, 174–5, 441, and 634); Clorinda is Marfisa and Camilla (G. 751 and 149). Numerous other parallels are discovered, of walk-on as well as of principal characters. Thirdly, individual passages and commonplace *concetti* are traced back to classical and Italian sources. Beni undertakes this with great gusto and performs his task with wide-ranging erudition: many pages of his long commentary are dedicated to lists of historically arranged commonplaces. As a source-gatherer he is often more efficient than modern critics: he treats the simile of the dog biting a stone (to take only one example) more completely and thoroughly than did Mario Praz (G. 1112–13).[14]

[13] S. Multineddu, *Le fonti della 'Gerusalemme liberata'* (Turin, 1895), see esp. pp. x–xi. Solerti (i. 447) described Beni's commentary as a 'bello ed accurato commento al poema'; and modern editors of the *Liberata* still use and quote Beni's commentary, for example Lanfranco Caretti (Turin, Einaudi, 1971).

[14] *Studies in Seventeenth-Century Imagery*, 2 vols. (Warburg Institute, 1939), i. 188–9.

Two things however limit the value for us of Beni's work on Tasso's literary imitation. The first is his source-hunting attitude. With the notion that 'nihil dictum quod non prius dictum' (G. 1044), Beni acts as a literary archaeologist; he sees poetry as a miraculous game of allusion which Tasso, to his great glory, played and which he (Beni) can now illustrate and explain. He rejoices in the fact that Tasso happily fished in the common pool of *topoi* and consecrated themes; and he underlines the unoriginality, for instance, of Tasso's description of dawn (G. 204). It is again revealing of a shift of taste to compare Beni's attitude with Multineddu's evident need to excuse Tasso's literary imitations and borrowings:

Le stesse imagini, le stesse invenzioni, le situazioni somiglianti ricorrono molte volte e inducono nel sospetto che l'autore avesse veramente quella povertà di fantasia di cui l'accusa il severo Galileo; ma in questo caso conviene ricordare che non può la fantasia muoversi liberamente quando ai suoi voli si oppongono limiti difficili ad essere rimossi, come quelli delle leggi arlstoteliche [sic] sul poema epico, e quando gl'intendenti tengono a queste leggi più che non all'arte, come appare ad evidenza delle tanto famose *Controversie* sulla *Gerusalemme* (Multineddu, p. 214).

Multineddu's post-Romantic plea for the freedom of the poet's imagination would never have appealed to Beni who has so often been held up as a champion of such freedom.

A further and equally surprising result of Beni's source-hunting is his neglect of Tasso's originality, and his failure to note how the poet transformed his sources. The succinct novelty of Tasso's metaphor

> Soli Argante e Clorinda argine e sponda
> Sono al furor che lor da tergo inonda   (G. 442)

is ignored when it is plainly confronted (without comment) with Homer's characteristic extended simile

> [. . .] et sicut in arva ruentes
> Sylvarum praerupta tenent, obiectaque totas
> Saxa morantur aquas, quae fluctibus omnia inundant,
> Et campis late stagnant, nec viribus ullis
> Saxa movere loco possunt, nec scindere rupes:
> Sic gemini Aiaces prohibent post terga suorum

Instantes Troas, qui non minus ultima Graium
Terga sequebantur.   (G. 442–3)[15]

Similarly, the pathetic antithesis between Erminia's physical
freedom from and spiritual bondage to Tancredi is overlooked
by Beni in favour of Tancredi's likeness to the merciful Alex-
ander (G. 766).

All of this is not to complain that Beni did not read Tasso as
modern critics such as Devoto, Ruggieri, and Chiappelli read
him: as a novel stylist. Rather it is simply to reveal that the
traditional champion of art and artifice, when examined in the
act of reading, shows no interest in the ornaments and poten-
tially 'Baroque' elements of the *Liberata*, save in so far as they
form a minor branch of literary imitation.

The second thing that limits the value of Beni's work on
Tasso's literary imitation is his comparative attitude (which is
symbolized by the very title of the *Comparatione*). Salviati had
placed Tasso far lower on the poetic league-table (epic division)
than Pulci and Boiardo.[16] Beni's self-imposed task was to prove
that Tasso should have been at the top. This influenced his
treatment of imitation in two ways. First, it led him to falsify the
range of Tasso's sources, as more recent work on the subject
allows us to judge. For, although Beni paid more attention to
modern sources than Gentili and Guastavini had done, yet he
did not pay sufficient attention to Tasso's use of medieval
chronicles (Solerti, i. 467). Secondly, Beni reveals, not how
Tasso was different, but how he was better, better than Trissino
(whose *Italia liberata dai Goti* suffered from excessive imitation
of Homer), better than Vida, Claudian, Statius, Ariosto, Valva-
sone, and so on. In a more constant fashion he maintains that
Tasso had beaten Homer and Virgil. But the principal battle for
the palm is no longer between Ariosto and Tasso, as it had been
for the Crusca and for Galileo, who all used Ariosto as their
poetic yardstick. Like Tasso, Beni shows no hostility towards
Ariosto's art (G. 43, 562, 845, and 856), and in the *Comparatione*
(VII and VIII) he shows Ariosto to be superior in most respects

---

[15] Quoted from Iliad XVII. Beni always quotes Homer in his own Latin translation.
[16] See L. Salviati, *Dello Infarinato Accademico della Crusca Risposta all'Apologia
di Torquato Tasso* (Florence, 1585), 10.

to Homer. As we shall see in Beni's linguistic writings, it is Dante who constituted the greatest threat to Tasso's reputation.

It is not always easy to define precisely why Beni thought Tasso better than all these other writers. But—leaving aside for the moment the question of language—we can discern three underlying criteria. First, using a critical commonplace, Beni argues that Tasso showed unique judgement in creating a unified work of art out of a variety of elements (G. 536, 1200–1, and 1034): Tasso gathered in the richest harvest that literature had to offer, and reorganized it 'imitando l'api le quali nel fare il mele raccolgon succhi da varii fiori: e pur imitando Zeusi, il qual nel formar Helena raccolse da varie parti varie bellezze' (G. 298). According to Beni, Tasso came closer than Homer or Virgil to fulfilling Aristotle's requirements for the unity of plot (Comp. II. 56); Homer had no notion of unity (Comp. II. 47–54) and Virgil produced two separate plots in the Aeneid (the first in Books One to Six, the second in the rest (Comp. II. 55)).

The second reason for Tasso's success in Beni's eyes is to be found in the decorum and Christian propriety of the Liberata. This view is a reaction to Salviati's definition of the work as 'lo 'mbrattare storia pia con sozzure di vizi carnali, e omicidi in persone di cristiani, e amici e sì fatti' (Stacciata prima, p. 130). Beni finds that Tasso perfected the characterization begun by Homer and developed further by Virgil: in the character of Goffredo Tasso gave us the perfect idea of the captain (G. 29). Not only are Achilles, Odysseus, and Aeneas without Christianity (which is enough in itself to disqualify them from the title of perfect hero), but none of them is completely virtuous even in a pagan sense; Achilles is cruel, Odysseus is cunning and thoughtless about his family, and Aeneas, who comes nearest to perfection, is flawed by his superstition and (above all) his love for Dido (of which Beni fails to see the literary aesthetic point, so blinded is he here in his literary judgement by moral Christian standards of behaviour). In Goffredo he finds moral perfection. As a Christian and a product of the Italian Counter-Reformation, he warmly rhapsodizes over Goffredo's resistance to Armida (Comp. I. 18–20), over his morning prayers (Comp. I. 25), and over his many other virtues. Beni clearly senses no hint of poetic frigidity in Tasso's portrayal of Goffredo (about which some modern critics have complained). Quite the opposite.

And Goffredo is seen as the central character in the poem (hence Beni's use of the title *Il Goffredo*), and is welcomed into Beni's heart and imagination as some sort of long-desired Christian fulfilment. From this point of view Beni's work could be seen as a Christian rather than a poetic or literary reading of Tasso: Goffredo becomes in Beni's eyes an icon rather than a real, living, fallible hero.

The third criterion used by Beni to assert Tasso's perfection is his *evidentia* or vividness of presentation. Salviati had compared Ariosto to the sun and Tasso to a glow-worm (*Stacciata prima*, pp. 227 and 232). Beni argues that Tasso is always visually vivid, especially in his similes (which are now noted on the contrary, not for their transparency, but for their vague musicality and for their complex blurring functions (*G*. 224 and 1135)).[17]

In Beni's defence of Tasso's imitation (both of life and of literature) there is a clear attempt to make Tasso conform to authority (Aristotle and the Church) as well as to precedence. The question of the relationship between the inner poetic world of the *Liberata* and the real physical historical and literary world outside the poem was the one that preoccupied Beni more and more as his commentary proceeded and which eventually swamped the question of *elocutio*.

IV

In the *Comparatione* (III, IV, and V) Beni relied on Aristotle to provide the ground rules for *dispositio*, or the arrangement of the plot. His detailed discussion, which relates very closely to his commentary on the *Poetics*, can be briefly summarized here. There are two possible narrative orders: first, the natural or historical where the beginning, middle, and end are narrated in that order; second, the artificial or *perturbato* or poetic where the actual order of events is altered in the narration. Aristotle, who otherwise separated history from poetry, is shown by Beni to have been in favour of the natural order. The *Iliad* and the

---

[17] See, for example, F. Chiappelli, *Studi sul linguaggio del Tasso epico* (Florence, 1957), 147; R. M. Ruggieri, 'Aspetti linguistici della polemica tassesca', *Lingua nostra*, 6 (1944–5), 47.

Goffredo adopt that order while the *Odyssey* and the *Aeneid* adopt the artificial order (*Comp.* III, *passim*).

The length of the epic should conform to Aristotle's two rules: first, that the reader should be able to hold in his mind all its constituent parts at any one time; and second, that it should amount to the length of several tragedies. From this second rule Beni ingeniously construes that the epic should take between ten and twelve hours to recite and that it should therefore contain between five and six thousand lines. The inconvenient fact that the *Goffredo* has fifteen thousand lines (more than the *Odyssey* or the *Aeneid*) is explained (by Beni) by the shortness of the Italian *endecasillabo*, and by the greater concision of Latin and Greek in comparison with Italian.

Finally, all the episodes of an epic should not, according to Beni's rules, exceed the length of the basic plot. They should be short, not interwoven, and they should appear once only. They should be appropriate to the main plot, but not so close to it in subject or theme that they cannot be distinguished from it (*Comp.* v. 186–91). Virgil and Tasso are judged to be equally successful here. However, Virgil is criticized for the lack of verisimilitude in some of his episodes, and Tasso is criticized for occasionally allowing his episodes to overlap (*Comp.* v. 211–12), no doubt in imitation of Ariosto whom he admired. The treatment of *dispositio* in the commentary adds little to the *Comparatione* and is largely unoriginal.

V

The question of *elocutio* was very much more important to Beni, and his commentary was ostensibly dedicated to it (*G.* 12). For Beni *elocutio* was the principal part of the epic; for Salviati and the Crusca it was (perhaps surprisingly given their linguistic bias) 'l'infima delle quattro parti' (*Stacciata prima*, p. 13). Yet, as the result of poor organization, *elocutio* does not receive pride of place in the commentary, though Beni constantly repeats that it should (*G.* 86, 394, 758, 1125, and 1207).

By *elocutio* Beni meant language rather than style. It is true that he interchanged the words *elocutione* and *stile* in the commentary, but he had no word for 'style', as used more recently by Chiappelli and Leo, to mean 'the manner of expression characteristic of the personality of a particular writer'. *Elocutio* never has such personal and aesthetic connotations in Beni, and his remarks on the subject constitute an apology in linguistic terms rather than an aesthetic appreciation of Tasso's style. A writer is seen simply as one who knows language and can manipulate words. And since Salviati and the Crusca had many a time spoken of Tasso's 'non intender la lingua' (*Stacciata prima*, p. 198), Beni was at pains to vindicate the correctness of Tasso's usage.

He defends Tasso's language in four distinct stages, which may be briefly summarized here. First, it is shown that the Italian language is inadequate and that Tasso was forced to resort to Latinisms and other linguistic borrowings in order to enrich his native tongue. Second, Tasso always followed the authority of *lodati scrittori*, which, as we shall see, included Latin, Greek, and Italian fourteenth-century writers. Third, Tasso obeyed the authority of *comune uso* (by which Beni meant, as we shall see, literary usage). And finally, Tasso always observed the more or less Bembist canons of linguistic taste, beauty, and sonority.[18]

VI

With the commentary on the *Goffredo* we can speak for the first time of the full acclimatization of Tasso's poem in all its aspects. The *Liberata* had been born into a hostile critical world, and even Tasso's most fervent champions had been unable to understand its apparent novelty. Tasso did not prove his own best apologist. He was incapable of answering Salviati in his own vituperative terms (he honestly admired both Florence and the Florentine language); and he weakly agreed to revise his poem. Salviati had complained that it took half an hour to make out the meaning of some lines of the *Liberata* (*Stacciata prima*, p. 221); and neither Pellegrino (*Il Carrafa*, pp. 154–7) nor Lombardelli (*Discorso*, p. 244), two of Tasso's most passionate admirers, had been able to deny the obscurity of the poem. Indeed Tasso admitted that some Latinisms were obscure and

---

[18] For a fuller discussion of this defence of Tasso's language in the context of Beni's linguistic ideas, see below, pp. 145–6, 149–56, and 161.

altered them accordingly in the *Conquistata* (see Brand, pp. 145, 147, and 149; and Ruggieri, 'Aspetti linguistici', pp. 45 and 49–50). Beni found no such obscurity in the poem: his ears and judgement and taste were quite inured to it. He accepted everything the *Liberata* had to offer. His 'complete' study of the work allowed him to demonstrate how Tasso brought to ultimate perfection what Homer began and Virgil continued (*G.* 699 and 909). And the novelty of the *Liberata*, which had baffled readers for more than thirty years, was interpreted by Beni as nothing less than classical epic grandeur. For Beni reached his acceptance of the *Liberata*, not by abandoning the old literary rhetorical linguistic and Christian standards, but by reasserting them. Refreshed with the authority of the *Poetics*, Beni turns out in his work on Tasso to be the champion of literary craftsmanship, linguistic authority and precedence, imitation and grave conformity.[19]

The criticism of Tasso combines all Beni's interests, linguistic, literary, rhetorical, and religious. His effort to justify Tasso's work turns into an exposition of all his own main preoccupations. In particular, his criticism of Tasso forms a bridge between his linguistic writings on the one hand, and the commentary on the *Poetics* on the other. It is to these otherwise unrelated subjects that we may now turn.

[19] See also what Beni says about Tasso and modern poetic style in his commentary on the *Rhetoric*, pp. 236–7 below.

11

THE LINGUISTIC WRITINGS

I

Beni's linguistic ideas have been more written about than any other aspect of his work, yet prejudices still go unquestioned, evidence unexamined, and books all too often unopened. And the fact that his ideas have been imperfectly understood is not solely attributable to the supposed loss of Parts Two, Three, and Four of the *Anticrusca,* now fortunately rediscovered by Casagrande. For that work, based largely as it is on the already published *Cavalcanti,* adds little to our knowledge of Beni's linguistic ideas, save in the important area of lexicographical theory. Furthermore, Casagrande's assessment of the work is principally based on the findings of earlier critics, notably Mazzacurati and Faithfull.[1] Thus, while he provides a reliable and valuable summary of Beni's views in relation to the sixteenth-century *questione della lingua,* Casagrande does not address himself to some of the fundamental problems of interpretation of Beni's linguistic theory with which I shall be concerned in the following pages. Of all Beni's linguistic critics, Faithfull still stands out as one of the most sensitive and perceptive; yet his study suffers, as we shall see, from his tendency to view Beni as part of an historical period rather than as an individual thinker.

What does emerge from the studies so far produced on Beni is a picture first, of a born polemicist, isolated by birth (in Greece) and profession (at Padua), without consistent aims or good sense, but goaded, as Dell'Aquila has it, by 'pura animosità' (p. 133); a lone soldier, rather than a scholar, who conducted various isolated campaigns: *Antiboccaccio, Antisalviati,* and *Antidante* are the titles which Migliorini preferred to give to the *Anticrusca* and the *Cavalcanti.*[2] Secondly, Beni (as linguist) is

[1] See the articles by Mazzacurati and Faithfull, already quoted.
[2] B. Migliorini, 'La questione della lingua', in *Questioni e correnti di storia letteraria,* ed. by A. Momigliano (Milan, 1949), 43.

portrayed as the furious and superstitious idolator of Tasso,[3] blind in consequence to the great charms of Homer and Dante; the despiser of *natura* (in Ariosto) and the hedonistic champion of *arte*, artifice, and ornament (in Tasso): 'puro Seicento' as Belloni puts it.[4] Thirdly, Beni is seen as the arch anti-authoritarian who judged all language by the hopelessly irrational and dubious standard of the ear (Belloni, 'Un professore', pp. 260–1), and who parochially defended Padua against the established authority of Florence.

The time is ripe for a re-examination of Beni's writings on the Italian language and a reassessment of these assumptions.

II

We may begin by establishing some basic external facts. Beni's professional interest in the *questione della lingua* can be traced as far back as around 1601: as we have seen,[5] his unpublished reply to Summo's *Discorso* announced some of his later linguistic views. But it was not until 1612, shortly after the appearance of the *Crusca* dictionary, that Beni began to publish his ideas on the Italian language. Although *Anticrusca I* (1612), the first of five projected dialogues, launched his campaign against the *Crusca*, it really consisted of a review of Francesco Alunno's *Le ricchezze della lingua volgare sopra il Boccaccio* (1543), in the form of a critique of Boccaccio's prose language and style. In 1613 Orlando Pescetti published his *Risposta all'Anticrusca*, in which the Florentine position is upheld against Beni by a non-Florentine. Beni's reply to Pescetti (*Il Cavalcanti*) came out in 1614. It was published under the fictitious name of Michelangelo Fonte,[6] and mysteriously presented as the work of the Florentine Bartolomeo Cavalcanti who provides, throughout the work, a personal defence of Beni and of his anti-Florentine, anti-

---

[3] See, for example, V. Vivaldi, *Storia delle controversie linguistiche in Italia da Dante ai nostri giorni* (Catanzaro, 1925), 154–5; and A. Belloni, 'Un professore anticruscante all'Università di Padova', *Archivio veneto-tridentino*, 1 (1922), 257.

[4] 'Un professore', pp. 258 and 254; see also C. Jannaco, 'Critici del primo Seicento', in *La critica stilistica e il barocco letterario: Atti del II Congresso Internazionale di Studi Italiani* (Florence, 1958), 228–9, and Dell'Aquila, 94.

[5] Chapter 5, Section VI, above.

[6] Giulio Negri describes him (as he emerges from Beni's *Cavalcanti*) as a real person in his *Istoria degli scrittori fiorentini* (Ferrara, 1722), 413.

Salviati linguistic position. Cavalcanti's works do not now seem fully to justify Beni's view of him; but it was evidently felt (by Tassoni, for instance) that Cavalcanti was anti-Florentine and anti-Boccaccian in his linguistic and stylistic choices, and that he would have been piqued by his exclusion from the *Crusca*'s modern linguistic authorities.[7] With the *Cavalcanti* Beni also published his *Rime varie*, which were intended to prove (against Pescetti's doubts) first that Beni was a poet and therefore qualified to speak about poetic language, and second that he was a poet long before 1612. Next, the imposing commentary on the *Liberata*—ostensibly, as we have seen, a linguistic commentary, but in effect much more than that—seeks to defend Tasso from the Crusca's linguistic attacks. And finally, the remaining three parts of the *Anticrusca* all hit out at the *Crusca* despite the fact that only Part Four is specifically dedicated to a review of that dictionary: Part Two reviews Alunno's *La fabbrica del mondo* (1546–8), and Part Three reviews Giacomo Pergamini's *Memoriale della lingua volgare* (1601).

This means that Beni's linguistic views are scattered throughout most of his vernacular writings after 1612: it is as if his feelings on the subject were so strong that they could not be contained or restricted to any one work. It would be impractical and tedious to examine these texts in chronological order, or even separately. They were all written within a relatively brief span of years (1612–17)[8] and all were written, if not directly against the Crusca's views, at least with them clearly in mind. Furthermore, it is characteristic of Beni to establish a polemical point in one work and to repeat it in subsequent ones (often indeed within the same work) *ad nauseam*. Such repetition of the same arguments (almost always with different examples and quotations) is attributable, not to forgetfulness on his part, but to a polemical need to hammer a point home, and to gain for it maximum coverage (in a way analogous to the use of media coverage in modern propaganda methods).

---

[7] Beni's view is shared by Alessandro Tassoni who singles out Cavalcanti for special praise as an eloquent Florentine writer who eschewed the influence of Boccaccio and who did not seek to force others to follow Boccaccio. See A. Tassoni, *Prose politiche e morali*, ed. by G. Rossi (1930), repr. ed. by P. Puliatti, 2 vols. (Bari, 1978), ii. 289. Tassoni is a possible source for Beni's view.

[8] The *Anticrusca* was slightly revised by Beni between 1617 and 1622. See ed. cit., p. lxii n. 1.

Yet, from the many words written in these works, a fairly coherent and consistent view of the Italian language emerges. This is not a view produced in a vacuum; and we will do well to remember that its every element was provoked by previous linguistic views, and that it rushes forth, not necessarily neatly or coherently, in a flood of vituperation or praise, detailed specific criticisms, and generalizations. However, the polemical purpose in his linguistic writings has often been noted, usually in dismissive terms. In what follows I wish to search out the guiding principles of his linguistic criticism, to explain them historically, to test their coherence, and to hint at their validity.

III

The main lines of Beni's ideas on the Italian language are as follows. He argues against the Crusca's view, namely that, after the Barbarian invasions, Italian was born, corrupt, from the ashes of Latin (which had reached perfection in Cicero and had then declined). From this humble origin (so ran the Crusca's argument) Italian steadily matured until, in the fourteenth century, it reached perfection in the writings of the *Tre Corone*, only to decline after Boccaccio's death, through the influence of Latin, down to the sixteenth century, when Bembo saved it from extinction. Beni accepts that Italian was born corrupt from Latin, but he refuses to allow that it reached maturity in the fourteenth century: he argues, with some logic and historical insight, that, the earlier the date, the more corrupt and 'incorrect' the Italian is likely to be (A. 196) and that, with the exception of Petrarch, fourteenth-century writers were mere babblers beside sixteenth-century ones.[9] Beni admits that the fifteenth century neglected the cultivation of Italian, yet he sees no evidence of Borghini's or Salviati's *peggioramento della favella*. In fact he notes a gradual improvement in the fifteenth century which reached its peak in Sannazaro, the 'novello cigno', as he calls him (A. 37), whose language and style mark a significant advance on Boccaccio's, foreshadowing the achievements of Bembo and Tasso (A. 37). Further steps were made, according to

[9] For Beni's parallel idea that all human institutions and customs (including language) gradually perfect themselves in time, see *Risp.* 201.

Beni, by Bembo's work; and Italy, having recovered in the early part of the sixteenth century from foreign invasions, settled down, founded various chairs of eloquence, and brought the Italian language to ultimate perfection.

So much for Beni's ideas on the development of Italian. But what of its status beside Latin and Greek? Whereas the Crusca had excluded the influence of Latin on Italian, Beni argued that nothing was more necessary to Italian (with its preponderance of *res* over *verba*) than the perfection of Latin and Greek. Echoing earlier arguments of Landino, he asserted that Latin was to Italian what Greek had been to Latin (*Cav.* 158; *G.* 15, 18, 58, 61, 239, 260, and 1051), and that in order to write good Italian you must be able to write good Latin (*Cav.* 36; *A.* 83). With Latin you will reduce Italian's natural aridity and poverty of words, you will increase its powers of expression, and, above all, you will regulate its grammar. Furthermore, since Italian is a language more suited to *dolcezza* than to *gravità* (AI 128), you will reduce its natural *languidezza* and strengthen it, thereby allowing it to achieve epic magnificence.

This is not to say that Beni sees Italian as a static fixed language like Latin or Greek (*Cav.* 157). For he constantly asserts the need for modest linguistic renewal which keeps abreast of current usage. However, as we shall see, by 'current usage' Beni does not intend to refer to regional dialects or to plebeian usage.[10] Nevertheless, within these limits, and unlike the Crusca and Bembo, he looks to the present and to the future in linguistic matters, and is confidently aware that perfect Italian is available.

But what is perfect Italian? According to Beni, it is a language acquired, not naturally in the cradle, but by constant study and observance of the best sixteenth- and early seventeenth-century writers (*Cav.* 126; *A.* 49–50). What matters is that it should be regular (*Cav.* 170; *A.* 17) and rationalized, especially in grammar, but also in pronunciation and orthography.

Where is such perfect Italian to be found? Beni's theoretical answer to this question is little different from Dante's and Trissino's: nowhere but everywhere. It is not to be found in any one Italian city (least of all in Florence, where the pronunciation is

---

[10] I shall develop this point in greater detail: see below, Section VII.

particularly guttural (AI 78)). Consequently, the speaker or writer of Italian will have to choose from all the best pronunciations and usages of all the principal Italian cities (A. 236). Beni has no doubt of the reality of such a common language, whose name (whether it be *volgare, italiana, cortigiana, toscana, illustre,* or *materna* (*Cav.* 193)) is unimportant. On the other side, Pescetti argues that such linguistic unity in Italy in the early Seicento is 'un mero sogno' (Pescetti, p. 15) and that, *faute de mieux*, Italian must be based on the usage of one city alone.

These arguments doubtless had a familiar ring, and had been aired many a time throughout the Cinquecento.[11] The logical conclusion for the Crusca was to turn more or less exclusively to the Trecento for linguistic models, and for Beni, with his ideal (he would say reality) of a modern language, rich but regulated, reasonably open to novelty and current usage, to decree that prose writers should imitate, not Boccaccio (who completeley lacks authority) but Guicciardini, Giraldi, and B. Cavalcanti, and that poets should imitate, not Dante and Pulci, but Petrarch, Tasso, and Ariosto.

IV

The foregoing account of Beni's linguistic ideas reveals many apparent contradictions, complications, and inconsistencies. These have proved a stumbling-block for most of Beni's critics, who have often concluded that he was an inconsistent ass, a militant with a bee in his bonnet, a man with more emotion than reason. How, for instance, can he dismiss the usage of the *volgo* and follow *comune uso* (AI 14)? How can he assert, with Salviati, the superiority of the spoken over the written word and yet claim, against Salviati, that the written word should be divorced from speech (A. 113)? Why does he affect to despise the Trecento, and yet follow Bembo, whose rules, as Pescetti astutely remarked (p. 111), are based upon fourteenth-century

---

[11] For general surveys of the *questione della lingua*, see B. Migliorini, *Storia della lingua italiana* (Florence, 1960); Migliorini and T. G. Griffith, *The Italian Language* (London, 1966); M. Vitale, *La questione della lingua*, new edn. (Palermo, 1978) and C. Grayson, 'Le Lingue del Rinascimento', in *Il Rinascimento: aspetti e problemi attuali*, ed. by V. Branca *et al.* (Florence, 1982), 135–52. Other more specific works will be cited where relevant.

usage? Then again, how can he praise in both Virgil and Tasso the poet's freedom to employ Latinisms and metaphors, and yet blame the same in Villani and Dante (AI 14)?

In order to begin answering these pressing questions, it is necessary first to explore in some depth four basic assumed distinctions, implicit or explicit in all his linguistic writings, which will help to show the consistency and logic of his views. These distinctions, though not new, are pointed up with great clarity in all his linguistic works.

The first is between lexis and grammar. It is clear that Beni applies two different standards here, and it is this difference of standards that Pescetti and the Crusca failed to understand. Lexis is made reliant in Beni upon the spoken word, and it is open to novelty of usage. In poetry, the importance of metaphor is particularly stressed, as is the importance of *peregrine voci* in general; and Bembo, Ariosto, and Tasso are praised for having enriched the Italian language by means of Latinisms (*Cav.* 157). Such lexical freedom, which will become a part of the Baroque poetic (see Migliorini and Griffith, pp. 261–2), is, however, carefully limited by the discretion ('elettione' (A. 81)) of the poet; and it is clearly misguided to overstress (with Jannaco and Doglio)[12] the anarchy implicit in such an attitude. Nevertheless, while Beni opens up the lexical doors he strongly locks the grammatical ones, and excludes all chances of grammatical novelty. He has great respect for Bembo's 'grammar', yet where Bembo (and Fortunio before him, in 1516) had offered a reasoned reduction of fourteenth-century usage, Beni suggests that his own grammatical rules are based not on any particular usage but on the laws of reason alone. He constantly equates *regola* with *ragione* (AI 104), and applies his universal standard of regularity to all authors. Such a belief in the ultimately rational nature of all language (which Pescetti did not share) enables Beni to rewrite Boccaccio, as we shall see. With this first distinction it is possible to see how Beni could criticize Boccaccio's grammatical freedom on the one hand and on the other praise Tasso's lexical freedom in the creation of metaphors.

The second distinction, no less potent in determining all Beni's linguistic comments, is that between verse and prose.

[12] Jannaco, art. cit., 227 and Doglio, 275; see also below, Chapter 13, Section VIII.

Here again the two things are kept so distinct that what applies to the one cannot be said to apply to the other (*AI* 116). And again, significantly, such a distinction is alien to the Crusca and to Pescetti (p. 52). Not only is poetry for Beni separate from prose, but it is also further divided into epic, lyric, and dramatic: each category is treated as a law unto itself, and like should only be compared with like (*Cav.* 13).

What makes poetry distinct from prose in Beni's mind is the greater freedom allowed to the poet, both in grammar and lexis (*AI* 14). Thus, while Dante and Petrarch are able to write 'in la' rather than 'nella', on no account should Boccaccio, as prose writer, do the same (*AI* 90–1). In all his works Beni returns to his notion that to write rhyming verse in Italian is harder than in other languages because Italian has so few rhyming alternatives. Thus, if you write in *terza rima* you are allowed greater latitude than if you write in *ottava rima*, rather less if you write in *verso sciolto*, and none at all if you write in prose (*Cav.* 119). Prose (and not only Boccaccio's) should be clear; it should be easy and natural to read, not pompous or periodic. It should avoid the strained rhythms of rhetorical prose (*AI* 25–6) and, above all, it should be prosaic, not poetic (for which fault Firenzuola is criticized (*A.* 218–19)). For prose is nothing more than 'un accurato parlare' (*A.* 129), and as such cannot be compared with poetry.

According to Beni, an Italian poetic tradition had been successfully established in the fourteenth century by Petrarch, while the Italian prose tradition had had to wait until the sixteenth century to be fully established. It is good, therefore, for Bembo and Sannazaro to imitate Petrarch, but bad for them to imitate Boccaccio as they did. This historical view of the development of Italian prose (as distinct from verse) has more recently been stated from a different angle by Kristeller, whose view of the matter is substantially that of Beni.[13]

A third distinction (that between *arte* and *natura*) has been understood even less by Beni's critics, and it requires considerable investigation here. Mazzacurati has written of Beni's 'avversione verso ogni forma di naturalismo letterario e

[13] See P. O. Kristeller, 'The Origin and Development of the Language of Italian Prose', in *Renaissance Thought and the Arts* (Princeton, 1980), 119–41.

linguistico' (art. cit., p. 497) and Casagrande, echoing him closely, has spoken of the 'linea maestra della sua inclinazione modernista [. . .] avversa ad ogni forma di naturalismo letterario e linguistico' (ed. cit., p. xvi). There is, of course, some truth in the view that Beni sometimes criticized *natura* and praised *arte* (*AI* 14 and 99). But it is far more often the case that he invokes nature as his linguistic and rhetorical yardstick. In the first place he puts the spoken above the written word: 'Insomma mentre ancor vive nella bocca de gli huomini la nostra lingua, convien seguir l'uso e costume di benigna Madre e non di crudel Noverca' (*G.* 17). And he makes the ear the arbiter of taste in linguistic matters (*AI* 77; *G.* 53, 139, and 326). The criterion of the ear was in no way new in Beni: he would have found it in Dionysius of Halicarnassus (whose works he knew) as well as in Vincenzio Borghini and Bembo.[14] Though it is the most prominent of his linguistic criteria, it is also one of the most elusive. For, being subjective and depending upon taste, it is difficult accurately to define:

Insomma l'orecchia per certo natural'instinto (siasi qual si vuol la cagione, che non è di questo luogo il ricercarla) suol ricevere alcune voci come dolci e grate, et alcun'altre come aspre et ingrate, e per dirla in breve, di alcune si rallegra, e d'altre ne resta offesa (*G.* 198).

Appella is harsh, *rappella* is good (*G.* 198); *disio* is not acceptable (it has too many 'i's) but *desio* is all right (*G.* 228); *destriero* and *cavaliero* are better than *destriere* and *cavaliere* (*G.* 614). Words are judged according as they are *dolci, gravi, piene, sonore, acute* (*G.* 324), *risonanti* (like 'involontario' (*G.* 701)).

Further evidence that Beni was more on the side of *natura* than has previously been thought is to be found in his criticism of Latinate syntax which he judged to be unnatural to Italian: effortful periods (such as he found in Boccaccio and Della Casa (*A.* 210)) and Latinate constructions (such as the accusative and infinitive construction) are unsuited to the Italian language, not naturally as concise as Latin (*AI* 72). Imitation is consequently judged according to its naturalness: Tasso successfully transferred Ovid into Italian terms (*AI* 123); Boccaccio's Italian, with its dependence upon Latinate constructions, remains synthetic.

---

[14] See Dionysius of Halicarnassus, 'La Composition stylistique', in *Opuscules rhétoriques*, ed. by G. Aujac and M. Lebel, iii (Paris, 1981), esp. 92–8.

It is also by nature's standard that Beni judges lexical Latin-isms and metaphors. This is best illustrated by his treatment of the opposite cases of Dante and Tasso. Beni describes Dante's Latinisms as unnatural; *pedantesco* and *fidenziano* are the adjectives Beni constantly employs to show that Dante's use of Latin went beyond acceptable limits, and against the natural grain of the Italian language. His criteria for the adoption of Latinisms are laid down no fewer than seven times in the commentary on the *Goffredo*. It is clear that he is in favour of using Latin to extend Italian, as we have seen, since the two languages stand in a close relation to each other. But this use of Latin must be made, as it was made by Petrarch, Bembo, and Ariosto 'con giu-ditio [. . .] et accortezza' (G. 1051). It is difficult to tell exactly what he means here by *giuditio* and *accortezza*: but the examples he offers of poets who successfully assimilated Latin elements into the fabric of their Italian suggest that Beni expected Latin-isms to widen the expressive powers of Italian without distort-ing or even altering the face of the language. Clearly, the mysterious chemistry of this process of linguistic transplan-tation is again difficult to define, and Beni, whenever he tries to explain it, falls back on such nebulous criteria as good sense, taste, instinct, nature, and the judgement of the ear. Dante's bold wholesale insertions of Latin lines and phrases in the *Comedy* were too much for Beni and for many of his contempor-aries, nurtured as they were on Petrarch's evenly assimilated Latinisms. Beni also criticizes single words in Dante for being Latin versions of perfectly acceptable and available Italian equivalents. Dante's *se mai continga*, for instance, could have been 'se mai avenga' or 'se fia giamai' (*Cav.* 26). Most of the single Latinisms which Beni finds objectionable in Dante are rhyme words. Clearly they all strike a jarring note for Beni: they are out of tune with the aesthetic criteria formulated by Bembo and exemplified by Petrarch.

A line is constantly drawn between Tasso's Latinisms and Dante's (G. 191, 584, 612, 1011, 1129, and 1133). Just as Salviati and the Crusca had found Ariosto's language artless, so Beni finds Tasso's (G. 1037). However, Beni does not have constant recourse to the comparison between Ariosto and Tasso which Salviati and his followers had used: for them, Ariosto was clear, Tasso was opaque; Ariosto was the sun, Tasso was a glow-worm; Ariosto was nature, Tasso was art. It is to Beni's credit that he avoids these facile comparisons; and he clearly sees, for instance, that Ariosto's poetry depends to a large extent on classical learning and precedence, and poetic and literary procedures derived therefrom. Thus, in his criticism of Tasso, Beni does not see him as the embodiment of *arte*. And, far from adopting the 'far mirar' aesthetic of Marino, Beni stresses the normality, uniformity, and acceptability of Tasso's *parole peregrine*:

Così voci che a qualche tempo poteron riputarsi a noi straniere, come *ange*, e di più dure, come *martira*, con l'uso si van mitigando e rendon [*sic*] quasi natie: in modo tale che usate poi opportunamente e da giuditioso Autore, massime nel verso che è povero di rime; si ricevon con lode (*G.* 89).

This may not tell us much about the poetry of the *Liberata*. But at least it shows how Beni was not the anti-naturalistic Baroque critic of the textbooks. In fact he sees Tasso as the embodiment of a happy balance between art and nature. In his unpublished 'Avvisi per ben comporre in prosa et in rima' (ASVB 129) he criticizes Baroque poets who destroyed the balance achieved *par excellence* by Tasso.[15] He judges the writings of such modern poets to be 'non solamente oscuri e turgidi in gran parte, ma ancora soverchiamente operosi e colmi d'artificio, sichè più tosto vi si scorge fatica e sforzo d'arte che benignità di Natura'. Tasso's poetry is praised for its *chiarezza*, *gentilezza*, and *leggiadria* (*G.* 120, 204, and 406). Whatever the truth of this view, it is obvious that the relationship between *natura* and *arte* in Beni's work is more balanced than has previously been noticed.[16]

Linked to this balance is the fourth and last distinction (between authority and reason) which is implicit in all Beni's linguistic criticism, and which has been the subject of some recent misunderstanding. Dell'Aquila (p. 17) has followed the common trend in contrasting *autorità* with *libertà*; and he has seen a struggle between these two in Tasso. However, Beni would never have made this distinction. For him (and it is clear

---

[15] Beni expresses the same view in the commentary on the *Rhetoric*, and there he quotes Aristotle in support of it: see pp. 236–7 below.

[16] See also below, Chapter 13, Section VI.

from all his works, literary, rhetorical, and theological) the opposite of authority is not liberty but reason. Thus, when he throws out authority (the great authority of Boccaccio, for instance), he replaces it, not with anarchy, but with a strict code based upon regulated usage. Though it is often the case with Beni that reason includes the ideas of liberty and authority, it also often excludes such ideas, as is clear from the balance between naturalism and regulation in his lexical and grammatical precepts.

V

It is Beni's faith in the reasonable nature of all language which leads him to his substantial critique of Italian lexicography. His ten highly theoretical conditions of a good dictionary, nourished as they are by his use and observance of Greek, Hebrew, and Latin lexicons, epitomize his strict application of reason over authority. It is this tough reasonableness that constitutes the striking novelty and far-sighted idealism of his ten lexicographical conditions. Briefly they are as follows. First, orthography should be standardized according to the dictates of etymology and the ear, so that entries should be easily found (*A.* 223–38).[17] Beni rightly saw that orthography was one of the major problems facing the lexicographer, and he accordingly gave it much space. There is a sane logicality in his answers to the problems: his insistence on etymology and the judgement of the ear constitutes a convincing alternative to Salviati's orthographical rules, and represents a fair attempt to decide the question without reference to any one geographical centre of Italy but, instead, according to reason. It is not surprising, given the cogency of his arguments, that Beni was brought back to life in 1641 as an interlocutor (with Celso Cittadini) in Diodato Franzoni's *L'oracolo della lingua d'Italia*, where he repeats his views on orthography.[18] Second, etymologies should be

---

[17] See Casagrande, ed. cit., pp. xlii–xlviii and xlix–l, for a good summary of Beni's views.
[18] Bologna, G. Monti and C. Zenero, 1641. The views expressed in this dialogue are remarkably similar to those in *Anticrusca* IV, and suggest that Franzoni (whoever he was) might have known the (then) unpublished work. I have failed to glean any information about this shadowy figure.

indicated in as scientifically accurate a way as possible
(A. 238–40). Third, parts of speech and genders should be indicated (A. 240–5). Four, synonyms should be indicated (A. 246).
Five, written examples should be presented in a rigorous order:
prose before verse usage; singular before plural; indicative
before subjunctive; the present before the other tenses
(A. 246–7). Six, spoken examples should be recorded in order to
clarify definitions (A. 247). Seven, as many different forms and
constructions as possible should be included in the examples
(A. 248). Eight, it is desirable, though not necessary, to include
Latin and Greek equivalents for the etymology thereby
revealed, for the stability of the definitions available in 'dead'
languages, and for the convenience to the non-Italian with a
classical background who wishes to learn Italian (A. 248–50).
Nine, a series of signs (similar to those now used by twentieth-
century lexicographers) should be evolved and consistently
applied in order to give some idea of the status of each word
(A. 250). Ten, the dictionary should include all words used by
eminent and authoritative writers, as well as all commonly
spoken words (whether or not they have been written down). It
is not the lexicographer's business to include words belonging
exclusively to the crafts; nor, since the lexicographer is not a
natural philosopher, a geographer, or an historian, should he
include all words belonging to such disciplines. Instead, the
business of the lexicographer is to 'ridurre in volume per ordine
d'alfabeto et insieme dichiarare e con essempi illustrare tutte
quelle voci che in buoni scrittori di sua lingua si ritrovino'
(A. 251; see also A. 91). This puts Beni's ideal dictionary firmly
on a literary footing. He does, however, allow spoken usage
some place: 'alle lingue che vivono il commune uso del parlare
serve in luogo di essempio'; but he goes on to say that 'poche
voci homai son dell'uso che appo qualche scrittore non se
n'habbia essempio' (A. 252).

VI

So far we have seen that Beni has a consistent historical view of
the Italian language and that his criticisms of the *Crusca* were
not, at least on his own terms, without foundation. His lexicographical norms are impressively idealistic. But do they not

sound too simple? What are the implications behind them? What, faced with the same linguistic situation as the Crusca had faced, would Beni do in compiling a dictionary? In particular, what, in his tenth condition, did he mean by *lodati scrittori* and by *comune uso*? Beni's critics have on the whole failed to address themselves to these key issues. For instance, Casagrande (ed. cit., pp. lv–lvi) briefly summarizes, but does not define or discuss Beni's problematic concept of *uso*.

Fortunately it is possible to find in Beni's writings answers to these realistic questions. The commentary on the *Goffredo*, because it is primarily a piece of practical criticism, provides a significant and striking extension of Beni's linguistic views. In that work it is possible to catch Beni, the critic, unawares, in the act of reading; and it is instructive to see how, at regular intervals throughout the 1214-page commentary, he defends Tasso's language against the Crusca's and Salviati's accusations, in the attempt to secure for Tasso the right to stand in the *Crusca* as a major modern linguistic authority. The words (of Tasso) which Beni had to defend in the commentary had been either criticized by the Crusca during the controversies over the *Liberata*, or omitted from the *Crusca*, usually both.

On the question of the authority of *lodati scrittori* the *Goffredo* commentary gives a view which complements that of the *Anticrusca* and the *Cavalcanti*. In the commentary, having established the need for a word, Beni attempts to prove, not Tasso's poetic freedom and novelty, but the very opposite: 'Torquato non fu il primo, o solo' (G. 321). In 1584 Pellegrino had announced Tasso's linguistic novelty; and Salviati had resented Pellegrino's frequent use of the word *nuovo* in respect of Tasso's language, maintaining that 'la importanza consiste nell'usar bene i vecchi' (*Stacciata prima*, p. 175). Beni forgets the idea that Tasso was novel and concentrates for the most part on proving linguistic precedence and conformity (a strategem Tasso himself adopted in his *Apologia*). His method is always to seek some authority, and that preferably written. In fact, if he fails to find a written authority for a word he generally assumes, not that there is none to find, but that it is unknown to him (G. 202 and 812). What are these authorities in the commentary?

First, Beni turns to Latin writers, delving deep in the resources of Italian's nearest and richest relative. One is constantly made aware here of Beni's vision of Italian as an extension of Latin. *Breve* used for 'picciolo' is justified, for instance, by Latin examples (G. 330); *fabro di calunnie*, harshly criticized by the Crusca and Salviati, is defended by Virgil's 'doli fabricator Epeus' (G. 383–4) and secondarily by Dante's 'fabro del parlar materno' (G. 384–5); *irrigiditi* is justified by Latin authorities and, since there were no Italian ones, Beni concludes:

Servaci l'autorità et il giuditio di Torquato, il qual sì leggiadramente arricchisce e c'insegna di arricchire la nostra lingua con le ricchezze della latina (G. 485).

Secondly he turns to Greek and even to Hebrew on occasion, though obviously less frequently than to Latin. Since Homer spoke of 'winged words' why should not Tasso be allowed *preghiere alate* (G. 885)? And though the Italian idiom is 'con lieta fronte' why should Tasso not follow the Hebrew, Greek, and Latin idiom and write *in lieta fronte* (G. 61–2)?

Thirdly, there are the Italian authorities. As we should expect, Beni makes extensive use of sixteenth-century writers, especially of Bembo and Ariosto; but he has recourse far more to the authority of the *Tre Corone*. Petrarch—predictably—figures on nearly every page; but the presence of Boccaccio and Dante as linguistic authorities is harder to explain.

Why Dante? Did he not represent for Beni everything that was bad in the Italian language? In order to understand Beni's attitude here we must first look at its direct cause: Salviati and the Crusca. For Salviati saw Dante ('quello stupore e quel miracolo')[19] as the ultimately perfect poet, able, with Petrarch, to rival if not beat all the ancient poets (*Orazione*, pp. 16 and 17). Unlike Bembo, Salviati placed Dante above Petrarch and all other Italian poets. His enthusiasm for Dante was transmitted to the Crusca, who, in their dictionary, placed Dante first and Petrarch second in their list of authorities. Tasso was passed over. Beni's attempt to refute the Crusca's view of Dante and Tasso formed the basis for all his comments on Dante's

[19] *Orazione di Lionardo Salviati nella quale si dimostra la fiorentina favella e i fiorentini autori essere a tutte l'altre lingue, così antiche come moderne, e a tutti gli altri scrittori di qual si vuol lingua di gran lunga superiori* (Florence, 1564), 19. In order to demonstrate the opposition between himself and Salviati, Beni reprinted in full Salviati's famous *Orazione* of 1564 with his *Cavalcanti* in 1614.

language. Beni evidently realized that the very linguistic criticisms with which the Crusca (through Salviati) had sought to devalue Tasso were applicable, and in larger measure, to Dante.

A brief summary of Salviati's linguistic criticisms of Tasso's language will show how Beni chose to attack Dante in the same terms. Salviati found Tasso's language so barbarous that, if Bembo, Molza, Della Casa, or any good Tuscan writer were to read him, they would be ashamed (*Risposta*, pp. 95 and 104). Salviati also resented what he described as Tasso's 'modi' and 'versi bassi' (*Stacciata prima*, p. 57; *Risposta*, p. 58); and he accused Tasso of having a poor ear and of producing cacophonous and unintelligible concatenations of sound (*Stacciata prima*, p. 155; *Risposta*, p. 139). He found Tasso's language ruined by forced obscurity (*Stacciata prima*, pp. 155, 221, and 227; *Risposta*, p. 99). And finally, Tasso's Latinisms struck Salviati as far too numerous and radical: of these he wrote (in the same terms as Beni was later to use in respect of Dante) that 'tante ne sono in quell'opera [*La Liberata*], che con poche più potrebbe parere dettato in lingua fidenziana' (*Stacciata prima*, pp. 169–70; see also *Risposta*, pp. 110–12).

It is clear that Beni, not wholly inappropriately, criticized Dante in the same terms. But he also realized that, if some linguistic licence or error were acceptable in Dante, then it must also be acceptable in Tasso. If you criticize Tasso's Latinisms, then you must criticize Boccaccio's and Dante's (*G.* 327); if you criticize Tasso for altering 'furono' to *foro* at the rhyme, then you must of necessity criticize many similar places in Dante (*G.* 138); if Tasso's metaphors are far-fetched, then how can Dante's allegorical fictions be excused (*G.* 886)? If Tasso's rhymes are sometimes obscure, and distort his thought, they never descend to Dante's low level (*G.* 55); let Salviati accuse Tasso of writing ill-sounding lines, they are sonorous beside Dante's (*G.* 324); finally, while Tasso combines beauty and erudition in his work, Dante had no beauty and his erudition is a sham ('sensi mistici o più tosto [. . .] chimere inventate da gl'Interpreti per colorir le costui vanità' (*G.* 129)).

But at the same time Beni could not avoid the fact that Tasso admired Dante's poetry,[20] and that in many places he imitated,

---

[20] There seems to be no comprehensive up-to-date study of Tasso and Dante. For some useful remarks and a select bibliography on the subject, see R. Negri and M. Fubini, 'Tasso, Torquato', in *Enciclopedia dantesca* (General Ed., U. Bosco), 5 vols. and 1 vol. (Appendix) (Rome, 1970–8), v (1976), 526–8.

not just words and phrases, but also ideas and situations which he found in the *Comedy*. Such imitation is more often than not interpreted by Beni as emendation rather than as imitation. Nevertheless, there are a substantial number of cases in which Beni states or implies that Tasso had used Dante's linguistic authority, or in which Beni, without adding adverse criticism, adduces Dante's language as authority for Tasso's. Since this use of Dante has not been previously noted by the critics, I list all the words in the *Goffredo* for which Beni gives Dante as an authority, with quotations where they are of significance:

---

brame (G. 89–90); *hoste*: 'E seben nè il Petrarca, ch'io sappia, nè Dante usò mai tal voce, usolla nondimeno frequentemente il Boccaccio e Giovan Villani con alcuni altri prosatori antichi, seguiti poi dal Bembo nella prosa, e nel verso dal nostro Tasso' (G. 93); *bisbiglio* (G. 117); *imperare* (G. 118); *innata* as an adjective (G. 120); *nulla* for 'alcuna cosa' (G. 139); *uffici* (G. 139–40); *rezzo* for 'ombra' in poetry (G. 155); *anche* and *anco* are not respectively prose and verse usages 'vedendosi che Dante nel verso usò l'una e l'altra voce secondo che li venne ad uopo' (G. 173); *lasso* for 'lascio' at the rhyme (G. 188); *t'avvalora* (G. 200); *alpestro/alpestre* (G. 231–2); *vendemmiare/mietere a* (G. 233–4); *prevenire* (G. 241); *apporsi* for 'to guess' (G. 323); *egregio* (G. 326 and 809); *ritorte* for 'legami', *corridor* for 'corsiero' (G. 329); *il die*, and *breve* for 'picciolo' (G. 330); *unqua* without the negative (G. 387); *affisse* for 'affise' at the rhyme (G. 388–9); *chere*, verb (G. 389); *accommiatar* (G. 390); *recare* for 'portare' (G. 392); *derivare* of tears (G. 477–8); *parenti* for 'genitori' (G. 604); *deluder* (G. 605); *vagante*: 'oltr'esser voce di Dante, è ricevuta da moderni, et usata con molta gratia' (G. 614); *colorare* (G. 615); *démon* instead of 'demònio' (G. 707); *torneamento* (G. 707); *divieto* (G. 708); *soi* for 'suoi' at the rhyme (G. 710); *eternare* (G. 711); *sermone* in verse (G. 712); *romita* as an adjective (G. 715); *rampognare* (G. 715); *pargoleggia* (G. 715–16); *desia* as a verb (G. 716); *instinto* (G. 716–17); *secretamente* and *hostello* (G. 717); *sorvenire* for 'sopravenire' and 'sopragiungere' (G. 718); *anhelante* (G. 718); *continuamente* (G. 801–2); *crescere* 'in significato immanente' (G. 808); *feruta* and *compiangere* (G. 809); *ministerio* and *invidiare* (G. 810); *imperare* (G. 813); *sublimare* for 'inalzare': 'non è voce inaudita, che usolla pur Dante oltre il Boccaccio' (G. 930); *pasturar la greggia* (G. 931); *historia* for 'storia', *dechina*, *corruccio*, or *coruccio*, *impaluda* as a verb, *rannicchia* for 'restringe e ritira', *eretto*: 'può parer non molto felicemente detto; ma pur'usollo Dante più d'una volta' (G. 932); *vetusto* (G. 933); *pondo* (G. 934–5); *vice* for 'vece' at the rhyme (G. 936); *pennuto* (G. 940); *spicciare* of blood (G. 941); *turbo* (G. 943); *ottuso* (G. 1123).

For most of these words Beni also adduces other authorities in addition to Dante's; and it is surprising that amongst these are such figures as Boccaccio and G. Villani. Beni's use of these fourteenth-century authorities (and especially of Dante) raises some problems of interpretation. For it is strange and unexpected to see a critic using as authorities fourteenth-century writers whom (with the exception of Petrarch) his linguistic principles appear to dismiss as mere babblers. Are we to interpret this as a sign of recognition of the historical value and continuity of the language of the Trecento? Or are we to interpret it merely as a polemical tactic aimed at defeating the Crusca with their own weapons? No doubt the answer lies partly in both solutions. For it is clear, on the one hand, that in using the authority of Dante and the others Beni hoped to show that, if Tasso erred, he erred together with the principal authorities of the *Crusca*. But it is equally true, on the other hand, that Beni was sincere in his belief that Tasso inherited from Dante and Boccaccio in linguistic matters.

It would be mistaken to conclude from this, however, that if he had been compiling his own dictionary of Italian Beni would have turned first to the fourteenth century for his authorities. Instead, it is legitimate to suggest that he would have put Tasso at the top of his list of authorities, not because he produced a new and different language (that is never Beni's claim), but precisely because he inherited and purified the best of fourteenth-century language. What makes Tasso more authoritative than Dante is that, in the work of Tasso and other sixteenth-century writers whom he admires, Beni finds the best of the Italian linguistic tradition embodied in a pure regular and accessible way, whereas in Dante 'pochi essempi si trovano [. . .] di alcuna parola buona e toscana che non ve ne sia mescolata alcun'altra rea e da fuggire' (*A.* 137).

VII

A more problematic area still is Beni's wish to include in his ideal dictionary all words in *comune uso*. What does this mean? Spoken or written *uso*? Spoken by all Italians or by one group only? Common to the whole of Italy? If so, then he is more than a little unrealistic. Did he not see that regional differences could not be totally ignored? Once again the *Goffredo* commentary allows us to answer these questions for, in addition to the authority of writers, Beni frequently calls on the authority of *comune uso* or *comune parlare* to defend Tasso's usage, even though he admits that it is the duty of the poet to rise above 'parlar commune' (G. 599).

A glance at the use of these terms in sixteenth- and seventeenth-century Italy shows that there was no widespread agreement as to their meaning. In his *Postille al Trissino* Tasso praises Petrarch's linguistic freedom in the following terms: 'Il Petrarca è molto più del parlar commune e poco del particular fiorentino'.[21] Here *parlar commune* refers to non-Florentine written or spoken usage of the past. In the *Apologia* Tasso uses the phrase *comune uso* to refer to present spoken or written usage.[22] Clearly Tasso believed in the existence of such common usage but restricted it to literary (or equivalent-to-literary) forms. Pellegrino uses the phrase *parlar comune* to mean 'literal' as opposed to 'modi di dir peregrini' (i.e. metaphoric or figurative usages), and he finds that the *Furioso* is all 'parlar commune' (*Il Carrafa*, p. 184). Here the distinguishing feature is not its non-Florentinity but its literalness.

The early seventeenth century still provides no consensus of what constitutes *comune uso*, as the very existence of the *Vocabolario della Crusca* indicates. Writers like Pescetti (p. 15) still strongly deny that there is any such thing. However, Faithfull has more recently detected in the early seventeenth century a development in the concept of *uso*: a new philological interest in the spoken language and an acceptance of *uso* as *uso parlato* rather than *uso letterario*.[23] To prove his point he cites Lombardelli's contemporary desire for a dictionary which includes ' "tutti i vocaboli del vulgo e de gli Antichi" ', and he suggests

---

[21] Quoted by B. T. Sozzi, 'Il Tasso estimatore del Petrarca', *Studi tassiani*, 11 (1961), 47.
[22] 'Apologia in difesa della Gerusalemme liberata', in T. Tasso, *Prose*, ed. by E. Mazzali (Milan–Naples, 1959), 479.
[23] R. G. Faithfull, 297–8. This interest in spoken Italian, which Faithfull wrongly attributes to Beni, can however be seen, though in an exclusively Florentine context, in the much earlier works of Giovan Battista Gelli and Benedetto Varchi.

that 'Paolo Beni [. . .] enuncia questo principio con notevole chiarezza'.[24]

But how far *is* Beni interested in spoken levels of Italian? It is true that, in theory at least, he speaks of an 'Italiano linguaggio, il quale de' attendersi al presente' (G. 583), and *comune uso* is often confronted with fourteenth-century usage. But an examination of the references in the *Goffredo* to *comune uso* reveals that in practice Beni's apparent interest in spoken Italian (which Faithfull made so much of) is very slight indeed. He argues from the authority of *comune uso* at least twelve times during the commentary:

1. *Absorto* is defended: 'nondimeno perchè nel commun parlare etiandio di huomini scientiati e dotti si ode *tutto absorto in Dio, absorto dal piacere*, e simili, io non ho per inconveniente il veder usata una tal voce' (G. 58).

2. He speaks of *comun parlare* in which 'non è cosa inaudita e nuova il dare il quarto caso al verbo persuadere' (G. 61).

3. *Acquisti* is used in *comun parlare* to mean 'worldly goods' (G. 143).

4. *Avventurieri*, not recorded in the *Crusca*, was of necessity derived by Tasso from *comun parlare* and *uso popolare* (G. 185).

5. *Apporsi* (='to guess') is defended: 'e pur communemente si suol dir Tu non ti apponghi al vero' (G. 323). The point is illustrated with examples from Dante and Ariosto.

6. '*Strage* e *decoro*, sono usitatissime, e tutto giorno s'odono in bocca di huomini eruditi e gravi e tra gente nobile. Contuttociò la Crusca non si degna di farne mentione' (G. 327–8). Here it is clear that spoken Italian is limited to what noble and educated men speak throughout Italy.

7. 'Decoro poi oltr'il venir usato alla giornata tanto in scrivendo quanto in parlando da persone gravi e giuditiose' (G. 328).

8. He invokes *comun parlare* only to illustrate it with a Latin quotation: 'avvertiscasi che seben nel commun parlare molti distinguono la rosa da i fiori, sì che etiandio da moderno Poeta si canta "*Oebalios flores Idaliasque rosas*" ' (G. 474). Here the reference is to written (not exclusively Italian) usage.

---

[24] Faithfull, 226; see also p. 218 and O. Lombardelli, *Fonti toscane* (Florence, 1598), 59.

9. *Nocente* and *innocente* are antonyms in *comun parlare*, and the point is clinched by a quotation from Boccaccio (G. 487).

10. 'Insomma nelle parole tratte in modo dal Latino che non men da intendenti che da' Idioti si leggono o pronunciano trasformate; come *fiore, acqua, braccio, nebbia, chiodo, fiume*, e simiglianti, non ha dubbio che debbiam seguir'il commun'uso: e non dir *flore*' etc. (G. 605). Here the concept is not exclusively that of spoken Italian.

11. *S'aspetta* (='appartiene') is 'voce nel commun parlare assai usata e trita: seben ne' Vocabolarii non se ne fa mention alcuna' (G. 708).

12. He defends Tasso's *imbasciata* (for 'ambasciata'): 'nel commun parlare etiandio in bocca di persone gravi e scientiate non meno Imbasciata s'oda che Ambasciata' (G. 805).

It has been necessary to explore these comments in some detail in order to show that in Beni's mind *comune uso* extended very little down the linguistic ladder. As often as not it refers to written usage (which is far preferable to him); and if it refers to spoken levels of language it is only to the very highest (witness examples 1, 6, 7, and 12 above). Altogether Beni betrays a narrower concept of *uso* than has previously been thought. His attitude to usage is predominantly literary: he stands apart both from fifteenth-century linguistic innovation and freedom and from the new Baroque lexical freedom as defined by Faithfull (p. 284). And it is interesting to note here that in the linguistic field (as in others, notably that of poetic theory) Beni's true cultural importance has been mistaken by critics intent on describing him as a Modern.

The commentary on the *Goffredo* thus allowed Beni to bring the theoretical conditions of his perfect dictionary more sharply into realistic focus: it would evidently be based on written sources, both Italian and Latin. It would pay very little attention to *comune uso* and spoken Italian, and even less to Lombardelli's 'vocaboli del vulgo'.

VIII

It would be foolish to pretend that everything in Beni's linguistic writings is logical and reasonable. For there remains, however one explains it, one apparent flaw which colours almost everything he wrote on the subject of language. This flaw springs from his aim in the *Anticrusca* (to compare and contrast the principal dictionaries of the Italian language). This he does mainly by going straight to what he considers the root of the problem, namely the literary texts on which such dictionaries were based. His most extensive section (*A.* IV 87–254) is devoted to criticism of the *Crusca*. Beni aims, as is his wont, to be exhaustive (but he mercifully gives up his attempt to review individually all the *Crusca*'s fourteenth-century sources). It would be tedious to summarize everything he wrote on the language of the numerous writers or groups of writers reviewed in the *Anticrusca*. Furthermore it would be exceedingly provocative. Anyone who is sensitive to literature and to the literary qualities in the works under review would be appalled by Beni's apparent lack of discernment and discretion. For, in all his linguistic works, Beni reads literature as language, and judges literature by misleading linguistic standards. This is best seen in his infamous treatment of Boccaccio and Dante, surely two of the most 'individual' voices in Italian literature.

Behind Beni's criticisms of Boccaccio's prose there lurks the ideal of a lucid regulated standard prose style. It is as if Beni thought that there was only one correct way of expressing any given object or idea in prose. If we wish to use labels, we might say that this is far more classical than Baroque. We can see this in Beni's comparison of Boccaccio with various historians. Tassoni had shown that Guicciardini was superior to G. Villani (a valid and justified comparison between two Italian historians);[25] but, more ambitious and less realistic, Beni sets out to show that Guicciardini was as good as, if not better than, Boccaccio (Boccaccio the *novelliere*). To prove this he lays end to end passages by Guicciardini, Sallust, Livy, and Boccaccio.[26] Guicciardini is shown to be equal to Livy and Sallust (*A.* 141). Boccaccio, on the contrary, is inferior to them in every respect (*A.* 142). His style is judged to be heavy and obscure, and his language is thought to be incorrect in such words as *richesto, saramenti, fedire, imbolava, coscienza, offer[r]ebbe* (*A.* 143). Beni

---

[25] For details of this, see Tassoni, *Prose politiche e morali*, ed. cit., ii. 283–8.
[26] Beni here quotes Sallust on Catiline and Jugurtha, Livy on Hannibal, Guicciardini on Alessandro Sesto, and Boccaccio on Ser Ciappelletto.

here falls into his perennial habit of reading an author not for his individual voice or style but for his correctness and conformity to an ideal model clarity. In comparing Boccaccio with Guicciardini Beni makes no attempt to see that the intentions of the two writers were vastly different: the idea of reading a writer on his own terms is foreign to his concept of standard language and style.

Elsewhere he uses as his *point de départ* a procedure adopted first by Salviati. But, unlike Salviati, his aim is unrealistic, and his results misleading. He takes and quotes *Decameron* 1. 9, which Salviati had translated into various Italian dialects,[27] and rewrites it (A. 162–8). With criticism of this type he intended to undermine the very foundations of the *Crusca*, to bring its authorities into disrepute, and suggest that, in placing Boccaccio higher on the league-table than Petrarch, the Crusca had got its linguistic (and by implication its literary and aesthetic) priorities wrong. Beni's treatment of *Decameron* 1. 9 provides a good example of how he failed in his linguistic criticism (because of his chosen point of view) to make the necessary distinction between language on the one hand and stylistic and literary qualities on the other. His most serious most persistent criticism is of the *Decameron*'s obscure involved syntax, which is considered to be too complicated to be credible in the mouths of the *brigata* (A. 165). Consequently, in his redaction of 1. 9 Beni simplifies the syntax, and, as in *Anticrusca* I, he is particularly concerned to regulate what he considers to be Boccaccio's loose use of relative pronouns. Thus, where Boccaccio had written

Ad Elisa restava l'ultimo commandamento della Reina, la quale, senza aspettarlo, tutta festevole cominciò

Beni clarifies what he considers the obscure *la quale*

Già l'ultimo commandamento della Regina toccava ad Elisa, la qual perciò senza aspettarlo, tutta festevole, così prese a ragionare (A. 168).

Conjunctions are altered and reduced to clarity; but altogether, Boccaccio's finely wrought and modulated style, hypotactic and capable of great nuances of light and shade, foreground and background, is disparaged and ignored. For Beni somehow expects—anachronistically and it must be said unartistically—

---

[27] *Avvertimenti*, Appendix to vol. i.

that the *novella* in question should conform to a modern regular standard as though its whole aim were merely to pronounce in simple transparent terms a bare factual message. Beni's comments are therefore inept as literary criticism of Boccaccio; as linguistic comments on the contemporary usefulness of Boccaccio as a model they are, however, significant and worthy of serious attention. But, because for Beni linguistic problems are necessarily literary problems, the two areas are never properly separated. For this reason Beni thinks nothing of bringing Boccaccio's language up to date and of criticizing it for being out of date (as if Boccaccio were guilty of writing without taking into account the needs of the seventeenth century: but Beni is criticizing the Crusca's mistaken use of outmoded models for the Italian language).

When Beni says that Boccaccio is of little use to modern writers and that he has been superseded by modern developments, he is of course saying nothing very new. His views on Boccaccio could, for example, be compared with Castiglione's.[28] But while Castiglione retains much respect for Boccaccio, claiming, not (like Beni) that he was all bad, but that it would be wrong to assume that there was no development in the Italian language after his death, Beni finds little to praise, and takes Boccaccio's linguistic faults as evidence of his failure in all other departments of writing.

More instructive in this respect is Beni's treatment of Dante's literary qualities, especially when we compare Beni's reactions to Bembo's.[29] For it was Bembo who supplied Beni not only with the seeds of his own critical ideas about Dante but also with a vocabulary capable of describing the apparent faults in Dante's language. Bembo's tactfully expressed views are well

[28] *Il Cortegiano*, I. xxxvi and I. xxxvii (*ad finem*).

[29] Earlier reactions to Dante (up to Bembo) are briefly examined in C. Grayson, 'Dante and the Renaissance', in *Italian Studies Presented to E. R. Vincent*, 57–75. The following studies mention Beni in general surveys of Dante's critical fortunes in the seventeenth century: U. Cosmo, *Con Dante attraverso il Seicento* (Bari, 1946), 21–7; U. Limentani, art. cit., 10–13; L. Martinelli, *Dante* (Storia della critica, 4) General Ed. G. Petronio (Palermo, 1966); A. Vallone, *L'interpretazione di Dante nel Cinquecento*, 2nd edn. (Florence, 1969), 277–82; R. Frattarolo, *Studi su Dante dal Trecento all'età romantica*, i (Ravenna, 1970); G. Tavani, *Dante nel Seicento: saggi su A. Guarini, N. Villani, L. Magalotti* (Florence, 1976), 42–5. The following studies are particularly hostile to Beni's views on Dante: C. Trabalza, *La critica letteraria* (Milan, 1915), 253; Belloni, 'Un professore', 265–9.

known, partly because they were symptomatic of a common critical reaction, and partly because they heralded much seventeenth-century reaction. Bembo's linguistic and stylistic criteria were based on Petrarch's achievement; and he clearly saw that Petrarch and Dante belonged to separate poetic traditions.[30] According to Bembo, Dante failed to observe grammatical rules and he abandoned essential criteria of beauty: Petrarch, by contrast, was 'osservantissimo [. . .] di tutte non solamente le regole, ma ancora le leggiadrie della lingua'.[31] Both Bembo and Beni found Dante's language crude, rough, primitive; but whereas Bembo felt that the subject-matter of the *Comedy* was to blame for this, Beni offered no such excuse and did not find in Dante that 'bello e spazioso campo' which Bembo so picturesquely described:

Con ciò sia cosa che a fine di poter di qualunque cosa scrivere, che ad animo gli veniva, quantunque poco acconcia e malagevole a caper nel verso, egli molto spesso ora le latine voci, ora le straniere, che non sono state dalla Toscana ricevute, ora le vecchie del tutto e tralasciate, ora le non usate e rozze, ora le immonde e brutte, ora le durissime usando, e allo 'ncontro le pure e gentili alcuna volta mutando e guastando, e talora, senza alcuna scelta o regola, da sé formandone e fingendone, ha in maniera operato, che si può la sua Comedia giustamente rassomigliare ad un bello e spazioso campo di grano, che sia tutto d'avene e di logli e d'erbe sterili e dannose mescolato, o ad alcuna non potata vite al suo tempo, la quale si vede essere poscia la state sì di foglie e di pampini e di viticci ripiena, che se ne offendono le belle uve (p. 89).

But Beni goes far beyond Bembo. Bembo attributed Dante's roughness to the very lofty and difficult subject of the *Comedy*. Beni conceives of this roughness as a personal fault, peculiar to Dante: 'Fu oltre modo rozzo; e [. . .] ciò avenne non tanto per l'altezza dell'argomento, o imperitia di que' tempi, quanto per mancamento d'ingegno (parlo nel poetare) e di giuditio' (*Cav.* 26). With his unartistic notion that there is a standard way of saying everything in prose and verse, Beni goes on to argue that Petrarch, given the same subject-matter, would have avoided Dante's *bassezze* (*Cav.* 26). These *bassezze* are words and phrases which, with their plebeian or highly realistic overtones, seem

[30] See C. Dionisotti, 'Bembo, Pietro', in *Enciclopedia dantesca*, i (1970), 568.
[31] P. Bembo, *Prose della volgar lingua*, ed. by M. Marti (Padua, 1955), 161.

inappropriate in a poem whose subject is a divine journey. Of the twenty examples of Dante's 'plebei, sozzi modi di parlare' which Beni cites, fifteen are from the *Inferno*. Evidently Beni was incapable of realizing that what he saw as a conflict between language and subject-matter was in fact an attempt on Dante's part to employ a low level of language to suit the low level of subject in the *Inferno*, and, elsewhere in the *Comedy*, as a means of increasing the realism of the work.

While Bembo traced Dante's linguistic faults to his subject-matter, Beni traces them to his choice of *terza rima*, the most difficult of forms (*A.* 204; *Cav.* 119). Unlike Petrarch in the *Trionfi* (*A.* 14) Dante showed no skill in handling his chosen metre: his rhymes are mostly 'sforzate'; his need to find rhymes led him into linguistic difficulties, unacceptable Latinisms (*Cav.* 24), neologisms (*G.* 685), and false metrical quantities (*G.* 685). In a clear effort to show that his linguistic faults led Dante into philosophical and theological faults, Beni suggests that the allegory of the *Comedy* was inadequate and wrong because Dante was constantly under pressure to obey his rhyme scheme (*G.* 104–5). This may seem an absurd and casuistical accusation; but it shows how, over a century, Beni's ideas about Dante had moved on from Bembo's. Beni reverses Bembo's equation, and suggests that Dante's failure as a theologian and philosopher was a direct result of his failure as a linguist. As in all Beni's linguistic criticism, Dante's specifically literary qualities are buried beneath a welter of linguistic comment. Such misguided literary judgements abound in Beni's linguistic writings. And not only in his adverse criticism (witness his treatment of Tasso).

I have dwelt at some length on this aspect of his work, partly because it has not been commented on before and partly because, if anything, it is the one area in which he can justifiably be faulted. It is easy to see what led him to this approach. Previous lexicographers had inevitably conducted literary *spogli*; yet their literary criticism was silent, tacit, apparent only in their adoption or rejection of this or that author (although Salviati and others had yoked together linguistic and literary considerations during the controversies over the *Liberata*). Beni was not satisfied with the criticism of individual entries in the dictionaries he reviewed (that might have been a more appropriate approach), and his desire to criticize the literary foundations of the dictionaries led him to denigrate style and content in the name of language.

Does this invalidate his linguistic criticism? For some, his lack of discernment must surely prove the ultimate stumbling-block. But if we remember how important it must have been to him, in the face of the *Crusca*, to make his point as strenuously as possible, it is not difficult to argue that his fault is only that he took a good point too far, partly as a result of his character, and partly as a result of his training. As linguistic criticism his work still stands; as literary criticism it appears maimed: like many before him, Beni read authors in order to learn how to write rather than to undergo some sort of literary experience. In order to understand his linguistic comments we must try to ignore his literary ones.

IX

There is a rigorous consistency as well as a remarkable urgency and intensity in his linguistic theory. That he should have resented the Crusca's archaic and authoritarian stand was only natural. His hostile reaction to the *Crusca* never developed or altered. Against the imperfections (as he saw them) of that dictionary he set his own ideal dictionary, with its logical and rational order, its underlying grammatical precepts based on reason, and its inclusion of all modern words in common use amongst 'good' writers or, at least, noble speakers. Clearly it would have nothing to do with the Florentine (or any other) dialect: it would be based on the vocabulary common to the whole of Italy, as used by the major Italian authors. Yet four-teenth-century writers would not be excluded: Petrarch would hold a pre-eminent place; and Dante and Boccaccio would no doubt be used. But the number of minor writings recorded in the *Crusca* would be reduced to make room for modern non-Florentine authorities. And although, as Ornella Olivieri has shown,[32] the *Crusca* was more modern than has often been thought, it did not satisfy Beni's need of an up-to-date diction-

---

[32] 'I primi vocabolari italiani fino alla prima edizione della Crusca', *Studi di filologia italiana*, 6 (1942), 64–192.

ary which could be trusted to include such basic and common written words as *stampare* (='to print (books)').[33] It was probably unrealistic in some ways to look for such a dictionary, but it was nevertheless an understandable and prophetic desire, as modern developments in Italian lexicography have shown. There is no evidence that Beni ever considered putting his own linguistic ideals into practice, thereby providing for Italy the sort of lexicographical tool whose lack (despite, or perhaps because of, the *Crusca*) was felt by many of his contemporaries, as well as by many eminent Italians during the following centuries.[34] His linguistic work was indeed only an interlude in his humanistic activities in Padua. It is to these that I now wish to turn.

[33] This example is quoted by Faithfull, 241–2.

[34] See, for example, V. Monti, 'Al Signor Marchese D. Gian Giacomo Trivulzio', in *Proposta di alcune correzioni ed aggiunte al Vocabolario della Crusca*, 3 vols. and 1 vol. (Appendix) (Milan, 1817–26), i (1817), pp. iii–lix, whose views are similar in many respects to Beni's, and whose dissatisfaction with the *Crusca*—though nourished in a different political climate—is not dissimilar in its intensity and sense of urgency. And Monti is only one of the dictionary's many critics throughout the centuries. I have made a separate study of the linguistic views of some of the other early critics of the *Crusca* (the Accademici della Crusca, A. Tassoni, and Giulio Ottonelli) which will be published soon as 'Some Early Critics of the First Edition of the *Vocabolario degli Accademici della Crusca* (1612)'.

12

THE COMMENTARY ON THE *POETICS* (I)

I

Beni's commentary on the *Poetics* (first published in 1613)[1] was the last complete formal commentary of its kind to be published in Italy, and comes at the end of a spate of such commentaries which had begun with Robortelli's in 1548. Like most of Beni's works, it is prolix and repetitive, occupying as it does more than six hundred folio pages, and offering a Greek text, two Latin translations (Pazzi's and Riccoboni's), as well as a thoroughgoing and meticulous commentary. In addition, Beni scattered throughout the work one hundred *controversiae* on key issues of poetic theory; and these are intended to provide definitive solutions to perennial problems of interpretation of Aristotle's text.

It is not proposed here to offer a complete, exhaustive critical examination of all aspects of the work. Nor is it proposed to give an account of its immediate impact either on Baroque poetic theory and practice in Italy (the comments of recent critics which will be surveyed in this chapter take it for granted that such an impact was decisive), or in France (where it is clear, after the briefest glance, that Beni's ideas were respected and well received).[2] Instead, in this and the following chapter, I shall limit myself to two complementary tasks. First, after some remarks on the work's modern critical fortunes, I shall examine in detail and in isolation Beni's pronouncements on two central issues arising from the *Poetics*: namely, imitation and the function of poetry. These two issues are, of course, very far from exhausting the content of Beni's commentary; but they

[1] *In Aristotelis Poeticam commentarii* (Padua, 1613) (hereafter *P.*). I quote throughout from this 1st edn. This chapter and the next are emended and slightly abridged versions of an article originally published in *Studi secenteschi*, 25 (1984), 53–100.
[2] See H. Phillips, *The Theatre and Its Critics in Seventeenth-Century France* (Oxford, 1980), 63.

represent some of his most fundamental preoccupations, and provide a good example of his characteristic method and manner. Secondly, I shall extend my field of vision in order to compare Beni's views on a wide variety of poetic issues (including imitation and the function of poetry) with those of earlier Italian commentators of the *Poetics*. By these means I hope both to clarify Beni's personal ideas and to replace them in their historical context: an exercise which will make it possible to judge aright the originality and cultural importance of Beni's work.

II

True modern critical attention can be said to begin (and in some ways finish) with J. E. Spingarn who, in 1899, called Beni's work 'the last of the great Italian commentaries on the *Poetics* to have a general European influence',[3] but did not consider it further because it fell outside his chronological range. Four years later, U. Cosmo, discussing Beni's anti-Dante pro-Tasso attitude, which was (he says) typical of the age, raises a question which has never been answered when he dismisses the possibility of Beni's vernacular literary criticism having in any way been influenced by his literary Aristotelianism: Cosmo mentions Beni's commentary on the *Poetics* only to show that it was irrelevant to his practical literary criticism (a view which is not convincing, given the links between the *Comparatione* and the commentary on the *Poetics*).[4] C. Trabalza's *La critica letteraria* of 1915 erroneously applies Spingarn's comment (quoted above) to the *Comparatione* instead of to the commentary on the *Poetics*, and is otherwise uninformative on the subject.[5]

It was not, therefore, until 1920 that Beni's work first received serious critical attention, from G. Toffanin who sees in the work all the characteristics of Secentismo. According to Toffanin, Beni's work—a distortion of Aristotle, written 'in Latino

[3] *A History of Literary Criticism in the Renaissance*, 2nd edn. (New York, 1908), 140.
[4] 'Le polemiche tassesche, la Crusca e Dante sullo scorcio del cinque e il principio del seicento', *Giornale storico della letteratura italiana*, 43 (1903), 112–60; also in id., *Con Dante attraverso il Seicento*, 1–75. On the links between Beni's commentary on the *Poetics* and his criticism of Tasso, see above, Chapter 10, Sections II and IV.
[5] Milan, 1915, 252.

marinista per isfoggio di sapienza'—characterizes poetry as a lovely vague and magnificent art, totally removed from moral preoccupations, towering above and divorced from politics, logic, grammar, history, and civil law. Toffanin's view—which shows evidence of his knowledge only of Beni's introductory *Oratio* where poetry is allegorically and extravagantly represented as the Queen of the Liberal Arts—seeks to integrate Beni's commentary into the cultural pattern of his times: and so Toffanin neatly links the *concetto predicabile* of Spanish and Italian preachers, the poetry of Marino, and Beni's commentary on the *Poetics* as three manifestations of the same cultural phenomenon: namely, decadence.[6]

Toffanin's interpretation caught on, and was substantially repeated by Belloni in an essay of 1922 in which it is said, clearly without a proper knowledge of the text, that Beni's definition of poetry 'racchiude in sè la quintessenza del secentismo: essa viene a dire che ciò che importa in arte è la forma esteriore, la decorazione, gli ornamenti: a questo deve tendere ogni sforzo dell'ingegno: ed ecco la virtuosità, l'artificio usurpare il posto dell'arte: ecco il secentismo' ('Un professore', p. 254).

Neither Toffanin nor Belloni attempted any detailed discussion of Beni's work: they were both at pains to map the outlines of a barely explored cultural territory. The same can be said of two later, and major, studies. The first, G. Zonta's 'Rinascimento, aristotelismo, e barocco', published in 1934,[7] attempts to trace the aesthetic transformation in Italy from Renaissance to Baroque. According to Zonta's theory, the Renaissance balance between Life and Art, Reason and Imagination, began to tilt around 1548 (the year of Robortelli's *Explicationes*) in favour of Art and Imagination. This shift in emphasis was effected (says Zonta) by means of the gradual distortion of Aristotle's *Poetics*, and especially the distortion in the commentators of its concepts of imitation (which became identified with *fictio fabulosa*) and catharsis (which became identified with *meraviglia*). Zonta does not hold Aristotle responsible for this shift in taste: he finds instead that the Church and Italy's spiritual tiredness around 1550 were the

---

[6] *La fine dell'Umanesimo* (Milan–Turin–Rome, 1920), 135–9.
[7] *Giornale storico della letteratura italiana*, 104 (1934), 1–63 and 185–240.

prime causes of cultural decline on all levels. By the beginning of the seventeenth century (continues Zonta) poetry had been totally divorced from Reason and Life; and the Imagination reigned supreme. Enter Paolo Beni, who clinches Zonta's argument for him: 'che tali conclusioni siano giuste ne dà la riprova l'ultimo commentatore della *Poetica*, il quale, in uno stile già del tutto barocco, non solo ripete tutte le opinioni anteriori, ma alla fine dà la più secentesca di tutte le definizioni' (p. 194). And, continues Zonta, following in the narrow wake of Toffanin, it is only a short step from this to fully fledged Baroque art which, cut off from ordinary Reason, could develop its own curious brand of Reason, namely, *ingegno*.

The second of these surveys of the cultural period comes from G. Morpurgo Tagliabue in his essay 'Aristotelismo e barocco' of 1955.[8] The details of his theory are not relevant here (for Beni is never inserted into the pattern of things) but an isolated comment makes it all too clear that, as in the previous work of Toffanin, Belloni, and Zonta, Beni's works had not been studied. For, in justification of the assertion that the Secentisti abandoned Aristotle's notion of the 'golden mean' in their attitude to metaphor, Morpurgo Tagliabue offers the following quotation from (as he mistakenly thinks) Beni's commentary on the *Poetics*: ' "La poesia non deve essere nè chiara nè precisa: deve essere soltanto magnifica" ' (quoted on p. 141). Now this is the very phrase which Toffanin and Belloni had quoted (inexplicably in Italian rather than Latin, and with no page reference); and, although it might have proved handy for the construction of a· makeshift theory, yet it did little justice, as we shall see, to Beni's painstaking and scholarly commentary.

In fact, it was not until 1958, with the publication of an article by C. Jannaco,[9] that Beni's commentary received any detailed consideration. Jannaco's work is pioneering, for it attempts to do more than merely accommodate Beni to a cultural pattern. Jannaco's general conclusion is that

l'*opus magnum* del Beni può essere considerato un deciso avvìo all'estetica del concettismo vero e proprio, in quanto viene a completare l'*ade-*

---

[8] In *Retorica e barocco: Atti del III Congresso Internazionale di Studi Umanistici*, ed. by E. Castelli (Rome, 1955), 119–95.

[9] 'Critici del primo Seicento', 219–44 (pp. 222–31 on Beni).

guamento d'Aristotele alla nuova sensibilità retorica della decadenza
rinascimentale e [. . .] della prima insorgenza barocca (p. 224).

It is shown, however, that Beni stood at a cultural crossroads: he
is neither at home with the new Baroque sensibility nor can he
understand 'la sostanza vera del pensiero antico' (p. 231). The
result of this is (for Jannaco) Beni's contradictory theorizing.
This view, which in essence is no more than an adaptation of
Toffanin's, Belloni's, and Zonta's, is supported, however, by a
closer reading of Beni's words in the attempt—admittedly not
completely fulfilled in only nine pages—to see the work in historical perspective. Jannaco reveals (as he sees it) Beni's distinction between poetry (*fictio fabulosa*) and history (truth), *poesia*
and *poetica*, his highly Baroque view of poetry, and his equally
Baroque interest in allegory, metaphor, and hyperbole, an interest which led Beni (according to Jannaco's interpretation) to
blur the line between truth and falsehood in poetry. *Horror* and
voluptas (rather than *utilitas*) are shown to be Beni's special preoccupations; and his interpretation of Aristotle's notion of catharsis (as well as of other central Aristotelian poetic issues) is
shown to be a pretext for 'edonismo, se non ancora di sensualismo' (p. 228). In Jannaco's presentation of him, Beni emerges
as a hedonist in classicist's clothing, and, as such, is judged to
be more culturally significant than such overt hedonists of the
Cinquecento as B. Tasso, Castelvetro, and Robortelli. Jannaco
also pays tribute to Beni's 'impegno e accuratezza—anche tipo-
grafica' (p. 223), admitting that there is more to Beni's work
than a distortion of Aristotle; but he does not enlarge on that
'more'. In the last analysis, it seems that, despite its closer attention to Beni's own words, Jannaco's interpretation does not
really go much beyond that of Toffanin, and does not bring us
to a new and deeper understanding of the significance of Beni's
work: for there remains something uncritically subjective about
Jannaco's essay. It is as if Jannaco read Beni merely to derive
from him those quotations which would support his general
(inherited) view of the Seicento, rather than vice versa.

The Americans, who are meanwhile at work on the critical
literature of the Italian Renaissance, tend (unlike the Italians we
have examined) to isolate literary criticism or theory from
broader cultural and aesthetic problems. B. Hathaway's *The Age*

of Criticism, published in 1962,[10] represents the most substantial, thorough, and objective account of Beni's commentary to date. It also provides a very different view from that of the Italians. Hathaway sees Beni's work against the background of Aristotelian literary scholarship in the sixteenth century, as the culmination of the arduous attempt to understand what Aristotle wrote about poetry. He is therefore more concerned to summarize what Beni said on various issues than to interpret what he said in the light of Secentismo or any other cultural abstraction. The problem here is that Hathaway's treatment of the issues tends to be more disjointed than Beni's, and so it fails to characterize Beni's ideas clearly enough. Hathaway discusses, for instance, all Beni's pronouncements on the thorny question of imitation, failing to relate them as he proceeds to any central argument, and leaving us in the end with a contradictory picture. In one place he tells us that Beni 'went beyond this point to develop one of the most comprehensive treatments of mimetic theory of the late Renaissance' (p. 20); this is later contradicted when it is said of Beni that 'unlike some of his predecessors, he failed to come forth with a clear theory of imitation because he refused to surrender anything' (p. 63). Similarly, we are told that Beni provided the last word on the question of catharsis for forty-seven years (up to the time of Corneille's *Discours*) (p. 284), but then this judgement is contradicted when we are told that Beni's theory of catharsis was weak and disappointing (p. 289). Despite this faultiness of organization, Beni's ideas—all of them carefully documented—do surface here and there in Hathaway's book: they are not only summarized, but extracted from their contexts, reshuffled, assorted into new categories, and mixed in with the pronouncements of all the other critics of the age. Beni emerges from all this as a Modern (pp. 62 and 430), a relativist (p. 62), something of a Platonist and a rationalist (p. 164), a wrathful professor, devoid of humour (pp. 275 and 428–9), and a 'conveyor of much of the late-sixteenth-century Italian literary speculation to France and the northern countries' (p. 290). Beni is seen as the finishing-post of sixty-five years of Aristotelian scholarship in Italy (p. 116), and not as the starting-post of a new 'Baroque' age

[10] Ithaca–New York, 1962.

(p. 459). Finally, it is interesting to note in Hathaway's work how a critic, cut off from, and apparently unaware of, twentieth-century Italian literary criticism, can see in Beni's theory of catharsis anything but the hedonist's delight, *meraviglia*, and *voluptas* which Jannaco and others in Italy have so clearly divined:

HATHAWAY. 'Beni's was (more than most) a rational rather than emotional interpretation of Catharsis' (pp. 289–90);

JANNACO. 'Il vero è che la spirituale catarsi aristotelica, arbitrariamente interpretata come mezzo di effetti stupefacenti, si è ormai snaturata intridendosi di edonismo, se non ancora di sensualismo' (p. 228).

The little done in Italy since 1962 on Beni's commentary (by Mazzacurati, Paparelli, Doglio, and others) generally reiterates Jannaco's words and ignores Hathaway's. This neglect, which has resulted in the premature fossilization of our understanding of Beni (if not also of his age), is perhaps not surprising given Mazzacurati's claim in 1966 (in no less a place than the *Dizionario biografico degli Italiani*) that Jannaco had already examined Beni's commentary 'in maniera esauriente'. Were nine pages adequate?

Before proceeding to give some account of the relationship between Beni and the earlier commentators, it is as well to try and remedy the relative neglect of his work in the remainder of this chapter with a detailed examination of his treatment of two major issues which most attracted his attention throughout the commentary.

III

Much of Beni's commentary is devoted to the discovery of what Aristotle had meant by imitation (which he had made the foundation of all poetry), and of what he had intended as the proper subject of such poetic imitation. At the end of his commentary on *Caput* I of the *Poetics*,[11] Beni concludes that Aristotle has tried to do three things: first, he has defined poetry as 'imitantium artium genus'; second, he has defined poetry's individual *formae* and *species*; and third, he has explored the threefold division of imitation according to instrument, subject-matter, and

[11] *Poetics*, 1447^a–1448^b 4 (the first three chapters in modern edns.).

mode. Beni finds Aristotle's treatment of all these subjects more or less unsatisfactory, partly because the *Poetics* is unfinished, partly because Aristotle is too concise, and partly because he wrote for an age which understood the basic assumptions beneath his precepts (p. 116–21). Consequently, thoughout his commentary, Beni stumbles again and again over one of the major inconveniences of the *Poetics*: namely, that it offers no clear definition of imitation even though it makes *imitatio* the corner-stone of poetic theory.

Beni valiantly faces up to the problem of definition early in his commentary, in *Controversia* XIV entitled bluntly 'Quid imitationis intelligat [Aristoteles] nomine' (*P*. 57–63). He begins by considering the sheer breadth of the term, which Aristotle interchanges with other similarly broad terms, and which simply means 'representationem alicuius rei'. Beni goes on to argue that *imitatio* is quintessentially a process whereby God, in Biblical terms, created the Word, his Son, in his own image; a process whereby, in Platonic terms, God created the world after Ideas in his mind. By analogy with God's relationship to the world (continues Beni) Nature imitates God, and Art in turn imitates Nature. Further down the scale it is seen that the 'Orator et Historicus et quisquis aliquid agit, aliquo modo imitatur, cum vel alterum, vel imaginem aliquam, sive externa illa sit sive mentis, exprimere nitatur'. However, this broad meaning which seems to inform the creative activity of anyone is felt by Beni not to bear directly enough on the definition of poetic imitation to be of any use. He consequently asks what Plutarch had meant by the term, and fails to discover an answer. He secondly asks what Aristotle had meant by it, and again discovers that Aristotle offered no definition, and used the term self-contradictorily: now saying that Homer does imitate when he speaks *ex propria persona*, now denying the same. (Beni later returned to this important contradiction.) Thirdly, he asks what Plato had meant by *imitatio*. And here he finds some satisfaction. For Plato clearly distinguished between, on the one hand, plain narration (*simplex narratio*) in which the writer speaks *ex propria persona* as in the dithyramb or the lyric, and which contains no imitation, and, on the other hand, imitation proper (*non simplex*) in which the poet makes others speak as in drama and some non-narrative parts of the epic.

With Plato's definition clearly in mind, Beni returns to Aristotle. It is obvious (he says) that Aristotle implicitly accepted Plato's definition of *imitatio* as 'narrationem, qua quis aut figura aut voce alterum representat': such an acceptance is clear from Aristotle's assertion that Homer was an imitator in so far as he made others speak, and not in so far as he himself spoke *in propria persona*. This part of Aristotle's definition is further brought into focus in *Controversia* xx (P. 91–4), where the important distinction is drawn between the vivid representation of inanimate objects (*enargeia*), which is shared by poets, historians, and orators alike, but which should be only incidental to the poet's work, and, on the other side, the form of imitation which is peculiar and exclusive to poets: namely the imitation of men in action.

So far then Beni has managed to cull from Aristotle the following definition of *imitatio*: 'the portrayal by voice or in person of a character in action'. Such, more or less, was Plato's definition in *Republic* III. But, as to Plato's other non-imitative type of poetry (*simplex narratio*), Aristotle seems to Beni ambivalent and self-contradictory. For in *Particula* xv he allows that Homer is imitating when he narrates *ex propria persona*, but in *Particula* CXXXI he denies this. Such a contradiction puzzles and worries Beni who realizes that if Homer, speaking *ex propria persona*, be conceded imitator status, then it follows that lyric poets, orators, and historians must also by the same token be called imitators, and therefore (in Aristotelian terms) poets (P. 109). Instead of dismissing Aristotle's contradiction as an oversight, Beni uses it as an opportunity for developing a neat theory of *imitatio* which he twice formulates in the course of his commentary (P. 61–3 and 105–12).

As we have seen, *imitatio* in the accepted poetic sense is only available to poets, and not to historians and such like. For if the historian (or the orator) were to imitate (represent men in action) as the poet must do rather than speak *in propria persona*, then his work would be suspect and lack credibility (P. 110). But, as far as Beni can see, there is no real difference between the narration *ex propria persona* of Virgil and that of Sallust, save in the former's use of verse which, *pace* Plato, is incidental (P. 109). Beni wishes to establish once and for all whether such narration *ex propria persona* can be granted the name of *imitatio*.

Aristotle, as we saw, answers both 'Yes' and 'No'. Beni's dissatisfaction with this leads him to define a secondary type of
imitation which the poet (as narrator) can share with the historian and the orator: namely the literary imitation of writers in
the same genre (*P.* 111). Beni warns, however, that the poet's
licence should be greater here than the historian's: for the literary imitation of the historian must be limited to form and style,
while that of the poet can include subject-matter as well as form
and style (*P.* 62). With this subtle refinement of Aristotle, Beni
contrives to allow poets (and to a lesser extent others) who
speak *ex propria persona* some share in the glorious name of
imitator, albeit only a minor share (*P.* 109).

Though Beni is unsure of the precise Aristotelian definition
of imitation, nevertheless he concurs (like most of his contemporaries) with Aristotle in seeing imitation rather than verse as
the essential ingredient of all poetry (*P.* 77 and 68–9). However,
he intuits that Aristotle's exaltation of imitation over verse as
poetry's defining feature was motivated by resentment against
his teacher, Plato. Accordingly, Beni refuses to be drawn into an
Aristotelian disregard for verse; and although he broadly agrees
with Aristotle's concentration of attention on imitation as
poetry's *genus*, yet he does not follow Aristotle's authority to its
logical conclusion. In the first place, he refuses to admit categor-
ically that Aristotle wished to deprive works in verse but without imitation of the status of poetry: for although Aristotle did
not call them 'good' poems, he might have called them poems
nevertheless. Secondly, Beni refuses to admit that an epic in
prose, but with imitation, could rank among the 'best' poems
(*P.* 81). Thirdly, Beni refuses to allow metre to be divorced from
any genre of poetry save the dramatic, where the convention of
declaiming in verse is thought to threaten verisimilitude (*P.*
82–3). Finally, Beni disagrees with Aristotle's notion that the
Platonic (and the Ciceronian) dialogues could be classed as
poetry, even though they contain much in the way of imitation
(*P.* 81).

The definition of imitation outlined above allowed Beni to
deal to some extent with the proper subject of poetic imitation:
the actions of men. But such a vague definition is not felt by
Beni to be informative enough. It does not tell us what sort of
actions should be imitated, whence they should be derived,

how they should be treated, and to what purpose. Accordingly, there is, throughout the commentary, a constant regard for the question: Should poetry's subject be falsehood, historical truth, verisimilitude, or universal ideals? In finding the theoretical answers to this question it will become apparent that these things are not mutually exclusive, for they all tend to resolve on the level of verisimilitude. But it is interesting to see how much relative weight Beni gives to each, and how often he differs from Aristotle in significant and unexpected ways.

Modern Italian critics have seen falsehood in Beni's commentary as the central subject for poetic imitation. For instance, Jannaco has written that

La poesia si diversifica anche dalla grammatica, dalla logica, dalla *civilis facultas*; ma più interessano gli sviluppi dell'estetica concettista e la violenta separazione della poesia stessa dalla storia e la sua conseguente identificazione con la *fictio fabulosa et dilectosa* [*sic; and Beni never used this phrase as far as I know*]. Mentre la storia è verità, la poesia è inganno: inganno di cui peraltro si afferma, con l'ingenua pretesa del suffragio ciceroniano, la piena legittimità (art. cit., p. 225).

There is much generally in the commentary to support this influential interpretation. First, there is the Aristotelian distinction between history (plain truth, plainly narrated) and poetry (verisimilitude), to which Beni, already the author of four books *de historia*,[12] constantly returns throughout the commentary on the *Poetics*. In the second place, because poetry does not have history's factual limitations it is free to use any form of embellishment it requires.[13]

Here Beni's generic claims might lead one to agree with Jannaco's view that, for Beni, poetry was a legitimate form of lying. But when Beni descends to particulars he makes it clear that, of the three literary genres which he considers (the epic, tragedy, and comedy), only comedy has an entirely free rein (*P.* 28). Invented names, for instance, are only wholly admissible in comedy; in tragedy, where the burden of credibility is greater, invented names are best avoided (*P.* 286).

If it is strange that a critic who is widely reputed to consider poetry as a form of lying should maintain, with Aristotle, that

---

[12] See below, Chapter 14.
[13] *P.* 4. See p. 181, below for a full quotation of the relevant passage.

tragedies are best limited to a few well-known, and therefore credible, historic family names, it is even more strange that the same critic should maintain, against Aristotle, that invented plots are out of place in tragedy. Yet it is so. Beni tells us that the question, first posed by Aristotle in the *Poetics*, as to whether the plot of a tragedy should be historical or invented was hotly debated in the sixteenth century, with Trissino on the side of historical plots and Giraldi, T. Tasso, and others on the side of invented plots (*P*. 289). Beni weighs up the arguments on both sides. He concedes that Aristotle made verisimilitude more important in poetry than factual truth, that a 'true' story is not obviously 'true' to an inexperienced audience, and that no one can possibly know all the by-ways of history (from which tragic plots might be derived). But Beni then puts the arguments in favour of the historical plot much more forcefully; and strongly concludes that truth of the historical kind is always preferable to falsehood in the plot of a tragedy. Beni finds himself forced to admit, therefore, that Tasso's *Torrismondo* and other fictitious tragedies are second class (*P*. 291). The advice with which Beni ends this debate very strongly belies his common image as a Tasso fanatic and the champion of the poetic lie. Furthermore, he decrees, following Aristotle, that an historical plot, once adopted (as it should be adopted), should not be altered except in its peripheral inessential parts. The same is also said of the epic, but not of comedy (which is always free to invent for itself) (*P*. 358).

It is clear from all this that Beni hovered between truth and falsehood in the commentary, as he did in his criticism of Tasso's *Liberata*. This appears to be an impossibly contradictory position. How, for instance, can he assert both that the poet, unlike the historian, is free to invent whatever he likes, and that Homer was wrong to tell lies (*mentiri*) in his quest for epic *admiratio* (*P*. 522–4)?

The partial resolution to this apparent contradiction lies in verisimilitude. Beni defines the poet, after Aristotle, as 'actionum verisimilium imitatorem' (*P*. 293), and verisimilitude, again after Aristotle, as 'poeticae actionis formam' (*P*. 295). According to Beni, verisimilitude is that broad stretch of territory which lies between truth and falsehood (*P*. 280), but, at the same time, verisimilitude is thought to be above the true–false dichotomy, for the historian narrates truth *qua* truth, while the poet relates truth (or indeed falsehoods) *qua* verisimilitude (*P*. 277).

In fact verisimilitude appears in Beni's commentary as his single most important guiding principle, and one that brings him closer to the French Classicists than to the Italian Baroque. For Beni, all poetic activity must depend on verisimilitude. This is so much the case that it is thought better, and here Beni is following Aristotle, to relate verisimilar lies than to tell inverisimilar truths (*P*. 277). The consideration of the audience's, or reader's, ability to believe in what it sees or hears informs all Beni's criticism. And the whole of his long campaign against verse in drama (which goes back to the *Disputatio* of 1600)[14] is based on the argument that it is not verisimilar (and therefore not beneficial to an audience) for actors to talk for hours on end in iambic metre, even though one or two iambuses might be expected to be thrown up during the normal course of conversation in Italian.

With the notion of verisimilitude always in the back of his mind, Beni never advocates the appearance of falsehood in poetry: for him poetry must always appear to be true. He does realize, however, that it is not possible for the poet always to preserve verisimilitude. He accordingly lists (in *Controversia* LII (*P*. 283–5)) six possible reasons for abandoning it. The most significant of these reasons is that the poet may sacrifice verisimilitude in order to excite (as excite he certainly must) *admiratio* (*P*. 284–5). But, far from allowing the poet a free licence or justifying Jannaco's conclusion that 'ora è chiaro che qui tenuissimo e trasparente diviene il limite che separa il vero dal falso, e che ormai l'assurdo ha piena cittadinanza in poesia' (art. cit., p. 227), Beni, like Aristotle, reminds us that any breach of verisimilitude should always be limited to the extrinsic inessential parts of a poem, and that it is always better avoided (*P*. 519). And the union of verisimilitude and *admiratio* can be effected by means of difficult but not impossible or incredible feats. This puts an extra burden on the poet to use his ingenuity and industry in exciting *admiratio* by the use of unexpected but logi-

---

[14] See Chapter 5, Section I for discussion of this *Disputatio*, and Chapter 5, Sections IV–VIII for discussion of its consequences.

cal steps in the plot (P. 284). *Admiratio* is completely out of place (according to Beni) in comedy; and it is to be used with care in tragedy because the eye (which watches tragedy) can spot inverisimilitude more readily than the ear (which listens to the epic) (P. 520).

Though Beni allows that the epic poet can go further than the tragic poet in breaching verisimilitude, yet he repeats throughout the commentary that the search for *admiratio* is not necessarily incompatible with the maintenance of verisimilitude, especially since the poet is free to invent. Indeed, it is in order to be able to preserve verisimilitude that the poet is so free to invent; and Beni only ever sanctions invention where verisimilitude is not thereby threatened (P. 526).

This general principle can be exemplified in his discussion of the place of *machina* (defined both as a stage contraption and as a general supernatural aid in tragedy and the epic), where the same conclusions are reached. *Machina* is totally out of place in comedy; more acceptable in the epic (which concerns both gods and men, and is heard, not seen) than in tragedy (which concerns only men, and is seen) (P. 526–7 and 396–7). Thus Beni follows Aristotle in restricting the use of *machina* to the inessential parts of the plot: it should not be used to supply the denouement (P. 409 and 527). This means that the poet (especially the tragic poet) should work hard to untie his own dramatic knot:

Ex quo fit, ut in Tragoedia ex iis quae ab actoribus geruntur dicunturve, sit fabulae peragendae hoc est nectendae, dilatandae, et solvendae, ratio ac modus derivandus; sigillatimque in totius fabulae nodo explicando, Poetae ipsius elucere debet ingenium: ne ad extremum iners atque artis expers et industriae videatur: praesertim quia misericordiae ac timori quae spectat Tragicus in nobis commovendis humanae actiones propter affinitatem plus valeant, quam quae extrinsecus et ex machina (hae enim plus novitatis habent quam probitatis et oculos magis capiunt quam afficiant animos) desumuntur praesidia (P. 396).

In the epic there is more room for *machina* because there the poet is not self-dependent, but can freely involve the Muses to aid him (P. 396).

In the passage quoted above Beni places greater emphasis on the poet's industry than on the use of mechanical aids. He does this for the sake of verisimilitude. What lies behind his thought is that an audience would not readily accept a *machina* as probable in a tragedy, and would not accept that a dramatic poet could reasonably invoke supernatural assistance in the form of the Muses. It is more than strange, therefore, that behind this same passage Jannaco has divined a Baroque deformation of Aristotle's spirit:

Si noti infatti con quanta sottigliezza il novello esegeta [. . .] cerchi di superare un ostacolo—*locus spinosus*—che malauguratamente trova in Aristotele, cioè il ripudio della *machina* nell'azione drammatica. Riconosce che la macchina è un mezzo 'estrinseco'; ma che cosa la sostituisce? Appunto la *ingeniosa solutio*, frutto *de propria industria* del poeta. In realtà è il gusto del complicato che si fa strada [. . .]. Così un'altra norma dell'estetica barocchista, quella della complicazione macchinosa, si è venuta laboriosamente formando nei *Commentarii* (art. cit., pp. 227–8).[15]

Jannaco's interpretation here seems very much further from the spirit of Beni than ever Beni's was from that of Aristotle: beneath Beni's words, as we have seen, there lies the Aristotelian notion of verisimilitude, and not the 'Baroque' notion of complication. Jannaco failed to relate the narrow issue of *machina* to the broader issue of the breach of verisimilitude.

The Aristotelian passages from which Beni derived his theory of verisimilitude also lent themselves to the formulation of a further theory, namely that poetic imitation should reduce or heighten reality to ideal exemplary proportions. Riccoboni's translation of the key passage, which Beni uses, is as follows: 'Manifestum autem est ex iis, quae dicta sunt, non esse poetae munus facta dicere, sed qualia fieri debent, et fieri possunt, secundum verisimile, vel necessarium'.[16] Beni provides a novel interpretation of the phrase *qualia fieri debent*. For, although it was generally acknowledged by most critics in the sixteenth century that poetry was more universal, ideal, and philosophi-

---

[15] Jannaco reached this conclusion after seriously misquoting (i.e. introducing and not signalling important omissions in) the passage from *P.* 396, quoted in full on p. 177 above.

[16] A. Riccoboni, *Poetica Aristotelis latine conversa* (Padua, 1587), 11. Bywater translates the passage (1451ᵃ 36–8) as follows: 'From what we have said it will be seen that the poet's function is to describe, not the thing that has happened, but a kind of thing that might happen', in Aristotle, *On the Art of Poetry*, a revised text with critical introduction, translation, and commentary by Ingram Bywater (Oxford, 1909), 27.

cal than history (which deals with single individual truths), yet
no critic made as precise a utilitarian doctrine out of it as did
Beni: he developed the notion that each literary genre was specifically designed to instruct, by the use of exemplary characters, a corresponding stratum of the population. Comedy will
instruct the 'cives et populares [. . .] in vita populari'; tragedy
will instruct the 'reges atque eos qui populis dominantur [. . .]
ut iuste ac moderate urbes administrent ac regna'; and the epic
will instruct the 'summum Ducem et Heroem' (*P.* 277). Accordingly, when Beni asks why Aristotle said that the historian
should relate what happened and the poet what ought to
happen, he answers confidently: 'quia Poetae est res quas
narrat, ad certam quandam ideam et formam revocare, unde
mortales in suo quique genere intueri possint quid sibi fugien-
dum, quid sequendum et imitandum' (*P.* 277). Beni justifies
this—and here we can speak properly of the deformation of
Aristotle's spirit—by reference to the final book of the *Politics*
where poetry and music are said to be useful as well as delightful. It may be doubted whether Aristotle intended to attribute
to poetry the specific utilitarian purpose that Beni divined in
the *Poetics*; but Beni nowhere shows any doubt about the precise message, neatly inserting it into his tripartite order, and
claiming that poetry, in its effort to teach, apes philosophy in
which it has its ancestral roots (*P.* 281–3 and 4).

In conclusion, therefore, the proper subject of poetic imitation
for Beni is both the verisimilar and the ideal. It is the poet's duty
to tidy up his subject-matter and to make it exemplary
(*P.* 548–50). Beni does not envisage any incompatibility between
the need for ideal imitation and verisimilitude (*P.* 550). In fact
both things spring from the same requirement in his thought,
namely that poetry should fulfil its moral function in society. For,
unless an imitated action is verisimilar, it will not be believed;
and if it is not believed, it will not teach. At the same time, if an
action is verisimilar but not exemplary of some moral standard,
then it will have nothing to teach the reader or audience.

IV

While the subject of poetic imitation is central to Aristotle's
poetic theory, that of the purpose and function of poetry is at

best incidental. Yet, in spite of the fact that Aristotle had given the subject short shrift, Beni and his immediate predecessors considered the moral effect of poetry to be a burning issue of poetic theory (and Beni's discussion of imitation necessarily involved, as we have seen, a discussion of the moral function of poetry). Various factors contribute to the inevitable preoccupation of the critics with the purpose and function of poetry: first, there is their knowledge of Horace's *Ars poetica* with its allusion to the usefulness of poetry; second, there is their considerable inheritance, which had accumulated over the centuries, of notions about poetry's didactic functions; and third, there is their awareness of the moral climate which followed upon the Counter-Reformation.

In fact, so important was the question of the function of poetry to Beni that he prefaced his discussion of it with a digression, completely unrelated to Aristotle's work, on the different aims of *poetica* (the study of poetry) and *poesis* (the reading of poetry). The purpose of *poetica* is fully expounded in *Controversia* IV (*P.* 22–3), where Beni reviews earlier commentators' definitions of the term: Robortelli, Maggi, and Castelvetro are all found to have mistaken poetics for poetry. Unlike these Beni makes a clear theoretical distinction; and he attributes to poetics a threefold purpose. First, it leads society to the 'beata vita'. Second, it purges the individual's soul. And third, its prime purpose ('proximus finis') is to teach men how to write and judge poetry. Neat though these distinctions are, they are none the less impractical and, as we shall see, they will be frequently disregarded in Beni's commentary. Their interest lies for us in the important fact that they aim to extract from the study of poetry the greatest possible moral usefulness, as if in justification of such study. So far, in 1613, was Beni from being prepared to give up his soul purely to the sensuous delight of poetry and to bathe in the hedonistic and heady pools of Secentistic *ingegno*.

Beni's theoretical distinction between *poetica* and *poesis* is never really put into practice, and already the introductory *oratio*, 'De Poesi atque Aristoteleae poeticae praestantia et utilitate' (*P.* 3–9), begins in a generic way to establish the delight and usefulness of both poetry and poetics. Delight *and* usefulness, it must be stressed: for if the Italian critics (Toffanin, Belloni, and

Jannaco amongst them) are to be believed, Beni's introductory is something of a hedonistic paradise where Secentismo is to be found in its purest essence. Such a view is apparently well supported by Beni's (unusual for him) extravagant picture of poetry as the gorgeously attired Queen of the Arts, rich in splendour, beauty, and freedom. Such a picture comes at the very beginning of Beni's commentary, and furnishes one of the rare purple passages in his work. Like a similar purple passage at the beginning of the *Comparatione*,[17] this one has also misled modern critics, who have read it as the key to Beni's commentary, and who have mistakenly allowed its matter and manner to influence their interpretation of Beni and of Baroque culture:

Etenim doctrinae ferme reliquae et facultates humili plane dictione pedestrique oratione utuntur; atque ita utuntur, ut non modo nitore careant et elegantia, sed munditia prope omni et cultu. Ita sane illarum sermo horridus passim apparet et squalore obsitus. Saepe etiam vulgi atque imperitissimae plebis oratione subdurior et inquinatior: Poesis contra admirabilem refert nitorem: nullam dicendi virtutem non sectatur: nullum orationis lumen et ornamentum non amplectitur. Denique quantum abundat Ver floribus, Autunnus [*sic*] pomis, Aurora coloribus, coelum luminibus, tantum suavissimis Orationis quasi floribus pomisque referta est Poesis, et pulcherrimis coloribus luminibusque distinguitur ac variatur. Ut mihi quidem caeterae illae artes atque doctrinae pedestres atque humiles incedere, Poesis veluti quadrigis invehi ac triumphum agere videatur [. . .]. Denique historia gravis matronae instar est, quae si paulo cultior appareat, ac munditiae nitorem addat, minus pudica, lasciva etiam et petulans, habeatur. At poesis quo magis coloribus distinguitur, et excolitur ornamentis, eo gratior accidit mortalium oculis atque iucundior. Est enim venustae puellae ac sponsae persimilis, quam nullum decus, nullum ornamentum, nullus splendor dedeceat: quin margaritis, auro, gemmis, purpura magna cum dignitate utitur ac laude (*P*. 4).

But this extravagance is balanced by poetry's serious nature. Beni reminds us that poetry is more difficult to understand than history or oratory, and that it is closer than these to philosophy. It is at this point also that Beni first introduces his novel and distorted interpretation of Aristotle's dictum (as Beni under-

---

[17] See my article in *Studi secenteschi*, 24 (1983), 51–5. Such purple passages at the beginning of some of Beni's works are to be read more as *captationes benevolentiae* than as profound and personal *confessions de foi*.

stood it) that the poet should imitate things not as they are but
as they ought to be; and his principle of ideal imitation, which
we have already examined, is brought out on the very first page
of the introductory *oratio* in the discussion of the function of
poetica, and it is a principle which Beni will never abandon
(*P*. 3).

He is only too well aware of the possible misinterpretation to
which his flamboyant picture of poetry is subject. Accordingly,
he formulates the hypothetical case against poetry, and claims
(as Plato, he says, claimed) that poetry 'ulcus est tota ac vene-
nato melle infecta', more suitable to which would be the image
of a wanton harlot than that of a dignified queen (*P*. 6). But Beni
defeats this view, in a dogmatic and generic way, claiming that
moderation is necessary in poetry, and attributing to poetry
('morum emendatricem vitaeque magistram optimam') a moral
role in society (*P*. 7; see also *P*. 33–4).

Such generic and dogmatic statements as we have so far
recorded were enough to allow Beni to proceed without too
many qualms through his commentary of the first *Caput* of the
Poetics. But by the time he reached page 179 of his commentary
he evidently felt the lack of Aristotle's blessing on his precise
belief in poetry's function. When, therefore, in *Controversia*
xxxv, 'De germana Poesis definitione ex Aristotelis initiis' (*P*.
179–85), he offers a full definition of poetry, he realizes that he
must fill in the gaps, and proposes to do so, first, according to
Aristotle's precepts, and secondly, according to the dictates of
reason (note how these two things remain separate here). The
definition which he proposes is as follows: 'Poesis est oratio
non exiguae magnitudinis actionem imitans, qua non sine
magna iucunditate ad virtutem excitentur et ad bene beateque
vivendum dirigantur mortales' (*P*. 181). Beni expounds the various parts of this definition, and briefly states, though with no
apparent justification from Aristotle, that the purpose of all
poetry is to instil virtue and expel vice by means of delight
('delectando prodesse mortalibus' (*P*. 184)). At this stage Beni
is still unspecific about how such delightful instruction should
be achieved, but he states firmly that in poetry delight is
achieved more from imitation and plot than from verse: a point
on which he is always a true Aristotelian.

Having produced this definition, apparently (though mistakenly) culled from the *Poetics*, Beni had to face, in *Controversia* xxxvi, 'De fine poesis' (*P*. 185–9), the further dilemma, from which no critic of the *Poetics* was immune, of having to decide between the rival claims of *utilitas* and *delectatio*. He begins by showing that some critics (following Horace) have given them equal weight, while others have made imitation the goal of poetry. Beni finds the conflicting opinions confusing, and proposes to discover once and for all what Aristotle thought on the matter. Beni submits seven hypothetical reasons why *voluptas* might be considered the chief end of poetry; but he immediately proves, against them, that *voluptas* can never be the end, and must always remain the means (*P*. 186). He also rejects Horace's notion (which was widely accepted in Beni's day) that both *utilitas* and *delectatio* can be served at once: for poetry, like everything else, can have only one end, and that must be usefulness (*P*. 188–9).[18]

It is not so much in his general view of poetry's function that Beni differs from earlier commentators, though his statement of the relationship between delight and profit is remarkable for its precision and clarity. But it is when he descends to particulars, and describes the specific purpose of individual poetic genres that we may find a certain individuality, even eccentricity, of interpretation.

Beni's discussions of the function of tragedy fall into two distinct areas which seem surprisingly independent of each other. In the first place he lists, here and there throughout the commentary, the pleasures of tragedy, defines them, and yokes them to their corresponding moral end. In the second place he debates the thorny issue of catharsis. What is strange in all this is that he seems incapable of linking the two areas, a point which will emerge (with an explanation) more clearly after a detailed examination of them.

Throughout the commentary, Beni's description of the function of tragedy is in line with his views about the relationship between *voluptas* and *utilitas* in poetry as outlined above: he shows that he is unprepared (as he thought Aristotle was

---

[18] In this doctrine Beni had the support of most of the previous commentators who more or less accept poetry's moral usefulness. See Spingarn, 58.

unprepared) to sanction any pleasure which is not also the instrument of some moral good. When commenting, for instance, on Aristotle's 'Not every kind of pleasure should be required of a tragedy, but only its own proper pleasure' (Bywater, ed. cit., p. 39), Beni does allow that tragedy has various pleasures (*sermo*, *rhythmus*, *harmonia*, metre, imitation, *peripeteia*, scenery, melody, chorus, plot, episodes, and denouement); but he is not content until, and quite contrary to anything Aristotle said, he has put *voluptas* in its proper (secondary) place (*P.* 352). Similarly, Beni shows himself willing to abandon any pleasure which is not harnessed to a useful end: it is decided, for instance, in *Controversia* XLI, 'An apparatus sit Tragoediae necessarius' (*P.* 226–9), that scenery and stage effects can be abandoned since tragedy can fulfil its (moral) function without them. And the delight engendered by the scenery (he says elsewhere) is best engendered by more 'difficult' means (*P.* 351). In the same way he concludes that Aristotle did not provide an unqualified recommendation of tragedy with a fictitious plot when he wrote in the *Poetics* 'And there are some [plays] without a single known name, e.g. Agathon's *Antheus*, in which both incidents and names are of the poet's invention; and it is no less delightful on that account' (Bywater, ed. cit., p. 29). For (argues Beni) Aristotle did not place such a play in the first rank for the simple reason that it delighted but did not instruct—a view which seems to go against the evidence of the text of the *Poetics*.

The notion that tragedy should use ideal examples to inculcate virtues will readily be seen to be out of step with the Aristotelian notion of catharsis. Nevertheless, Beni provided a thorough treatment of the problem; but ultimately he failed to assimilate catharsis or to see it clearly, partly because he always felt that poetry should be directly didactic rather than spiritually influential, and partly because, even if he admitted that tragic catharsis might be useful, he could never see how it might be pleasurable. For these reasons Beni is prevented, like many of his contemporaries, from any proper realization of Aristotle's elusive concept.

The question of catharsis is mainly treated in *Controversia* XXXIX, 'Num recte de Tragica purgatione praeceperit Aristoteles' (*P.* 201–12). Beni begins by framing seven key questions about Aristotle's concept. The answers to these questions are not to be had from the *Poetics*, however; for the parts which contained them are now lost.[19] Instead (continues Beni), the meaning of catharsis will have to be gleaned from other sources. Predictably he finds no satisfactory definition wherever he looks; and, after reviewing all the earlier commentators, he proceeds to expound in detail his own view, which is as follows: tragedy, though it had humble beginnings and was at first without didatic purpose, soon reached perfection and turned to kings for both its subject-matter and its audience. Beni considers that Aristotle's notion of tragic catharsis took for granted the fact that tragedy was originally and principally aimed at the instruction of kings, and of no other social group.

With this as his premiss, he goes on to argue that it is easy to see what Aristotle meant when he referred to pity and fear. For if pity and fear are aroused (as they should be aroused) in kings, then the right kingly virtues will be inculcated in the kings in the audience:

Dum enim rex regem videt ob superbiam aut rapacitatem vel libidinem et intemperantiam e foelici illo statu in calamitatem deturbari, similis exemplo sibi ipse timet; omninoque statuit ea declinare vitia et moderari perturbationes, unde illae calamitosus factus est. [. . .] Ita sane perspicuum videri potest cur Aristoteles timorem maxime, et misericordiam purgandis perturbationibus adhibuerit, et quam iure adhibuerit (P. 209).

It is of little use to excite pity and fear in ordinary citizens. In this way Beni is forced to restrict tragedy's usefulness to an absurdly small number of the population: 'Nam revera non omnibus mortalibus timor utiliter incutitur et misericordia, sed Regibus ac potentibus' (P. 209). Such are Beni's conclusions in *Controversia* XXXIX. However, there is, elsewhere, strong evidence to suggest that Beni was not in fact willing to restrict the usefulness of tragedy to kings alone. Such evidence is contained in *Controversia* LXIV, 'Utra fabula sit magis probanda, simplex ne an duplex' (P. 366–71), in which Beni relates the question of whether the tragic plot should be single or double to the question of catharsis. He argues that, if you believe (with Aristotle) that tragedy should benefit only kings, then the single plot is to

[19] The notion that the *Poetics* was incomplete seems to have begun with Vettori.

be recommended, as Aristotle recommended it (*P.* 369). But—
and here Beni seems to be throwing the Aristotelian notion of
catharsis, even as it is distorted by him, out of the window—if
you believe that tragedy should benefit the whole of society,
then the double plot is to be recommended. In such a way (Beni
argues) you can derive from poetry the same moral usefulness
as from history, where good behaviour is rewarded and bad
punished (*P.* 370).

The forcefulness with which Beni makes this point proves
two things. First, that when he restricts the cathartic principle
to kings alone he is expressing, not his own, but what he considers (quite wrongly) to be Aristotle's views,[20] and is explaining why, historically, Aristotle should have mentioned pity and
fear in relation to catharsis. Secondly, it proves that for Beni,
influenced as he undoubtedly was by Christian thought, the
cathartic principle had little or no relevance, and seemed outmoded. For he does not understand how the excitement of pity
and fear can be of use to ordinary citizens, while he does understand the Christian principle that moral examples shown on
stage can be of benefit to the audience. Beni's implied doubts
about the relevance of tragic catharsis were boldly stated some
years before by G. B. Guarini in his *Verrato primo*, where it was
argued that conventional classical comedy and tragedy were no
longer necessary to a Christian society: 'E per venire all'età nostra, che bisogno abbiamo noi oggi di purgar il terrore, e la com-
miserazione con le Tragiche viste? avendo i precetti santissimi
della nostra religione, che ce l'insegna con la parola evange-
lica?'[21] Beni's position on this is the same as Guarini's. In both,
as well as in the majority of men of their age, the inability properly to understand Aristotle's concept is largely due to their
awareness of its irrelevance.

When we turn to Beni's discussion of the function of comedy
and the epic we find that (like Aristotle) he says considerably
less. As has already been stated, Beni assumed that Aristotle
had restricted the usefulness of the epic to leaders and heroes
(*P.* 483). The epic is thought to have no purgative powers. Com-

[20] He found his justification for this in *Poetics*, 1453[a].
[21] 'Il Verrato ovvero difesa di quanto ha scritto Messer Jason Denores contra
le tragicommedie, e le pastorali, in un suo discorso di poesia', in Guarini, *Opere*,
ed. cit., ii (1737), 261.

edy has cathartic powers (Beni does not describe them) through which the souls of ordinary mortals are cleansed (*P.* 210).

It is not always easy to discern in the foregoing discussion which are Beni's views, and which are Aristotle's (in Beni's often distorted interpretation and reconstruction of them). None the less, it is easy to see that, where in the *Poetics* Aristotle had stressed delight and pleasure, Beni stressed utility. The very idea of art for art's sake was unthinkable to him; and all his earnest and Christian efforts were directed to finding some moral justification for poetry and for the study of poetry. As we saw, such efforts often led him into thoroughly un-Aristotelian territory: they led him, in the first place, to lend catharsis a narrowly moral interpretation; and, in the second place, to undervalue catharsis in the name of an even greater moral utility; finally, they led him to see poetry as a pleasant channel through which specific virtues can be pumped into specific groups of men.

13

THE COMMENTARY ON THE *POETICS* (II)

So far I have made little attempt to relate what Beni wrote on the *Poetics* to what the earlier commentators had written. The reasons for thus isolating Beni's ideas and treating them (so to speak) in a vacuum are obvious: for such a treatment allowed us to clarify his ideas and to reassemble them according to an ideal aesthetic philosophy. But, at the same time, Beni was aware, as we must be, that such ideas were not produced in a vacuum. Not only did he relate his own work to that of the earlier commentators in the preface to the commentary, and throughout repeatedly summarize and quote the earlier opinions, most often in order to refute them; but he also included in the catalogue of his private library a list of the most important *Poetics* commentaries which he owned: Robortelli, Maggi/Lombardi, Vettori, Castelvetro, and Piccolomini (BB 94–5). Furthermore, the problem of Beni's relationship to earlier critics is aggravated by the related problem of Beni's relationship to Aristotle; and the need to individualize and to relate historically the ideas which began with Aristotle, filtered through the major sixteenth-century commentaries, and finally came to rest in Beni's work can easily prove overwhelmingly difficult and baffling. The man who tries to write the history of such ideas (I am thinking of Weinberg in his monumental *History of Literary Criticism in the Italian Renaissance*) will, if he is not careful, unwittingly fall into the trap of treating as individual and personal, utterances in the commentators which were merely paraphrases of the *Poetics*. Thus, throughout his chronological treatment of the commentators before 1600, Weinberg unnecessarily repeats Aristotle's rules for verisimilitude in poetry without acknowledging the Aristotelian origin of such a body of thought; and his book has other similar needless and unrelated repetitions of unacknowledged Aristotelian doctrine. More-

over, this method of treating the Renaissance critics can be misleading, as, for instance, when H. B. Charlton says of Castelvetro that 'He alone held that tragedy is the supreme poetic
species'.[1] Surely it is fair to wonder how Charlton could believe
that Castelvetro was alone in this view when it had been clearly
expressed in the *Poetics* by Aristotle himself, and many times
repeated by the commentators.

Conversely, the man who sets out with a theory of the cultural development of the period, and the man who wishes to
make of Beni the missing link between Rinascimento and
Barocco (I am thinking of Jannaco, Mazzacurati, Toffanin, Belloni, and many others) is likely to fall into the trap of making
the facts fit the theory.

I hope in what follows to steer a course between Weinberg's
and Jannaco's opposite approaches by comparing what Beni
says on the key issues of the *Poetics* with what the earlier principal commentators (Robortelli, Maggi, Vettori, and Castelvetro)
had to say.[2] I shall consider the matter under the following
heads: general attitudes towards the *Poetics*; imitation; the
place of verse in poetry; the proper subject of poetic imitation;
the *meraviglioso* and the verisimilar; the relationship between
pleasure and usefulness; language (with metaphor). My aim
will be to discover—empirically, so far as that is possible, and
with no particular axe to grind—the answers to two related
questions: first, how far were Beni's ideas derivative and how
far original; and second, does his originality (if any) tend, as it
is thought by many to tend,[3] in the direction of what could be

---

[1] *Castelvetro's Theory of Poetry* (Manchester, 1913), 141.

[2] It would be impossible and unnecessarily tedious to conduct here a detailed
survey of all previous critics who touched on subjects relating to the *Poetics*, for
almost every critic did this. Furthermore, the general positions of all the critics
(up to 1600) are summarized by B. Weinberg, *A History of Literary Criticism in the
Italian Renaissance*, and such positions are well represented by the principal
commentators discussed in this chapter. I refer throughout to the following
edns: F. Robortelli, *In librum Aristotelis de arte poetica, explicationes*, 2nd edn.
(Basel, 1555; 1st edn. 1548); V. Maggi and B. Lombardi, *In Aristotelis librum de
poetica communes explicationes* (Venice, 1550); P. Vettori, *Commentarii in primum
librum Aristotelis de arte poetarum* (Florence, 1560); L. Castelvetro, *Poetica d'Aristotele vulgarizzata et sposta*, 2nd edn. (Basel, 1576; 1st edn. 1570). In what follows
I shall refer to all these commentaries by quoting only the author's surname and
page number(s). For a full bibliography of works on poetic theory in this period
(up to 1600), see Weinberg, ii.

[3] See above, Chapter 12, Section II.

called a Baroque aesthetic? The answers to these questions should have significant implications both for the history of literary Aristotelianism in Italy and for the phenomenon of the Baroque.

II

The first difference amongst the critics springs from the sort of questions they ask about the *Poetics*: for the early commentators (Robortelli, Maggi, and Vettori) many of the most pressing questions were textual. It was natural that they should attempt first to emend what was clearly a faulty text, to discover intelligent readings for the many obscure parts, before they could enter fully into deep critical discussions on the meaning and validity of the *Poetics*. Vettori was especially scrupulous over the text, and considered in detail all the available variants. As a result of this adherence to the text, these early critics meekly accept whatever doctrines the *Poetics* throws in their way; they are not inclined to disagree with Aristotle's word; and, although they find the text full of problems, they do not find its dogmas difficult to accept. In many cases, indeed, they are content merely to paraphrase Aristotle's words without evaluating their validity or practicality (Maggi (p. 187) and Vettori (pp. 167–8), for instance, on poetic fury, and all three critics on iambics in drama (Robortelli, pp. 39, 242, and 243; Maggi, p. 85; Vettori, pp. 45–6 and 251–3)). In these early critics it would be difficult to find a place where Aristotle's authority is questioned and not vindicated. It is true that there are distortions of Aristotle's meaning (as far as modern scholarship can tell what was his meaning), but these are never openly presented as disagreements. Throughout, Aristotle is synonymous with reason: if anything is lacking for these critics, it is the text, and not Aristotle's reason or authority.

This emphasis changes with Castelvetro. For him, the first to publish a major commentary on the *Poetics* in Italian, the text is still faulty, but so also is the reasoning behind it. Castelvetro is the first of the commentators to ask fundamental and searching questions about the deep meaning of the text; and, in doing this, he assumes a superior attitude towards Aristotle, often

undermining the whole edifice of his poetic theory: 'Ammaes-
tramenti suoi non paiono buoni per la poesia, poi che non
suono [sic] buoni per l'historia' (pp. 6–7 and *ad indicem*). On
occasion Castelvetro will relentlessly find fault with the logic (or
absence of it) in Aristotle's similes and so squash his message
(e.g. p. 504), and whenever Aristotle is mentioned he is criticized (witness the two hundred or so entries in the index under
'Aristotele').

Beni is to be seen as the heir to the practical and doubting
realism of Castelvetro. For him, as for Castelvetro, there is no
longer a case, in the field of poetic theory, for the identification
of Aristotle with reason (*P*. 180), and we do not find, in either
Beni or Castelvetro, the syncretistical desire to discover a consensus amongst ancient literary authorities that we find in
Robortelli, Maggi, and Vettori. On the contrary, both Castelvetro and Beni enjoy a good *dubitatio*, but Beni will make more of a
meal of it than Castelvetro. For, although both writers are more
verbose than their predecessors (and that is partly because they
had more material to cover), their works are cast in different
moulds: Castelvetro's is quite outside the scholastic world, and
avoids, with its fluent discursive Italian, the chop-logic of the
Schools where Beni's commentary, as we have seen, found its
origins. This means that Beni's work is harder to interpret than
Castelvetro's: Beni argues hypothetically, weighing carefully
both sides of a question, and is often very good at, and fond of,
constructing a plausible argument only afterwards to demolish
it. The unsuspecting and cursory reader, not used to Beni's
manner, but used to reading the one-sided accounts of the
earlier commentators, will easily be led into mistaking the pros-
ecution for the defence, so to speak.[4]

It is no doubt the highly scholastic nature of Beni's commentary which leads him to see in Aristotle an inconsistent, parti-
san academical critic. This is most clearly evidenced in his
presentation of Aristotle's relationship to Plato, and of his
championing of Homer. Robortelli, Maggi, Vettori, and Castelvetro all (following Aristotle) accept that Homer was in some
sense divine, the fountainhead of all poetic wisdom, and the

[4] This, I think, is one of the principal sources of recent misinterpretations of
Beni's commentary.

key to the *Poetics* (Robortelli, pp. 2 and 246; Maggi, pp. 10, 145, 250–2, and 254; Vettori, p. 37; Castelvetro, pp. 545 and 576). They rightly see that Aristotle made some effort in the *Poetics*, especially in his defence of Homer and in his concept of catharsis, to answer Plato's case against poetry. Yet, while they all accept Homer's 'divinity', Beni completely rejects it, as he did in the *Comparatione*, maintaining that Aristotle's whole purpose in writing the *Poetics* was a polemical one: namely to discredit Plato's criticisms of poetry, and to patch together a set of rules which would defend Homer's poetic integrity. This criticism of Aristotle runs through Beni's commentary, and constitutes his particular way of undermining Aristotle's dogmas. Thus, many of the major problems of interpretation in the *Poetics* spring (in Beni's view) not from the text so much as from Aristotle's theoretical inconsistency, and from his now leaning in one direction, now in another, always according to Homer's practice (e.g. *P.* 534).

In this way Beni makes of Aristotle a fellow academic and polemicist; and he treats the *Poetics* with some scepticism. Beni is to some extent open in his commentary to the implications for modern vernacular literature; but, like Robortelli, Maggi, and Vettori (and unlike the more practical Castelvetro), he almost always gives examples from ancient literature. He makes surprisingly little effort therefore to praise Tasso or to prove the latter's conformity to Aristotelian precepts (this absence of Tasso worship in the commentary is surprising in one who is widely supposed to be a fanatical champion of Tasso); and while Beni was clearly a Modern[5] in his linguistic works, his instinct in the commentary on the *Poetics*, as elsewhere in his Latin commentaries, is to put the old before the new.

III

Beni's views on the nature of poetic imitation have already been examined. It was discovered that he was dissatisfied with Aristotle's treatment of the subject, and was particularly concerned to know whether narration *ex propria persona* (in history,

[5] By 'Modern' I mean a supporter of sixteenth- and seventeenth-century linguistic achievements rather than of those of the *buon secolo*.

for instance) could be termed poetic imitation. The apparent contradictions over this question in the *Poetics* led Beni (as we saw) to expand Aristotle's notion of imitation to include the literary imitation of other writers. It was clear in what Beni wrote that he was keenly alive to the practical implications of the Aristotelian theory of imitation, and he managed subtly to draw out of Aristotle's concept the acceptance as true poets of those (such as lyricists) who speak *ex propria persona*.

Beni was led to this substantial enlargement and distortion of Aristotle's theory by the unquestioning and impractical repetition of the concepts of the *Poetics* in the earlier commentators. For Robortelli, Maggi, and Vettori all slavishly accept Aristotle's contradictions on the subject. Hence, when Aristotle says that narration can be imitation, so also does Robortelli: 'Epopoeia [. . .] inducit narrationem, per quam imitatur'; but when Aristotle, contradicting himself, makes imitation and narration mutually exclusive, so also does Robortelli: 'Narrationes imitatione carentes' (pp. 33 and 247). The same pattern of contradiction is evident in Maggi (pp. 93 and 261) and Vettori (pp. 52 and 254–5). In these three critics the practical implications of such a contradiction are ignored: Aristotle's dicta are explored philologically, but left unexplored semantically and aesthetically. Robortelli, for example, like Maggi and Vettori, gives a clear and accurate paraphrase of Aristotle's notion that objects can be imitated only as they were, as they are, or as they seem to be or should be (Robortelli, p. 253). But Beni's literary experience shows this not to be true in practice (*P.* 533).

The case is different with Castelvetro. He draws up, as is his wont, long and complicated tables of all the different imitative permutations which Aristotle allows (Castelvetro, pp. 47–50). But when he comes to develop his own interpretation of imitation he seems to part company with Aristotle:

Questa rassomiglianza richiesta alla poesia non è, nè si dee, o si può appellare dirittamente, o propriamente rassomiglianza, ma è, o si dee, o si può appellare gareggiamento del poeta, e della dispositione della fortuna, o del corso delle mondane cose in trovare uno accidente d'attione humana più dilettevole ad ascoltare, e più maraviglioso (pp. 68–9).

And the idea of literary imitation of other writers (which Beni was to develop extensively) is firmly rejected by Castelvetro in his prophetic quest for originality (p. 67).

In all this, if one is looking for Baroque tendencies, they are easily to be found in Castelvetro and not in Beni. For it is Castelvetro's standard of original invention to produce delight and *meraviglia* that Marino and others might have adopted, and not Beni's subtle distinction between narration and imitation.

IV

Like Beni, all the critics acknowledge Aristotle's claim that the essence of poetry lies in imitation rather than in verse. But, when pushed, they all maintain that Aristotle thought the perfect essence of poetry to lie in a mixture of imitation *and* verse. Robortelli writes: 'Sed verius, magisque proprie appellatur poesis, quae et imitatione, et metro conflata fuerit' (p. 79). Maggi is more decided on the matter when he says that there are 'tria Poetarum genera ex Aristotele reperiri. Primum illorum est, qui tum imitantur, tum etiam carmine utuntur. Atque hi proprie poetae nomen merentur' (p. 57). And Vettori is the most positive of all:

Ut autem penitus, quod sentio, de hac re, testificer, arbitror alterum eorum, quae reddunt aliquos proprie poetas, esse orationem metricam. Nec posse quempiam vere vocari poetam, quamvis imitetur: eximieque exprimat, quod vult, nisi utatur hac oratione. [. . .] Nec me latet habere me multos, qui aliter de hac re sentiant; nec defuerint etiam nostra aetate viri acuti lepidique ingenii, qui comoedias scripserint soluta oratione. Quod (ut opinor) veteres nunquam tentarunt (p. 12).

Now it is on this last point that Beni and Castelvetro part company with Robortelli, Maggi, and Vettori. The earlier critics accept Aristotle's Greek notion that drama should be written in iambic metre (which most resembled everyday speech); but Beni and Castelvetro, with greater practical insight, realized that contemporary Italian had no metre as informal (and, therefore, as verisimilar) as the Greek iambic metre (Castelvetro, pp. 90–1). Beni develops this point in much greater depth than Castelvetro; he had already dedicated his *Disputatio* of 1600 to the problem, and there, and throughout his commentary on the

Poetics, his arguments were based on a strictly classical (and in no way Baroque) regard for verisimilitude and decorum.

V

If we do not find Beni assuming a Baroque position over the issue of verse in poetry, we find him taking an even less Baroque position over the subject of poetic imitation. For, as I have already tried to show, against the opinion of historians of the Baroque, Beni never openly advocates the false as a subject for poetry, and more often than not recommends historical subjects. So much is clear from a careful reading of Beni in isolation from his predecessors. But when his strict and classical rules are set beside Robortelli's, Maggi's, Vettori's, and Castelvetro's, we can see that the presumed Baroque elements which the critics have divined in Beni's work were present, and present in greater intensity, in the earlier commentators. The point can be simply illustrated. I have already quoted Jannaco's (in my view mistaken) notion of Beni's 'estetica concettista e la violenta separazione della poesia stessa dalla storia e la sua conseguente identificazione con la *fictio fabulosa et dilectosa*'.[6] Other critics, notably Mazzacurati, have accepted Jannaco's influential view of Beni as the official Aristotelian broadcaster of the Baroque aesthetic in Italy. But against this view there are two very strong arguments. First, Beni never used the phrase *fictio fabulosa et dilectosa* in his commentary or anywhere else (as far as I know); and, as we have seen, he never described poetry as falsehood. Secondly, and more importantly, Jannaco's phrase (or its very near equivalent), *fictio fabulosa et dilectosa*, was used by Robortelli in his commentary as early as 1548: that is, sixty-five years before Beni is thought (mistakenly) to have made cultural history with the phrase.[7] What could be more Baroque than the following quotation from Robortelli?

Cum igitur poetice subiectam sibi habeat pro materie *orationem fictam*

---

[6] See p. 174 above. The quotation comes from Jannaco, art. cit., 225.
[7] Robortelli was clearly not the only commentator to have seen poetry as a sort of delightful lie: Riccoboni, for instance, also claimed that the end of poetry is 'fabulosa delectatio' (see Weinberg, i. 604).

et fabulosam: patet ad poeticen pertinere, ut fabulam, et mendacium
apte confingat: nulliusque alterius artis proprium magis esse: menda-
cia comminisci, quam huius. Homerum, a quo omnis poetice derivata
est, testatur Aristoteles primum docuisse, qua ratione esset mendacium apte dicendum. Nihil vero hoc esse aliud, quam paralogismum.
[. . .] Iam satis (uti puto) declaratum est, qualem habeat sibi subiectam materiem poetica facultas; *orationem scilicet falsam, seu fabulosam,
et mendaciorum plenam* (p. 2; my italics).

And it is not only in this passage that Robortelli shows closer
sympathies than Beni towards the Baroque. For instance, on the
question (raised by Aristotle in the *Poetics*) as to whether a tragedy should have an historical basis Robortelli assumes a
lenient attitude and, like Aristotle, uses delight rather than historical truth as his criterion of a successful tragedy (Robortelli,
pp. 82–3). Contrary to this, Beni had argued, as we saw, against
invented tragic plots. In all this it is true that all the commentators resolve the difference between true and false in verisimilitude; but Robortelli allows the poet significantly more freedom
than does Beni (Robortelli, pp. 75, 76–7, 248, and 263–4). As far
as Robortelli is concerned the historian must alter nothing
while the poet 'autem actionem mutat, auget, minuit, exornat,
amplificat, narrat demum potius, ut agi debuerit, quam ut acta
fuerit' (p. 78).

Similarly, Maggi argues that the poet abandons truth for verisimilitude, and that a poetic action 'secundum id, quod verisimile, aut necessarium est exprimatur, *posthabita veritatis ratione*'
(p. 131; my italics). Maggi also appears more to approve of the
false poetic subject than Beni because he, unlike Beni, accepts
Aristotle's praise of Homer as an exemplary poet-liar (Maggi,
p. 265). And all the commentators, except Beni, accept this argument.

Like Beni, Vettori separates poetry from history, as do all
Aristotelian critics of the time (Vettori, pp. 92–3). But, unlike
Beni, Vettori allows a complete divorce between the two disciplines: he tells poets to forget all about historical names and
plots when they compose tragedies, and he points out that the
tragic pleasure (whatever that is) has nothing to do with historical truth (Vettori, p.97). He too evens out the distinction
between true and false by raising them both onto the level of
verisimilitude and decorum; but he always vindicates the

poet's right to invent and distort reality (Vettori, pp. 24–5 and 275).

Castelvetro predictably begins with the Aristotelian distinction between poetry and history, but goes on to develop it in a personal and confusing way. He is struck by the similarity between the two disciplines (p. 5), and, like Beni, he finds that poetry should be built upon historical fact (Castelvetro, pp. 193–4 and 212). According to Castelvetro, the poet's inventiveness, once allowed a free rein, would know no end (what could it not invent?) and so must be strictly curbed (p. 212). For this reason Castelvetro argues that the historical tragedy or epic is possibly better than the imagined (p. 214). But elsewhere in his commentary he betrays an uneasy doubt (which he shared with many of his age, including Beni) about the relative status of fact and fiction. Thus, while he has argued that poetry should be made out of history, he now argues that it should be similar to, but distinct from, history (p. 28). Then, again shifting his ground, he argues that poetry should not be made out of well-known history, but instead out of a vaguer less well-known type of history (p. 72; see also pp. 187 and 210). Castelvetro's uncertainty over this issue helps to put into perspective Beni's relative certainty in his theoretical work. In both writers one might be tempted to see the dim foreshadowing of a Baroque aesthetic; but it is strange that the critics who most slavishly follow Aristotle—Vettori and Robortelli—come much closer to describing a Baroque aesthetic than do Castelvetro and Beni.

VI

As we have seen, Beni gave the *admirabile* in poetry an important place but, by making it dependent on the poet's skill or craft (his *ingenium*), he did not allow it to conflict with the verisimilar. Consequently, while Aristotle had said that poets are either *furore perciti* or *ingeniosi*, Beni rejected the first idea (that poets were inspired by a poetic fury) and accepted the second (that they could gain sufficient competence through study and art). The modern critics who take Beni's word *ingenium* out of context and hold it up as a novel Baroque notion are lending the word anachronistic connotations: for the word is associated in Beni's mind with the poet's hard work and effort to marry manner to matter, form to content, and not with firework displays of Baroque 'wit' and complication.

In all this Beni is not alone. All the commentators acknowledge (after Aristotle) the necessity for the *admirabile* in poetry. Robortelli writes a lot about it, and relates it to the wonder engendered by unexpected turns in the plot (pp. 86, 87, 143 and 53–4). He is aware of the great pleasure and wonder which poetry can arouse, but he makes *admiratio* dependent on the self-control and skill of the learned poet (p. 247). Like Beni, he does not allow the wonder to arise from the indiscriminate use of *machina* or from the external addition of complication (pp. 154–5 and 91). In short, Robortelli, like Beni, uses the words *artificium* and *ingenium* to describe the poet's skill and craft. He always sets the poet's *ingenium* and *artificium* against the easily won popularity and applause of the *vulgus*. And, echoing Aristotle, he says that the poet who takes short cuts to the achievement of wonder in his reader 'propriam [. . .] magis respicit voluptatem, quam artificium, quod requiritur in tali poematum genere' (p. 149).

Maggi also lends *admiratio* an important place in poetry. He relates it, as Aristotle had related it, to the complication of the plot: 'Cum in Peripetiis, et Agnitionibus tum discere, tum admirari contingat, haudquaquam dubium, quin ex iis maxima voluptas capiatur' (p. 111). Indeed, Maggi seems to argue for the highest degree of complication in tragedy when he paraphrases Aristotle as follows: 'Eas Tragoedias Philosophus [*Aristoteles*], quae peripetiam agnitioni iunctam habent, pulcherrimas appellat, quoniam et summopere delectant, et animum a perturbationibus magna cum voluptate repurgant' (p. 143). But, like Aristotle, Maggi stresses the need for *artificium* and *ars*: Aristotle (he argues) set no great store either by his first type of *agnitio* (for 'id [. . .] artificio caret' (p. 177)), or by his second type (for it was an obvious construction or contrivance of the poet rather than a logical outcome of the plot; and it is therefore said to 'carere arte' (pp. 178–9)). Here *ars* is used to mean 'the art that conceals the art' and has nothing to do with Secentistic displays of 'wit'.

The same pattern is more clearly evident in Vettori's commentary. The absolute necessity of *admiratio* in tragedy and comedy is acknowledged (p. 256). And, as if to add grist to the

Secentistic mill, Vettori underlines the necessarily irrational nature of the *admirabile* (p. 257). In Vettori's commentary complication is placed before simplicity, as it was in the *Poetics*:

Oportet pulcherrimae tragoediae compositionem esse, non simplicem, sed plexam [. . .]: supra autem probavit [*Aristoteles*], fabulas, rerumque coagmentationes, involutas et in quibus agnitio peripetiaque existeret, anteponendas esse simplicibus argumentis: quamvis enim ex simplici apertoque argumento fabula confici possit non mala, cum tamen hic de pulcherrima, omnibusque rebus ornata tragoedia loquatur, merito illam removet (Vettori, p. 119; see also pp. 107, 108, and 69).

Like Maggi, Vettori makes the poet's *ingenium* and *ars* the source of *admiratio*; and, again, *ars* is for him the art that conceals the art (Vettori, pp. 154 and 158). Throughout, *ingenium* is associated with brains and hard work ('mentis lumina' and 'labor' (Vettori, p. 303)).

Enough has now been said to show the particular way in which these commentators (including Beni) viewed the *ingenium* and *ars* of the poet. It can be seen that the words were used in the commentaries to mean something quite different from the associations which the words *ingegno* and *arte* presently enjoy in modern criticism of the Italian Baroque. The problem of defining the term *arte* in Beni's criticism is, however, far from simple. For, although he implies in the commentary on the *Poetics* that it is a good desirable thing, yet he is capable in his practical literary and linguistic criticism of using it in a pejorative sense, to mean something false and unnatural and forced.[8] The problem is here that he uses the same term (*arte*) to designate both art which is properly balanced with nature, and which is present but not obtrusive (which is good for him), and art which outweighs and denies nature (which is bad for him). 'Art' in poetry can thus be either good or bad.

Further investigation into the precise connotations of the word *ingenium* in sixteenth- and seventeenth-century criticism would no doubt shed much light on the culture of the period. C. S. Lewis wisely wrote that 'if a man had time to study the history of one word only, *wit* would perhaps be the best word he could choose'.[9] In this case, we cannot hope to understand

---

[8] See above, pp. 143–6.
[9] *Studies in Words* (Cambridge, 1960), 86.

the critical literature of the period, and its wider implications, until we have passed beyond the limited sphere of purely literary theory, and explore the wider semantic and conceptual fields in which the terms of sixteenth- and seventeenth-century poetic theory operated. For not until the connotations of individual terms like *ingenium* have been carefully examined and defined will we be able to write a history of the ideas behind such words.

VII

It has already been shown in the last chapter that Beni moved substantially away from the *Poetics* in his stress on the useful nature of all poetry, and that he was responsible for novel interpretations of the concepts of ideal reality and catharsis, interpretations which he reached by restricting the usefulness of tragedy, comedy, and the epic respectively to kings, ordinary citizens, and leaders. All this was seen to be far removed from the Baroque.

The other commentators provide a cross-section of the variety of thought on this question of the relationship between *voluptas* and *utilitas* in poetry. Wholly and extremely on the side of pleasure sits Castelvetro. For him the only aim of poetry worth consideration is *diletto*: for him there can be no doubt that 'la poesia sia stata trovata solamente per dilettare, e per ricreare, io dico per dilettare e per ricreare gli animi della rozza moltitudine' (p. 29; see also pp. 549 and 552, etc.). Consequently, Castelvetro accepts whatever gives pleasure in poetry (multiple actions, for instance (p. 504)), and ignores or discredits whatever is thought only to offer instruction (catharsis, for instance (pp. 117 and 275)).

Next to Castelvetro sits Robortelli, still firmly on the side of pleasure, but with some acceptance of poetry's moral value: 'Poetice, si quis diligenter attendat, omnem suam vim confert ad oblectandum, etsi prodest quoque. [. . .] Quem igitur alium finem poetices facultatis esse dicemus, quam oblectare per repraesentationem, descriptionem, et imitationem omnium actionum humanarum, omnium motionum, omnium rerum tum animatarum, tum inanimutarum [*sic*]?' (p. 2). Like Beni, and unlike Castelvetro, Robortelli accepts the concepts of ideal imitation and catharsis; but his interpretation of them is more aesthetic than moral. Thus, while Beni considered that poetry should supply moral exemplars, Robortelli thought that it should provide aesthetic examplars; and he related the duty of poets to that of painters, who should always 'ad Ideam respicere, et pulchriora omnia pingere, quam sint' (p. 79; see also pp. 158–9). Similarly, Robortelli, again unlike Beni, lends catharsis a predominantly aesthetic function, relating it to the pleasures principally, and only incidentally to the utility, of poetry. For in catharsis 'Plane [. . .] idem contingit iis, qui commiseratione, et metu detinentur gravissimis animi perturbationibus: ut leventur, et purgentur cum voluptate: non secus ac devoti, ac supplices homines, cum carminibus sacris expiantibus animum utuntur' (Robortelli, p. 46).

The obvious stress on delight in Castelvetro and Robortelli is enough to put Beni in the shade as a theoretical precursor of Secentismo. And the two remaining commentators, though they are both on the side of utility (Maggi, p. 299; Vettori, Preface), yet place more stress than did Beni on pleasure (Maggi, p. 299; Vettori, pp. 303–4). Both Maggi and Vettori develop a theory of catharsis which is more orthodox, less bizarre, than Beni's; but both, like Beni, allow that catharsis in tragedy should purge, through pity and fear, other emotions as well as pity and fear. But neither Maggi nor Vettori restricted (as Beni restricted) the usefulness of tragedy to kings alone (Maggi, pp. 97–8; Vettori, pp. 56 and 101). Similarly, Vettori develops the concept (only vaguely perceptible in Aristotle) of poetry's ideal imitation: and, like Beni, he accords to poetry a substantial civic role, but does not develop this in Beni's oversubtle way (Vettori, p. 292).

Clearly then, Beni has inherited from the Aristotelian critical tradition, and especially from Vettori, the need and ability to make poetry theoretically useful to society. But, equally clearly, he has taken Vettori's moderate position (where pleasure and utility were balanced) to extreme limits. On this issue, therefore, Beni sits directly opposite to Castelvetro. One wonders consequently how recent critics have concluded that Beni was the champion of *voluptas* in his commentary on the *Poetics*. Can there be any truth in M. L. Doglio's statement (an echo of a similar earlier statement by Jannaco, already quoted) about

Beni: 'Nel lungo corso della trattazione (nei *Commentarii*) acquista sempre maggior rilievo la *voluptas*, che da semplice mezzo finisce col diventare scopo essenziale dell'attività artistica, "condimentum" di ogni forma di poesia' (art. cit., p. 275; see also, for the same view, Jannaco, art. cit., p. 228)? And is it any longer possible to follow Benedetto Croce in grouping together Riccoboni, Castelvetro, and Beni as critics who 'avevano o apertamente o tortuosamente asserito o per le forze delle loro premesse preparato la conclusione, che la poesia non ha altro fine che il diletto'?[10] Does it make sense to link Castelvetro (or even Robortelli) with Beni here?

VIII

The critics who have seen new Baroque tendencies in Beni's commentary have predictably stressed his predilection for metaphor:

Matrice inesauribile di meraviglia e strumento precipuo del 'novus Protheus' (dove già il traslato allude al processo reversibile, tipicamente barocco, del mito che origina la metafora) è appunto la metafora, che il B. tende a fondere con l'allegoria, in un chiaro esempio di trasformazione metamorfica della retorica medioevale (Doglio, p. 275).

Aristotle treats metaphor in some detail in the *Poetics* (1457^b 6–33), and so, even if Beni had not a special regard for it, he might still be expected to give it wide coverage in the commentary. But the truth is that he almost ignores it, along with other linguistic and stylistic devices mentioned in the *Poetics*, and gives it the most summary treatment. He yokes together all the sections of the *Poetics* which deal with metaphor and skips over them, arguing that they have already been fully explained by previous commentators (P. 463^v–64^r). The same comment—hardly that of a concettistic pioneer of metaphor—is offered when the next group of *Particulae* (cxvi–cxxiii)[11] is explained. How could Beni read Aristotle's clear exaltation of metaphor above all other stylistic and linguistic devices, and yet pass over it with the following dismissive comment: 'nos tamen vel quia Interpretes locum hunc universum explicant accurate, vel quia

[10] *Storia della età barocca in Italia* (Bari, 1929), 163.
[11] *Poetics*, 1458^a 18–1459^a 16.

de Dictione multa diximus antea, plura etiam in libris de Historia [. . .] de Dictione silebimus in praesentia' (*P.* 465ᵛ)?
Further proof—if it were needed—of Beni's classically res-
trained attitude to style and language is provided in his comment on Aristotle's attempt to grant poetry special stylistic and
linguistic licence. For Beni discredits such an attempt by inter-
preting it as yet another example of Aristotle's special pleading
on Homer's behalf: 'A qua tamen licentia Latini et Italici longe
absunt, qui nihil nisi diligentius consultis auribus faciunt.
Malunt enim castiores Poetae pauca et convenienti dictione seu
carmine scribere quam per nimiam licentiam permulta pangere'
(*P.* 534). And so Beni completely ignores Aristotle's invitation
to, and potential theoretical sanction of, Baroque linguistic freedom.[12]

When we turn from Beni to the earlier commentators the now
familiar pattern of things asserts itself. For, without exception,
all the commentators, taking their legitimate lead from Aristotle, make more of metaphor and linguistic freedom than did
Beni. We can compare, for instance, Beni's strict criticism of
poetic licence (quoted above) with the following libertarian
interpretation of the same passage from Robortelli: 'Praeterea
videre est apud poetas saepissime, nova confingi nomina ex
apta syllabarum connexione, vel ut sonum, vel ut temporis lon-
gitudinem, et intervallum, vet ut corporis magnitudinem, vel
perturbationis alicuius vim exprimant: sicuti Homerus facit'
(p. 201). Furthermore, Robortelli devotes many pages of commentary, as well as a diagram, to Aristotle's theory of metaphor;
and, though much of what he writes consists of the scholarly
dredging up of parallels and sources, yet it is all symptomatic of
an interest which was completely absent from Beni's commentary. Similarly, Maggi amplifies and expands Aristotle's
thoughts on metaphor, quoting Cicero, Quintilian, and Demet-
rius (pp. 227–9). Vettori devotes fourteen pages to metaphor,
and although much of his treatment concerns textual problems,
it nevertheless satisfied Beni, who gave the matter a mere para-
graph and referred to Vettori (Vettori, pp. 209–23). Finally, Castelvetro gives a very full account of figurative language. He
explores territory left uncharted by Aristotle's already

---

[12] For the same conclusion in the linguistic works, see above, p. 156.

expansive treatment, and lists, for example, eight occasions when similes might be used (pp. 448–9).

Of all the commentators under review Beni is the only one who does not enthusiastically schematize and reorganize Aristotle's categories of metaphor. So much for his Baroque interest in it.

IX

The foregoing survey of Beni's commentary in relation to previous commentaries has been necessarily destructive. It has destroyed, or tried to destroy, the widespread notion that Beni's commentary was the first to open the floodgates to Secentismo, or, in the words of a recent critic, that it 'fu pure il primo segno del trapasso a una diversa sensibilità, la necessaria premessa alle teorie del concettismo e alle poetiche del Peregrini del Pallavicino e del Tesauro' (Doglio, p. 274). On the contrary, there can be no doubt that the markedly Baroque tendencies which the critics have thought to see in Beni are not there. Indeed it is at times incomprehensible that he could ever have been saddled with such an inappropriate cultural role. You might just as well look at a bishop and describe a clown as look at Beni and describe a Baroque sensibility. His work may enshrine some seventeenth-century ideals, but these are clearly more classical than Baroque; and where they could be called Baroque, they are always present, and more markedly present, in the earlier commentators. Does this mean that the theory of the Baroque began in 1548 with the publication of Robortelli's commentary? Or did it begin with Aristotle's *Poetics*? And, if it did begin in 1548, why had it declined by 1613 when Beni published his commentary? Or, as is perhaps more likely, is the whole Aristotelian tradition of literary theory, up to and including Beni, only incidentally related to the so-called Baroque movement in literature? Whatever the answers to these pressing questions, it is certain that our view of Secentismo and of the period in which it flourished still requires review. My purpose has not been to defend Beni from the taint of Secentismo or decadence, still less to sully the reputation and scholarly integrity of the earlier commentators. In fact the very word *taint* symbolizes an inappropriate attitude towards the literature and the literary theory of the period. It is perhaps time that we finally relinquished the convenient and makeshift idea of a marked cultural and moral decadence between Rinascimento and Barocco, and instead addressed ourselves to the positive discovery, description, and interpretation of the culture of the period.

14

THE THEORY AND PRACTICE OF HISTORY

I

As we have seen, Beni did not turn seriously to the problem of history until around Christmas 1609. He wrote on 19 February 1610 to Marc'Antonio Bonciario in Perugia, telling him how the *De historia libri quatuor*[1] were conceived and written:

> ma l'offesa della gamba la qual mi occorse apunto sul principio delle dette vacanze, m'impedì, e non so in qual modo poi m'indusse a mutar pensiero. Perciochè per la noia dell'otio e delle notti sì lunghe m'addussi (giachè nel Timeo e nella detta Comparatione convien pur trattenersi in speculationi e rivolger copia di libri) a farmi leggere alcuni Historici: donde fui anco tirato a dettar un libro o più tosto quattro libri *De Historia*.[2]

Beni's next historical work was a commentary on Sallust's *Catiline*, with an edition of the *Jugurtha*.[3] It is not certain when the commentary was written, but it could not have been written before the treatise *De historia* (1610–11) partly because it is not mentioned there in the many places one would expect it to be mentioned, and partly because, as we saw, the *De historia* was Beni's first work on history. The catalogue of Beni's library lists two editions of the commentary on the *Catiline*, 1622 and 1612 (BB 66). I have not discovered a 1612 edition, and it is impossible, in the muddle of Beni's literary production of this period, to be certain that there was such an edition. Internal evidence (apart from the absence of references to the *De historia*) is of little assistance here: for references to the commentaries on the first book of the *Rhetoric* (published in 1624) and the *Aeneid* (published in 1622) (*S.* 47, 53, and 179) do not prove that the

---

[1] Venice, 1611 (hereafter *DH*). There was a 2nd edn. in 1622.

[2] Letter, dated Padua, 19 February 1610, printed in *Lettere di uomini illustri scritte a M. Antonio Bonciario perugino*, 11–14 (pp. 12–13). See also above, p. 96 and Chapter 7 n.5.

[3] *In Sallustii Catilinariam commentarii . . . His additur Iugurthinum Bellum: cui Annuae Literae quaedam subiiciuntur* (Venice, 1622) (hereafter *S.*).

work was one of Beni's last, for we know that these commentaries had been written (though not necessarily in their published form) before 1610 (in the case of the commentary on the *Rhetoric* (see *Lettere . . . a . . . Bonciario*, p. 12)) and before 1613 (in the case of the commentary on the *Aeneid* (see Dedicatory Letter in *P.*)). However, the possibility of a 1612 edition of the commentary on the *Catiline* is rendered extremely unlikely by the fact that Beni did not lecture at the Studio on Sallust until 1615.[4] And it is impossible to believe that he would have published such a commentary (clearly the outcome of a lecture course) before he had delivered it, probably several times, before his pupils. At any rate, the *De historia* and the *Catiline* commentary present themselves as companion works, as we shall see, and are closely related in their ideas about history.

The question of history's identity and function was a central one in discussions about the arts. History provided, in Beni's time as it had since Aristotle's, a comparison with poetry and rhetoric: each of the three cognate disciplines was regularly used to define the others (see Weinberg, i. 1–37). Yet the theoretical problems of history had never been thoroughly explored in the Middle Ages or in the Renaissance (up to the period of Machiavelli and Guicciardini). Soon after Guicciardini's death, 'Arts' of history began to appear with the first (poorly focused) attempt coming from Padua in Speroni's *Dialoghi* (1542). Somewhat more systematic was (still from Padua) Robortelli's *De historica facultate* (1548: the famous year of the commentary on the *Poetics* from the same pen). But it was Robortelli's 'heretical' pupil, Francesco Patrizi, who was the first to ask deep searching questions about the nature of history in his *Della historia diece dialoghi* (1560); and although his mercurial manner led to inconsistencies and contradictions, Patrizi's doubts could not afterwards be ignored by anyone seriously interested in the theory of history. Numerous 'Arts' followed these early Paduan productions; and the theories of history, poetry, and rhetoric in many ways ran parallel courses. Unlike poetics and rhetoric, however, the theory of history had no authoritative classical text on which to base its discussions, and it took some time for

---

[4] See 'Oratio LII. Habuit hanc Patavii Anno 1615 cum primo Sallustium explicare aggrederetur', in *OQS* 132–53 (=35).

the most pertinent questions to be asked, and even longer for them to be answered. Up to Patrizi, Cicero's brief characterization of history in the *De oratore* (II. v; II. ix; III. x) formed the basis for most discussion (though Cicero's ideas were more often paraphrased and repeated than examined); but after Patrizi discussion was placed on a new, freer footing.

Beni is to be seen as the heir to both approaches, conservative and free-thinking. His *De historia* is the most comprehensive 'Art': it takes all previous approaches into account (tacitly as a rule), and addresses itself to both the Ciceronian and the Patrizian positions. Differing views of the importance of Beni's theory are offered by modern critics. In a pioneering study of the theory of history in the Italian Counter-Reformation, Giorgio Spini[5] has placed Beni against the background of writers from Speroni to the eighteenth-century Muratori, and has seen him specifically as the link between Patrizi and Campanella in the successive working out of modern historical method, and in the freeing of historical theory from the 'shackles' of 'Ciceronian orthodoxy'. Spini sees Beni as repudiating the notions of the Ciceronians in his reasoned attitude to the definition of history and of its sources, as well as in his separation of history from poetry and rhetoric. Beni's infamous attack on Livy is seen as symptomatic of his anti-Ciceronianism: for Livy (according to Spini) was 'the historian par excellence of the Ciceronians' (p. 111). At the same time (argues Spini) Beni shows, in his linguistic and stylistic observations on the historians, that he was a traditionalist, a 'professor of stylistics', more interested in how the historians expressed themselves than in what they said (p. 112). Without prejudging Spini's interesting thesis, some preliminary objections might be raised. First, the group which Spini calls 'Ciceronians' and which he presents as homogeneous ('to read one of these orthodox writers is not much different from reading them all' (p. 100)) do not in fact always agree on major issues, as we shall see. Secondly, Beni's rejection of Livy can hardly be said to prove him anti-Ciceronian since it

[5] 'Historiography: The Art of History in the Italian Counter Reformation', in *The Late Italian Renaissance, 1525–1630*, ed. by E. Cochrane (London, 1970), 91–133. This is Cochrane's translation of Spini's already quoted article. 'I trattatisti dell'arte storica nella Controriforma italiana'. In what follows I use the English version.

is justified by a comparison with Cicero, who is found to be superior as a linguistic and stylistic model. Evidently, therefore, there is a danger here (as in the parallel case of poetics) of schematically classifying without proper justification individual writers (such as Beni) in terms of general cultural trends. Such schemes and pictures of cultural trends, which are useful at the beginning of an enquiry as makeshifts, are all too often retained against the evidence, and are very rarely and reluctantly abandoned. Another recent critic, and one who cannot but be familiar with Spini's ideas, Eric Cochrane, has provided a view which seems both self-contradictory and at odds with Spini's view, as the following quotation shows: 'Even the vociferous linguistic iconoclast Paolo Beni [. . .] has nothing to add [to the theory of history], in the first decades of the next century, except a few more nasty words about Livy's style.'[6]

With these two divergent views of Beni's contribution in mind, I shall examine the principal issues of historical theory in order to discover, first, what Beni said about them, secondly, whether his views were original, and thirdly, in what direction such originality tends.[7]

II

The most important aspect of history for Beni was its usefulness. The first page of the *De historia* proclaims this, as does the

---

[6] *Historians and Historiography in the Italian Renaissance*, 484. In his 'Prologue' Cochrane alludes to the mass of material which he has had to consider in preparing his book, and he admits to having developed a method of skimming rather than reading the texts. He seems to damn his own achievement, even allowing for false modesty, and does not inspire confidence when he writes: 'Similarly, even a well-trained skimmer cannot grasp what is really evident to someone who reads in depth; and there is nothing I say about any single text that could not be modified or rejected after a more careful scrutiny' (p. xvii). Is it unfair to ask why such an unrealistically large project was ever undertaken? See Introduction above.

[7] I take into account the following 'Arts' of history: S. Speroni, 'Dialogo dell'historia', in *Dialoghi del sig. Speron Speroni* (Venice, 1596; 1st edn. 1542); F. Robortelli, *De historica facultate, disputatio* (Florence, 1548); F. Patrizi, *Della historia diece dialoghi* (Venice, 1560); L. Ducci, *Ars historica* (Ferrara, 1604); T. Campanella, 'Historiographiae liber unus iuxta propria principia', in *Tutte le opere*, ed. by L. Firpo (Milan–Verona, 1954), 1221–55. This last work was circulated in MS in 1612 (ed. cit., p. lxxxiii). Beni had copies in his library of all these works (except of course Campanella's). See BB 79 ff. In what follows I refer to all these works by quoting only the authors' names and page numbers.

whole of Book Four, which is dedicated to the subject. Beni accepted Cicero's definition of history as 'magistra vitae' (*De oratore*, II. ix) and expanded it to include all conceivable practical, moral, academic, and spiritual uses. For him, history was not merely a record of events, but also the teacher of prudence through examples (*DH* 23, 245 and 20–1). It teaches not only about public institutions and figures, but also about personal afflictions, how to cope with them, and how to maintain a family ('universae familiae gubernandae rationem') (*DH* 250=248–52). The lessons learned from history are more valuable than those derived from personal experience or travel: for lessons from history are easier to come by, more quickly learned, and more richly diverse (*DH* 245–7). History is useful also to other disciplines: it provides the orator and the poet with material (for all poetry, except the comic, should be based largely on history, according to Beni); and history usefully records the origins and early growth of theology, natural philosophy, mathematics, jurisprudence, medicine, and agriculture (*DH* 219^2–244). Finally, Beni accords to history a full spiritual role, and argues that 'quoniam ad veram immortalitatem nobis aspirandum est, eo etiam dirigenda est rerum gestarum cognitio, ut tum mortalitatis perfugium, tum, Numine aspirante, immortalitatis ac beatae vitae incitamentum sit ac subsidium' (*DH* 23). It might reasonably be asked whether such a lofty aim can be ascribed to a discipline which can include annals and similarly sub-literary documents: Beni's fervent intention to justify spiritually the study of history may have led him into an exaggeration here.

In spite of this implicit exaggeration Beni, of all the theorists, gives the fullest and most enthusiastic account of history's uses. This is a fact which Spini's argument seems to obscure. For, according to him, Patrizi made an attempt to destroy the Ciceronian concept of history as *magistra vitae*, while Campanella freed history 'from every remnant of moral and pedagogic ends' (Spini, pp. 102–3; see also p. 112). Beni, who (in Spini's view) is the link between Patrizi and Campanella, is conveniently omitted from consideration on this score. It is not clear, however, that Patrizi and Campanella *did* divest history of its usefulness: Patrizi twice formulates the theory that happiness consists in temporal and spiritual peace (to be found in the

Republic and in God, respectively). Such peace (according to Patrizi) depends on good laws and their observance. Philosophy offers universal ideal solutions to this problem of peace while history offers valuable particular experiences of it (Patrizi, fos. 24^r and 51^r–54^r). Thus, the use of history which Patrizi envisages is principally political. Similarly, Campanella places the usefulness of history in the examples it presents to present-day law-maker:

Cum enim noverimus quid veteres bene, quidque male egerint, et quibus artibus rempublicam et rem familiarem et se ipsos natosque rexerunt, nos similiter discimus quae nobis prosunt obsuntque, et regulas ex tot experimentis eliciemus, et scientias reformamus et leges, et quomodo cum singulis nationibus agere oporteat intelligemus (p. 1246).

Patrizi and Campanella may have stopped repeating *ad nauseam* the *magistra vitae* dictum of the earlier theorists; but there can be no doubt that Cicero's idea was in the back of their minds when they conceived of history's usefulness. Unlike them, Beni brought it out into the open, and cultivated it as no one had previously done.

III

In a further area of debate (what constitutes the proper subject of history), the ideas of Patrizi and Campanella can properly be said to move far away from the traditional view. All the theorists described history as narration or memory, or both. But the question arose: narration of what? Up to Patrizi's time the answer was simply: the past deeds of famous men (see, for example, Robortelli, pp. 8 and 25–6). Patrizi breaks down such narrowness and defines history as 'il narramento adunque degli effetti, che caggiono sotto alla cognition de' sentimenti, & degli occhi sopra tutto' (fo. 8^v). With this he includes future as well as past events (fo. 13^v), non-human elements (such as natural history), as well as painting and sculpture (fo. 14r). Campanella further extends the breadth of historical inquiry, and writes that 'omnis narrator, sive per epistolam, sive ore tenus, sive motibus, historicus est' (p. 1228).

Beside these spacious panoramic views of history's territory Beni defines a circumscribed and tiny area. He takes Patrizi's arguments fully into account (he could not have known Campanella's), and provides a logical and consistent answer to them. For Beni, history is the chronological written narration of particular human events in the past. Thus history cannot include paintings, for they do not narrate chronologically (*DH* 54). Nor can it include future events. Natural events cannot be the central subject of history for Beni since they are not human (except by reflection) and because natural phenomena are usually treated by philosophers in a universal rather than a particular manner (*DH* 62–7). It is mistaken to claim that Beni's view was original, as Spini (pp. 110–11) has done, for Lorenzo Ducci had already used the same arguments to separate natural history from history proper in his *Ars historica* (pp. 20 and 177–8).

So much for what is excluded from history. What did Beni include in it? The answer is straightforward: all facts which further history's end, that is to say, which teach prudence. Here again Ducci (p. 20) had already made the same point. Beni goes beyond the traditionalists in including private as well as public material, but he warns that the historian should choose from the former only those things which will benefit humanity and teach prudence (*DH* 29). Similarly, history is permitted to relate bad, ugly, or immoral matter, but this purely in order that the reader should be warned realistically of life's dangers (*DH* 31, 217–18[2]=222).

However, side by side with this ideal theory, which is not original, Beni shows, in his practical criticism of the *Catiline*, that he wanted from history a more objective record of the truth, such as Patrizi had ideated, irrespective of its moral, spiritual, and practical usefulness. This can be seen in the following comment, where he comes close to Patrizi's all-inclusiveness:

Res praesentes quo magis in promptu sunt omnibus, et exploratae, eo magis narrandae; etenim ea in primis quae vera sunt, et explorata literis sunt consignanda, siquidem veritas quaerenda est in historia. Certe si hoc coluisset praeceptum antiquitas, ut ea ipsa quae in omnium oculis oreque vigebant, ac nemini non explorata erant, scripsisset, sexcenta nosceremus, quae nunc vehementer requirimus, ut de armis, de vestibus, de insignibus, deque huiusmodi aliis (*S.* 31; see also *S.* 146).

Yet one important difference still exists here between Beni and Patrizi (as well as Campanella): history, for Beni, is always human and has no business, except incidentally, with the non-human; for Patrizi and Campanella its horizons are limitless. In the end, therefore, although Beni betrays a slightly wider view than his pure theory indicates, his ideas of what the proper subject-matter of history should be are conservative.

IV

Beni's contribution to the definition of history's subject-matter is small beside his contribution to what might be called the methodology of history.

All the theorists agree that the historian's job is to follow the truth. Beni calls truth the *puppis et prora* of history, and follows word for word the laws which Cicero had laid down on the matter in the *De oratore*, II. v (*DH* 75–8; *S*. 24, 86, and 117). History is described, as it was in the commentary on the *Poetics*,[8] as a 'pudica matrona' (*DH* 43).

So much is simple to state. But how was truth to be established? The traditionalists tended to take Cicero's *leges* for granted, assuming that the truth was easy of access. Patrizi gives the impression of being consciously heretical when he casts melancholy doubts on the possibility of the historian ever reaching the truth (though he never denies that the truth exists) (fos. 25^r–30^r). Nevertheless, and despite his professed doubts, Patrizi does list the sources upon which the historian should draw: for past events, documents and eyewitnesses; for present or recent events, eyewitnesses and reports of eyewitnesses (fo. 26^{r-v}). But, for the history of nations and cities (*historia universale*), sources should include: (1) witnesses and actors on all sides of the event; (2) contemporaries not directly involved; (3) writers of the same nation; and (4) foreign histories of the nation in question (fo. 31^v). These two lists of sources do not seem consistent with each other; and it was left to Beni to provide a more rigorous treatment of the problem of historical sources. He grades them according to importance, as follows: (1) what the writer or historian witnessed or did; (2) what

---

[8] See above, p. 181. The idea that history was a 'pudica matrona' and poetry a bejewelled virgin was a critical commonplace, and not Beni's personal vision of the Baroque (*pace* Toffanin, Belloni, Jannaco, Mazzacurati, etc.). On this commonplace, see Trabalza, 148 and Cochrane, *Historians and Historiography*, 485.

annals and other documents say; (3) what other eyewitnesses say; and (4) what *fama* reports (*DH* 27; see also *DH* 93). In effect this might not be more than a description of what historians had been doing in practice for some time, but it is novel in the relatively immature theory of history.

Confident that the truth could be discovered, Beni went on to give a comprehensive account of how it should be presented. His criteria were, not beauty, artifice, or persuasiveness, but intelligibility, clarity, and faithfulness. In this, history is distinct from poetry and rhetoric, as it had traditionally been for numerous theorists since Speroni.[9] But it is only with Patrizi that a clean and consistent break is made between history and oratory. This is followed through by Beni and Campanella. The problem of speeches in history provides a good example of the practical workings of such a break: Speroni, though aware of the grave dangers (of untruthfulness) in allowing rhetorical speeches in history, allowed them all the same, albeit in a grudging fashion (pp. 494–6); Patrizi finds orations in history totally out of place, and bans them (fos. 58^v–59^r); Beni reaches the same conclusion, but differs from Patrizi in that he provides a full practical demonstration of the possibilities of speeches in the writing of history (*DH* 34–42) as well as criticism of Sallust's oratorical use of delightful but untrue and unbelievable speeches in the *Catiline* (*S.* 35, 86–91, 170 ff., 176, 187, and 195). In this, as in other matters of historical theory, Beni has taken the view of an earlier critic (Patrizi), and fleshed it out to provide one of the most systematic treatments of the subject.

The same is true of Beni's acute observations on compositional procedures in history. He begins with what Patrizi had written, and adds to it: he adopts the Aristotelian notion of unity of period (*DH* 87): the historian should choose a period (day, year, etc.) and treat it in such a way that all the events contained in it can be maintained at once in the reader's memory (*DH* 92).[10] Beni adduces the same Aristotelian criteria to impose

---

[9] It is interesting to see that Speroni separates history from oratory (pp. 488–90) while Robortelli (with whom Speroni is classed by Spini) connects the two disciplines ('historica facultas rhetoricae pars est quaedam' (p. 26)).

[10] Baronio's *Annales* come in here for some adverse criticism. This is in contrast to the flattery which Beni had deployed in his early occasional and hasty *Disputatio* of 1596: see above, Chapter 3, Section IV.

unity of place and of people (*personarum*)[11] in history (*DH* 88–9). Historical narration should proceed in a clear, natural, and uncluttered manner (*DH* 105–7); and, armed with a strict criterion of relevance, Beni outlaws all digressions (*DH* 99–100). Such theories are further worked out in his criticism of the *Catiline*. For, as with the prose of Boccaccio, he rearranges and rewrites much of Sallust's work according to his own rules of historical composition. In this, Sallust is treated as a model of how not to compose history. For example, Beni condenses the first nineteen chapters of the *Catiline* into one page of factual impartial and concise historical narration (*S.* 83–4). He shows that Sallust paid too much attention to unimportant and irrelevant matters (*S.* 116, and 182–3), and that his narration turned the natural order of events topsy-turvy (*S.* 71).

V

The clear-sightedness with which Beni illustrated his ideas on the composition of history is equally apparent in his observations on language and style. Since the first duty of the historian is to tell the truth, it follows that the language (*oratio*) of history should be above all clear (*perspicua*). It should be correct and regular in its forms (*pura, emendata*), free of metaphor (*propria*), charged with meaning (*significantissima*), natural (*naturalis*) and concise (but not so concise as to be obscure) (*DH* 42–6 and 109 ff.; *S.* 118). It should attract no attention to itself, for 'historica locutio matrem familias exprimat, quae ubi munditiam retinuerit, maiora ornamenta non quaeret' (*DH* 43).[12]

No other theorist got as close as Beni to defining the stylistic and linguistic problem, a fact which will emerge more clearly after a brief review of what some previous theorists had said on the subject. Speroni discusses at length whether history should be written in Latin or Italian, but does not tackle the other

[11] By this he means nations as opposed to larger groups of people, like Europeans, Asians, etc.

[12] Mazzacurati and Casagrande see in Beni's criticism of Livy (as well as in his linguistic ideas generally) evidence of his 'generale avversione verso ogni forma di naturalismo letterario e linguistico' (Mazzacurati, art. cit., 497; see also Casagrande, ed. cit., p. xvi). This judgement does not appear to be accurate for either Beni's linguistic or his literary criticism. In both, nature plays a strong, often dominant role. See above, pp. 143–6.

linguistic and stylistic problems of writing history. Robortelli follows Cicero, and makes historical style dependent upon rhetorical ideals: 'huiusmodi orationis genus, huiusmodi, inquam, requirit historia: apertum, grave, politum, ornatum; splendidum' (Robortelli, p. 28). Patrizi says little about this problem. And Ducci still retains a rhetorical concept of historical style: 'ita quoque de elocutione sentiendum, est autem commendabilior ornata quam inculta: igitur Historicum ornata locutione uti decet: sunt autem ornamenta orationis perspicuitas, suavitas, gravitas' (p. 190). Beni appears far more practically aware than these writers of the need for a set of trusty linguistic and stylistic rules. Not only does he sever all links with traditionally rhetorical style, but, in his search for a model, and in his criticism of Sallust, he clarifies and exemplifies his notion of a clear unadorned style.

The model had to be Latin: for Beni, despite his later and not fully deserved reputation as a *moderne* in the *Querelle des anciens et des modernes*, never considers the idea that history might be written in the vernacular.[13] But, of all the Roman historians (Beni short-lists Caesar, Livy, Sallust, and Curtius for consideration as models), not one is perfect in matters of language and style, though all, except Livy (*poeticus, horridus, quodam veluti squalore obsitus, tortuosus, inaequabilis, longior, incompositus, inconcinnus, turgidus, spinosus, durus* (DH 136)), have some qualities worthy of imitation.[14] These Roman writers should be imitated only briefly, therefore. They are best used to provide variety in long historical compositions. But, in all other cases, Cicero is the only fit model, for he is reliable, regulated in usage, and has numerous passages in a middle style (which is eminently suitable for historical narration) (DH 139–40; S. 14–15 and 56–7). These criteria, and their application, recall Beni's

---

[13] Again his linguistic views here—like his views on poetic theory—have been taken by Mazzacurati and Casagrande as evidence of his 'modernismo' (Mazzacurati, art. cit., 497) and 'inclinazione modernista' (Casagrande, ed. cit., p. xvi). This seems inaccurate.

[14] Predictably Beni's condemnation of Livy was rebuffed by Paduan writers, amongst whom we can mention L. Pignoria, 'L. P. Balthassari Bonifacio archidiacono tarvisino, viro reverendissimo. Epist. XLIV', in *Symbolarum epistolicarum liber* (Padua, 1628), 174–90; and I. Ph. Tomasini, *T. Livius patavinus* (Padua, 1630), 34–7. Other writers have deplored Beni's criticism of Livy, such as Tiraboschi, vii. 1059.

criticism of the *Crusca* dictionary. Similarities are especially evident in Beni's detailed and almost totally adverse criticism of Sallust's language. Sallust is shown to furnish in the *Catiline* a linguistic and stylistic model of what not to do. Beni treats this work exactly as he treated Boccaccio's in the *Anticrusca*, rewriting it according to criteria of clarity, regularity, and decorum (see *S.* 14–16, for example).[15]

What did Beni find objectionable in Sallust's Latin? First, his concision and obscurity. For example, of the words 'Mihi a spe, metu, partibus Reipublicae, animus liber erat' (*Catiline* IV) Beni writes 'ad aenigma potius vergunt quam serviant perspicuitati: Itaque hoc quoque dicendi genus historico vitandum vel maxime' (*S.* 25; see also *S.* 97, 118, 123, 138, and 152). Here Beni would no doubt have sacrificed Sallust's extremely neat clear compressed formulation for an expansive treatment of each separate idea in the marvellously concise sentence. Secondly, Beni objected to the obsolete nature of much of Sallust's language, which seemed barbarous and unregulated in comparison with Cicero's: such forms as *omnis homines, inter mortalis* (*S.* 16), *colos* (for 'color'), *labos* (for 'labor'), *lubidine* (for 'libidine'), *veget* (for 'viget'), *flagitiorum* and *facinorum* (for 'flagitiosorum' and 'facinorosum') (*S.* 14) are a few of the many words cited by Beni in order to deter historians from slavish imitation of Sallust (see also *S.* 25, 66, 72, and 188). Thirdly, Sallust was criticized for employing inappropriate oratorical and poetic devices (*S.* 25 and 85). And, finally, he was accused of possessing a poor ear (*S.* 118), a criterion Beni might have derived from Dionysius of Halicarnassus (whom he cites, along with Aristotle and Cicero, as the three principal influences on his concept of historical writing (*DH* 107–9)).[16]

In all these linguistic criticisms, it is not the originality of Beni's ideas that is striking, so much as the close connection between his criticism of Sallust on the one hand, and of Dante, Boccaccio, and G. Villani on the other. This is further proof that Beni's anti-Cruscan campaign was not motivated solely (or at all) by personal hatred, fanatical passion for Tasso, and *campanilismo*, but instead by a deep-rooted conviction

---

[15] See above, pp. 158–9.

[16] For Beni's reliance on the criterion of the ear in his linguistic writings, see above, p. 144.

about the nature of language and style. For there is no polemical thrust in Beni's criticisms of Sallust: he seems merely to be searching objectively for a reliable linguistic and stylistic model, as in the *Anticrusca*. Of course, here (as there) he is hampered by his inability to separate linguistic from stylistic and aesthetic considerations; here (as there) he is reading in order to learn how to write rather than in order to experience a literary work.

<h1 style="text-align:center">VI</h1>

A striking feature of all Beni's historical theory is its lack of interest in the question of vernacular Italian history. As we have seen, Speroni was interested almost exclusively in this problem; and other theorists were more clearly aware of it than Beni. Ducci, for example, illustrates his theoretical points with classical and modern Italian historians (amongst them Guicciardini and C. Campana), and relates the problem of including direct speeches in history to that of Italy's different dialects (*idiomata*) (p. 161). Beni's omission here is the more remarkable since, in the *Anticrusca*, he lays end to end passages from Sallust, Livy, Guicciardini, and Boccaccio in order to prove (as we saw in an earlier chapter) that Guicciardini was more successful than Boccaccio.[17]

Equally surprising is the discrepancy between the not unfavourable comments on Sallust in the *Anticrusca* and the wholesale criticism of him in the commentary on the *Catiline*. Not only does Beni attack Sallust's composition, style, and language, but he also disagrees with many of the moral assumptions in the *Catiline*. Most noticeably, he objects to Sallust's depiction of *Fortuna* as a powerful and capricious ruler of men's affairs, and prefers to see it as a form of Divine Providence (S. 44–7, 56, and 154). Sallust's portrait of the voluptuous and learned Sempronia (which Beni finds distasteful) provides Beni with the opportunity for stressing that a woman's place is in the home (S. 111). And, similarly, he produces homilies against Sallust on the nobility of hunting and agriculture (S. 24–5) and the benefits of keeping silent (S. 105).

---

[17] A. 140–5. For further discussion of this, see above, p. 157.

What should we make of this apparent discrepancy between the *Anticrusca* and the commentary on the *Catiline*? Was Beni merely inconsistent here? If we remember from an earlier chapter his ideal of a single standard invariable prose style as well as his consequently comparative criticism of language and style, his apparent change of view in respect of Sallust becomes understandable. For in the *Anticrusca* Sallust and Livy were thought—rightly or wrongly—to be better than Boccaccio (who in any case was more or less worthless to Beni); in the commentary on the *Catiline* Sallust was judged, and found wanting, according to the much higher (indeed the highest) standard of Cicero. Thus the two different contexts of the works help to explain Beni's apparent contradiction: he did not change his mind about Sallust so much as his terms of reference.

However, since he finds so little to admire in the *Catiline*, it has to be asked why he chose to write a commentary on it. Was it purely an academic exercise, a part of his teaching programme? Or was he influenced in his choice by the fact that, from the time of its *editio princeps* of 1470, the *Catiline* had gone through more editions than any other work of ancient history, and had retained a consistently high level of popularity?[18] Clearly, these two factors played their part in Beni's choice of a text. But perhaps more potent was his desire to use Sallust's failure as an object-lesson in historical composition (and this explains why he produced no commentary on the *Jugurtha*, which he thought was better than the *Catiline* in every respect). He could use Sallust's linguistic defects to develop positive linguistic rules, just as he did at length with Dante and Boccaccio in the *Anticrusca* and the *Cavalcanti*.

VII

When we turn to Beni's practice as an historian it is a surprise to find that he wrote nothing in Latin. His treatise 'Della veneta

[18] See P. Burke, 'A Survey of the Popularity of Ancient Historians, 1450–1700', *History and Theory*, 5 (1966), 136–7; and E. Bolaffi, *Sallustio e la sua fortuna nei secoli* (Rome, 1949), 258. This last work covers a very wide field sketchily.

libertà'[19] has two unequal parts: the first and shortest consists of a history of the Venetian Republic, and the second provides a very long and unfavourable review of the anonymous *Squitinio della libertà veneta* (1612). In his review Beni quotes the *Squitinio* word for word, fiercely refuting it as he goes along, arguing that Venice was born free, without a town, but with a body of citizens, long before the foundation of the Roman Empire, to which it (*pace* the author of the *Squitinio*) has never bowed. Characteristically, Beni runs out of time and energy in the review, and impatiently dismisses the final three chapters of the *Squitinio* as 'Vanità' (BN 324, fo. 277[r]). This work is to be seen in the context of the long and flourishing line of Venetian histories which were politically motivated and dominated by notions of the myth of Venice. Beni's work is not original, but is (as he says in the catalogue of his library (BB 77)) a compendium of facts culled from various published histories of Venice, including that of Bembo.[20] It is not unlikely that, in writing this work, Beni hoped to achieve Bembo's former position as official Venetian historian. He says in the catalogue of his library (ibid.) that he was asked to write the treatise by the Republic; but nothing seems to have come of the finished product, and it was never published.

Beni's other historical work is also presumably a commission. It is a history of the Trissino family from its origins to 1624 (the year of the first publication of Book One; Book Two remains unpublished).[21] The work comprises a chronological list of

---

[19] This exists in two autograph MS versions: (*a*) Paris, Bibliothèque nationale (hereafter BN), MS 324, and (*b*) PU MS 412. (*a*) is a slightly fuller version of (*b*). There is scope for further work on these MSS. Internal evidence suggests that this work was composed, at least in part, after 1616 (for there are references to Beni's own printed commentary on the *Goffredo*, eg. on p. 6 of (*b*), mentioned above).

[20] On the flourishing state of Venetian historiography at this time, see W. J. Bouwsma, 'Three Types of Historiography in Post-Renaissance Italy', *History and Theory*, 4 (1964), 309 ff.

[21] The first book was published as *Trattato dell'origine et fatti della famiglia Trissina* (Padua, in casa dell'auttore, 1624). There was another edition—with the same dedication however—*Trattato dell'origine, et fatti illustri della famiglia Trissina* (Milan, M. Malatesta, 1626). The second book exists now in a nineteenth-century copy as 'Trattato dell'origine della famiglia Trissina, libro secondo' in Vicenza, Biblioteca Bertoliana, G.21.11.20* (=2830), pp. 1–37. B. Morsolin uses Beni's first book in his *Giangiorgio Trissino* (Florence, 1894) but does not mention the second book.

famous and not so famous members of the family, in the manner of Francesco Sansovino.[22] In its brief and factual potted biographies it draws on a very large variety of sources: personal
documents then in the possession of the Trissino family, medieval chronicles, annals, and other documents scattered throughout the Italian libraries. Indeed it is hard to believe that Beni, in
very old age and infirm, could have amassed such a bulk of
archival and other material, or that he felt sufficient enthusiasm
(never expressed elsewhere) for the Trissino family to carry out
such a project. Yet the work was unmistakably dedicated to
Conte Bonifacio Trissino on 21 March 1624 by Beni; and there is
no circumstantial evidence of any sort to suggest that the work is
not actually by Beni. However, it remains thoroughly uncharac-
teristic, and reads more like a work of minute local history than
as one of the last works of a professor of humanities. In fact,
even if the work is Beni's own, it can be assumed that the
material was gathered mainly from correspondence with members of the Trissino family and others, and that Beni simply
arranged the material in chronological order, added a few notes
of praise, and put his name to the title-page.

VIII

The foregoing survey has shown that there are few connections
between Beni's theory and practice as an historian. Indeed,
there is little evidence that he ever tried to practise what he
preached. His two works of history are occasional, encomiastic,
and (in one case at least) polemical; and they bear little resemblance to his high theoretical ideal of objective truth-telling. It is
as if critical theory exists here by and for itself. It is an auton-
omous subject which survives and blossoms solely in its own
essentially theoretical element. The same can be said (in a similar field) of Beni's small quantity of unimpressive verse, all of
which is occasional, and none of which has anything to do with
his complex Aristotelian teachings on the subject of poetic
theory.[23]

   At the same time, as we have seen, his historical theory is full

---

[22] *Della origine & de' fatti delle famiglie illustri d'Italia* (Venice, 1582).
[23] See above, pp. 25–6 and 204.

of practical advice on how to compose history and how to find the correct Latin style. Beni did not stop, as most of his predecessors had stopped, with theoretical rules: he went further and demonstrated in his treatment of Sallust how such rules can be put into practice. All this is addressed primarily to his Paduan pupils. Yet it is tempting to wonder whether any of them ever thought of putting Beni's advice and admonitions to the practical test. Is it not possible that his practical rules were merely speculated on, criticized, and discussed by his pupils and colleagues, only to pass directly into the realms of academic theory without achieving any practical results? The choice of Latin as a medium for theory (and teaching), and of Italian as a medium for more practical (especially polemical) criticism, no doubt plays a part (and not in Beni's case alone) in this remarkable divorce between theory and practice.

But, putting aside this puzzling discrepancy, we can say in conclusion that the picture of Beni's theory of history which has emerged from this study differs from Spini's picture: Spini called Beni 'that incorrigible *enfant terrible* of the age' (p. 109), and saw him in consequence as an important link between Patrizi and Campanella in the development of modern historical theory and method. This study has not confirmed such a clear outline, but has shown instead that Beni's position is delicately nuanced. For although Beni came close to Patrizi and Campanella in his views of compositional procedures, yet he was far from them in other ways. First, he demonstrated none of their anti-authoritarianism (he derived many of his rules from Cicero, and was often dependent on earlier critics for his views). Secondly, he fully accepted Cicero's *magistra vitae* thesis, and gladly and perhaps too ambitiously expanded it. Thirdly, he rejected Patrizi's (and by implication Campanella's) arguments in favour of extending the breadth of history's subject-matter. And finally, he provided, what no other theorist had done, a comprehensive account of the linguistic and stylistic problem of writing Latin history.

Beni came late to the theory of history. There was hardly a time when he was not in some way involved with the theory and practice of rhetoric, and it is to those that the next, and final, chapter will be dedicated.

15

THE WRITINGS ON RHETORIC

I

The basic classical writings on rhetoric had never been lost, for rhetoric had been an essential part of medieval education.[1] But well before the middle of the sixteenth century such writings were being made increasingly available to a wider audience. Aristotle's *Rhetoric* which, during the Middle Ages, had been less often consulted by rhetoricians than Cicero's rhetorical works, the *Ad Herennium*, and the works of the Sophists, was now presented to the public in published commentaries, lectures, and translations; and during the century or so before Beni published his commentary Aristotle's text had received a good deal of scholarly attention, as had other classical rhetorical texts.[2]

Side by side with these versions and commentaries of the

---

[1] For a general account of rhetoric since classical times, see C. S. Baldwin, *Ancient Rhetoric and Poetic* (New York, 1924), *Medieval Rhetoric and Poetic* (New York, 1928) and *Renaissance Literary Theory and Practice* (New York, 1939) (a sketchy and sometimes inaccurate work). For more general works, see Trabalza, *La critica letteraria*; Spingarn, *A History*; Toffanin, *La fine*, and *Il Cinquecento*, 6th edn. (Milan, 1960); E. Garin, 'Note su alcune retoriche rinascimentali', in *Testi umanistici su la retorica* (Milan, 1953), 7–55; E. R. Curtius, *European Literature and the Latin Middle Ages*, trans. by W. R. Trask (London and Henley, 1953); R. R. Bolgar, *The Classical Heritage and Its Beneficiaries* (Cambridge, 1954); Weinberg, *A History*; P. O. Kristeller, 'Philosophy and Rhetoric from Antiquity to the Renaissance', in *Renaissance Thought and Its Sources*, ed. by M. Mooney (New York, 1979), 211–59; B. Vickers, 'On the Practicalities of Renaissance Rhetoric' and 'Territorial Disputes: Philosophy *versus* Rhetoric', both in *Rhetoric Revalued: Papers from the International Society for the History of Rhetoric*, ed. by B. Vickers (Binghamton, New York, 1982), 133–41 and 247–66 respectively.

[2] There is no satisfactory bibliography of translations and commentaries on the *Rhetoric*. For my research I have used, but supplemented, the following: R. C. Williams, 'Italian Critical Treatises of the Sixteenth Century', *Modern Language Notes*, 35 (1920), 506–7; W. L. Bullock, 'Italian Sixteenth Century Criticism', *Modern Language Notes*, 41 (1926), 254–63; Roaf, thesis cit., pp. 358–60; F. E. Cranz, *A Bibliography of Aristotle Editions 1501–1600* (Baden-Baden, 1971); J. J. Murphy, *Renaissance Rhetoric: A Short-Title Catalogue of Works on Rhetorical Theory from the Beginning of Printing to A.D. 1700* (New York and London, 1981).

Rhetoric went original Italian works on rhetoric and poetry which grew and flourished throughout the sixteenth century. Perhaps the most exhaustive treatment of rhetoric was provided by Bartolomeo Cavalcanti, whose aim was to form a compendium of everything that had ever been written on the subject.[3] The subject of rhetoric also found its way into other disciplines. Few 'Arts' of poetry omit to mention the rhetorical rules of style, and practical literary criticism made free use of the rhetorical categories of *inventio*, *dispositio*, and *elocutio*. Discussions about the role of the historian or the philosopher led to comparisons with the role of the orator; and it was widely acknowledged that rhetoric shaded into many other disciplines, including art. This means that when Beni sat down to write about Aristotle's *Rhetoric* he had before him a vast quantity of secondary material and a proliferation of varying approaches to the subject.

His commentary on the *Rhetoric* was published (with its companion works)[4] as part of his unfinished *Opera omnia* in 1624 and 1625. It is not certain when he wrote the commentary, but a passage in Book Two (p. 121) tells us that he was nearly seventy as he wrote. It can safely be conjectured therefore that Beni was working on the commentary in the early 1620s and, more precisely, that he was well over half way through the final draft towards the end of 1622.

Though Beni was old when he wrote the commentary, the work had its genesis far back in his early career (the early 1590s and possibly even before) and, in many ways, it comes as the logical conclusion to that career. For he had held, since 1600, one of the most renowned chairs of eloquence in Italy, and had taught rhetoric in a place where, as he says in the *Oratoriae disputationes* (pp. 1–2), rhetoric had been long and successfully

---

[3] *La retorica* (Venice 1559) went through ten edns. in the sixteenth century and was clearly the most popular amongst similar general Italian works on rhetoric by Speroni, Giulio Camillo Delminio, D. Barbaro, F. Sansovino, F. Patrizi, G. Denores, etc. See C. Roaf's introduction to B. Cavalcanti's *Lettere edite e inedite* (Bologna, 1967), pp. xxxix–xlvi.

[4] *In Aristotelis libros rhetoricorum commentarii* (Venice, I, 1624; II and III, 1625) (hereafter *R.*). The companion works are: *Oratoriae disputationes seu rhetoricae controversiae* (Venice, 1624) (hereafter *OD*); *In M. T. Ciceronis Orationem Pro Lege Manilia commentarii . . .* (Venice, 1625); *Orationes quinque et septuaginta* (Venice, 1625) (hereafter *OQS*).

cultivated. Thus, and it is clear from the commentary itself, the work was first cast in the lecture mould (*R.* I. 66 and 369: II. 149). Beni was not only a theorist: for theoretical and practical rhetoric were taught simultaneously,[5] and he was thus the author of a number of rhetorical compositions: *Orationes quinquaginta* and *Orationes quinque et septuaginta*, various *discorsi* addressed to the pope, panegyrics upon St Thomas Aquinas[6] and Cesare Baronio, several sermons, orations, and many dedicatory and other letters written on others' behalf. Furthermore, Beni's even earlier career in the Ricovrati, where (as we saw) he was required to argue and refute cases, contributed to his knowledge of rhetoric. As a result of all this, Beni writes throughout his commentary on the *Rhetoric* as a seasoned speaker (*R.* III. 105, for instance). Finally it would not be an exaggeration to say that Beni never composed any work of whatever kind which did not bear a strong rhetorical stamp. Whether he is writing a poem in praise of someone, or commenting on Guarini, Tasso, or Aristotle, or criticizing the *Crusca*, or preaching from the pulpit, or even writing a letter, he is always passionately and meticulously arguing a case. He rarely (as we have seen) writes a word which is not directed for or against some cause. Hence his reputation as a born polemicist and fighter, and, of course, the misunderstandings to which his work has often fallen prey.[7] Clearly, Beni was not alone in his use of rhetoric: it was a powerful influence in one way or another on many aspects of the culture and writing of his day (as well as before and after). But it would be hard to find a writer who more nearly embodied what could be called a rhetorical approach to writing (by which I mean that he wrote to persuade, though not however to be oratorical in terms of style and language).

II

If it is obvious why Beni wrote theoretically about rhetoric, it is equally clear why he should have chosen to expound the

---

[5] See P. France, *Rhetoric and Truth in France: Descartes to Diderot* (Oxford, 1972), 17.

[6] Beni mentions it in *R.* III. 99. It was published in *OQS* 153–7 as 'Oratio LXII habita Patavii in B. Thomae Aquinatis Natali die'.

[7] For example, when he argues other people's causes or when critics have taken at face value his convincing but hypothetical arguments.

Rhetoric: first, because he considered it Aristotle's best work
(*R.*, Dedicatory Letter), and second, because it remained for him
the fount of all rhetorical knowledge (*R.*, Preface). This praise
heralds a new respect in Beni for Aristotle: for, while in the
commentary on the *Poetics* he was careful to distinguish Aristotle from reason (*P.* 180), here he clearly and confidently identi-
fies Aristotle with reason (*R.* I. 420).

Despite this fresh confidence in Aristotle, Beni still finds him
tortuous to understand, partly because he was too concise and
obscure, and did not observe his own stylistic principles (*R.* II.
181; III. 54), and partly because he wrote for learned men of his
time. And although many modern critics had expounded the
Rhetoric, Beni did not find that they had solved all the problems.
In his Preface and throughout the commentary, he mentions
and evaluates many previous writers on rhetoric. Of these he
sees that Riccoboni, Maioragius (Antonio Maria de' Conti),[8]
and Vettori[9] were the most important: the first two for their
translations, and the third for his textual criticism. But none of
them addressed themselves (as Beni intends to do) to all the difficulties in the text. In his commentary he gives a Greek text and
Riccoboni's and Maioragius' translations ('illam quod verbis
haereat fideliter, hanc quod elegans sit et copiosa' (*R.* I. 12)). He
then paraphrases what Aristotle wrote, explains its meaning,
relates it to its context (thereby clarifying the intellectual structure of the work), expands it, fills in the gaps around it, questions it (in numerous *controversiae*), and sometimes disagrees
with it. Throughout he quotes freely from Maioragius and
Vettori to agree or disagree.

This method has its obvious disadvantages. First, it is over-
ambitious. With so much material to sift, and such high ideals
of accuracy and thoroughness, Beni was bound to fail. His commentary on Book One is inordinately long (566 pages), that on
Book Two is shorter (264 pages), and that on Book Three is possibly inadequate (164 pages). As so often in his works, Beni ran

---

[8] (1514–55). He was a scholar, a popular teacher, and a writer, who shows in
his Latin works clear affinities with Beni. His *Orationes, et praefationes omnes*
(Venice, 1582) might well have been the model for Beni's later *Orationes* (1613
and 1625). There is quite a lot of information on M. in *Notizie intorno alla vita di
Primo del Conte* [M.'s teacher] *milanese della Congregazione di Somasca teologo al
Concilio di Trento* (Rome, 1805), 61–9.

[9] See, on Vettori, F. Niccolai, *Pier Vettori (1499–1585)* (Florence, 1912).

out of energy and enthusiasm; and he promised more than he could realistically fulfil. Secondly, the organization of the work is faulty: he raises doubts as and when they arise, but has often to postpone answering them fully until further relevant passages occur (see, for example, *R.* 1. 166–7). This makes for repetitiousness. Thirdly, in his effort to be clear, he indulges in prolix summaries of almost everything Aristotle says. And finally, since Aristotle's is a work which Beni largely admires and supports, his numerous *controversiae* and *dubitationes* strike a bombastic and otiose note. They sound too much like exercises in rhetorical skill as, for instance, in *Controversiae* XVIII and XIX where he questions whether Chapter One of Book One should be read as a *proemium*.

The characteristics which give rise to the defects also give rise to the qualities in the commentary. As was seen in the commentary on the *Liberata*, Beni is very good at tracing sources and analogues. So in this commentary. He demonstrates throughout the points where Cicero (the pinnacle of all oratory for Beni (*R.* 1. 9–10)) followed Aristotle; and a passage in the *Rhetoric* will draw from Beni analogous passages from Aristotle's other works, from Quintilian, and the *Ad Herennium*. The result is, as in Vettori, a sort of compilation of classical commonplaces. Rarely does Beni move outside the ancient classical world; and it is symptomatic of his classical interest that he exemplifies the best of each branch of rhetoric with classical models (*R.* 1. 175–6). His searching thoroughness allows him, where appropriate, to run Aristotle to ground on central issues (as we shall see) and to define key terms (see, for example, *R.* 1. 154 and 158–9). It also enables him to handle complex technical matters lucidly, simply, and meticulously (for example in his long *controversia* on the enthymeme (*R.* 1. 129–42)). His respect for the truth and his rational optimism about the reality of answers leads him to some modest but sound advances in the translation of the *Rhetoric*. He conducts a careful comparison of all available translations and, on occasion, his accuracy leads him convincingly to disagree with the principal translators (see, for example, *R.* 1. 170–1 and 416; II. 36). Such moments are rare, however, as are those when his textual criticism amounts to very much. For he realized that Vettori had done most of the work in that field, leaving him free to explore the larger problems and questions raised by the *Rhetoric*.

III

Since the commentary begins with a show of respect for Aristotle, it is not surprising to find that Beni agrees with Aristotle on the basics of rhetoric. He accepts Aristotle's threefold division of rhetoric into deliberative, judicial, and demonstrative, and disagrees with Quintilian's opinion that there should be more branches (*R.* I. 171–3). On the different aims of each branch Beni again sides with Aristotle (against Cicero and Quintilian in the case of deliberative rhetoric (*R.* I. 181)). Like Aristotle, Beni describes oratory's aim as persuasion ('facultas videndi quae sint ad fidem faciendam accommodata' (*R.* II. 7)), and, like Cicero, he likens the power of oratory to that of music (*R.* II. 155); but he goes further and interprets the Orpheus myth as an allegorical statement about the persuasive powers of rhetoric (*R.* II. 156).

Despite some doubts (which Beni disperses) that Aristotle restricted rhetoric to *inventio*, Beni shows that he also included the two other main parts (*dispositio* and *elocutio*) in his definition as essential ingredients (*R.* I. 28–31 and 75; III. 5). (He approves of Aristotle's exclusion of *pronuntiatio* and *memoria*.) Against the background of Giason Denores' attempt to wrest Book Three (which deals with *dispositio* and *elocutio*) from the *Rhetoric* on the grounds that its subjects were irrelevant to Aristotle's purpose (on this see Weinberg, i. 204–5), Beni asserts that *dispositio* and *elocutio* belong more to the orator than to anyone else, because, without them, he would be powerless to move people (*R.* II. 185–6; III. 7). However, like Aristotle, Beni shows far less interest in these two parts than in *inventio* (Books One and Two); and the commentary on Book Three, apart from being uncharacteristically short (as we saw), also lacks the wide-ranging introduction which Beni gave to the other two books. This lack of concern with the problems of *elocutio* and (to some extent) *dispositio* in the commentary is reflected in their absence from the *Oratoriae disputatiònes*, surely a significant omission.

The subject-matter of rhetoric is another important issue on

which Beni agreed with Aristotle. Critics had traditionally
found the limitless breadth of rhetoric difficult to define, and,
taking their cue from Aristotle, had drawn comparisons
between it and other similar disciplines (principally those
which engaged in reasoning (*ratiocinatio*) through the medium
of speech or words) such as history, poetry, grammar, and dialectics.[10]

Aristotle linked rhetoric mainly with dialectics and politics.
So did Beni. In his discussion of the relationship between rhetoric and dialectics he follows a long line of critics who had
drawn similar parallels.[11] Both disciplines have limitless subjects, and can be argued on both sides. (However, Beni
attempts to make a subtle distinction here (as he had done for
poetics) between the art of rhetoric, which has a limited subject-matter (the rules of oratory), and rhetoric itself, which is
indeed infinite (*R*. I. 5).) But, echoing earlier arguments of Valla
(see Garin, p. 9), Beni finds that there are essential differences
between the two disciplines: dialectics does not have ornaments and blandishments, rhetoric does; dialectics uses the
hard syllogism, rhetoric uses the softer enthymeme; dialectics
must above all tell the truth, rhetoric can use verisimilitude
(*R*. I. 17–18).

The relationship between rhetoric and politics is not so
close.[12] Beni sees the orator as serving the health of the republic, and he agrees with Aristotle that deliberative (political) oratory is of the greatest value (*R*. I. 76). For this reason the orator
should be acquainted with the various forms of government
(Beni advises study of Aristotle's *Politics* III (*R*. I. 214)) and with
the law (*R*. I. 211). But although the orator is 'Politici quasi
administer', the subject-matter with which he has to deal is
quite other than that of politics proper (*R*. I. 7).

Both Aristotle and Beni describe similar links between history and rhetoric, and both acknowledge the great value of history to the orator (*R*. I. 22–4). But, again, Beni stresses the

[10] On the general relationship, see Weinberg, i. 1–37.

[11] On the relationship between rhetoric and dialectics, see Garin, 15–18 and
31–2; B. Vickers, 'Territorial Disputes', 247–66; and Kristeller, 'Philosophy and
Rhetoric'.

[12] On the relationship between rhetoric and politics, see Garin, 13–15;
D. Cantimori, 'Rhetoric and Politics in Italian Humanism', *Journal of the Warburg and Courtauld Institutes*, 1 (1937–8), 83–102.

differences: the orator is free to alter the facts and use ornament while the historian is tied to the simple unadorned truth (*R.* I. 404 and 525).

In all these inter-disciplinary relationships the same difference occurs: namely, that the orator is free to use the subject-matter of each, yet he cannot thereby become a dialectician, a politician, or an historian. For the orator handles all subjects *populariter* or *probabiliter* (*R.* I. 5 and 161), and produces a sort of commoner's vulgarized philosophy (*R.* I. 228). Beni here defines the cultural role of rhetoric in a way which suggests analogies with the present-day role of the television: a more or less persuasive medium which can handle most subjects, but always on a necessarily vulgarized level. It is not perhaps surprising, therefore, that Renaissance philosophers had little or no interest in rhetoric and poetics, and left these to humanists and literary critics (Kristeller, 'Philosophy and Rhetoric', p. 252), though doubtless the orators felt a good deal of interest in philosophy.[13]

A further discipline to which rhetoric had been traditionally linked was poetry. Following Aristotle and Cicero, Beni explains that poets appeared on the scene before orators, and that orators took certain stylistic hints from them (*R.* III. 13). But, like Aristotle, Beni is at pains to separate rhetoric from poetry. He maintains that there are differences in *dispositio* and *elocutio* and (to some extent) in *inventio* (*R.* II. 185–6). This clearly limits the usefulness of rhetoric to poetry and vice versa, especially in the field of stylistics: for both Aristotle and Beni see *elocutio* in Book Three as referring principally to prose style (poetic style was treated in the *Poetics* as far as Beni was concerned), and comparisons between the two disciplines are mostly in the form of contrasts (see, for example, *R.* III. 16). This dismissal of the possible links between rhetoric and poetry extends throughout the whole commentary: Beni virtually ignores areas in which fruitful parallels could be drawn, as, for instance, when Aristotle speaks of pity and terror in Book Two (*R.* II. 123).[14] This lack of concern is the more surprising in view

[13] Perhaps the dividing line between philosophy and oratory (in Beni, at any rate) was not so clear as Kristeller here suggests.
[14] The relevant passage is in *The 'Art' of Rhetoric*, trans. by J. H. Freese (The Loeb Classical Library: Cambridge, Mass. and London, 1926), 229.

of Beni's use of rhetorical categories in his writings on the *Liberata*.[15] No doubt this is yet another case of conflict between theory and practice; and, to judge by a comment in his inaugural lecture of 1600, Beni always found it desirable but often difficult to separate out the various disciplines which went under the collective name of *studia humanitatis* (*DHS*, fo. 5ʳ).

These are some of the points on which Beni agrees with Aristotle. Others could be added, but they would not add significantly to the picture. We can now turn to the important issues about which Beni differed from Aristotle.

I V

Unlike the commentary on the *Poetics*, that on the *Rhetoric* leaves an impression of consensus. This is very largely because many potential disagreements are averted by Beni's saying that Aristotle spoke *populariter* in the *Rhetoric*, or by referring to Aristotle's more specialized works where a better treatment of the subject under discussion is available. In this way Aristotle is often let off the hook. But on two related and central matters there is a real difference of opinion: first, on whether rhetoric should tell the truth, and in what circumstances; and secondly, what sort of goodness (if any) the orator should possess or demonstrate.

Where possible, Beni presents as Aristotle's, his own (and Plato's) view that oratory is a truth-finding and a truth-telling function, the Christian's moral protection against evil (*R. 1. 52, 54*, and *57–8*). But elsewhere he has to face the fact that the aim Aristotle gave rhetoric (persuasion) and the aim Plato ideally gave it (truth-telling) were discordant. Predictably, Beni sides here (like Patrizi)[16] with Plato (*R. 1. 81–2*). And while no reasonable commentator would bluntly advocate dishonesty in rhetorical practice (Aristotle himself was far from doing that), yet few would go as far as Beni in order to clear rhetoric of blame. His fervent advice to the orator faced with the option of speaking dishonestly is as follows:

---

[15] In his commentary on the poem Beni holds up the speeches which Tasso puts into the mouths of his characters as exemplary models of their kind, worthy of a Cicero or a Demosthenes (see, for example, *G*. 346 and 648).

[16] F. Patrizi, *Della retorica dieci dialoghi* (Venice, 1562).

satius est honeste silere quam turpiter loqui et iniquum consilium dare. Imo vero si forte sine culpa nequaquam scilere [sic] liceat, ac summatim ut sententiam proferamus oporteat, ingenue fatendum rem indignam esse quam amplectamur. Quin si eo evadat turpitudo ut aperte iustitia ac Religio violetur, satius est honeste mori sive ad honeste occumbendum auditores hortari, quam se atque alios flagitio ullo foedare et obstringere (R. I. 181).

Earlier, on whether the orator should employ false verisimilitude, Beni clearly sided with Plato and Christianity in refusing to allow any lies (R. I. 84). Similarly, he argued against the use of the apparent enthymeme or fallacy, both in dialectics and rhetoric, though he admitted that it is better to use it in rhetoric than in dialectics (R. I. 102 and 400). Finally, though Beni accepted the idea that virtues (of someone about whom one is speaking) can be legitimately magnified in a speech, he resented Aristotle's view that the orator can describe some vices as virtues (R. I. 398–400).

A related issue, which again pushed Beni towards Plato, was whether the orator should be an innately and irreproachably 'good' man (Plato's view) or whether he should merely be able to appear a 'good' man when speaking as an orator (Aristotle's view). Though Beni long postponed deciding this, he concludes that both things are desirable (R. I. 87 and 373). He finds that Aristotle did not say enough about the mores of the orator, and he offers his own advice on the subject (R. II. 12 and 14–15). Unlike Aristotle, he expects the orator to live a good life. A typical case of the clash between Aristotle and Beni occurs when the latter contradicts and idealistically reshapes the former's realistic advice on how the orator should cope with slander and prejudice:

Sed commodius ac praestabilius ut qui frequentare decreverit forum, ita vivat, ita se gerat, ut nullum de eo crimen excitari possit, nulla criminis opinio, nulla suspicio suboriri: satius enim est culpa carere quam culpam depraecari sive eruere: satius inter pugnandum vulnera devitare, quam vulneri sanando aut cicatrici eluendae medicamentum adhibere (R. III. 122).

V

The most interesting and absorbing aspect of Beni's commentary is to be found in the expansions and asides which he includes, in those passages where he deviates from Aristotle's line of argument and adds something of his own. Such asides are far more numerous here than in the commentary on the *Poetics*: for the *Rhetoric* covers an immense area of human experience (especially in the first two books) and demands and invites a more wide-ranging commentary. The significance of what Beni chooses to expatiate upon is obvious; and his digressions provide a good indication of the preoccupations of the intellectual and moral man. Though these asides come perilously close to contradicting Aristotle on occasion, they never make such contradiction explicit.

Most of Beni's asides can be called moral, both in that they show an interest in humanity and in that they tend to moralize (often Christianize) Aristotle's pagan view of the world. Aristotle's confidence about good fortune in old age pushes Beni to present, in truly eloquent prose, his own view of the great fragility of our life on earth, in terms reminiscent of his Ash Wednesday sermon of 1594 (*R.* I. 280).

A large number of these moral asides are provoked by anything in the text which smacks of hedonism. It is characteristic of Beni, and no doubt of many who lived through the Counter-Reformation in Italy, to shy away from anything which has only physical pleasure as its aim (in theory, at least). Thus, when Aristotle says that all men naturally desire pleasure (*The 'Art' of Rhetoric*, ed. cit., p. 61), Beni quickly excludes from this all bodily pleasures (*R.* I. 297–8); and he argues elsewhere, irrespective of Aristotle, that irrational pleasures should not be allowed (*R.* I. 448). The pleasure which is aroused by artistic beauty is acceptable to Beni because it inspires men with wonder (*admiratio*), and thence leads them to learning, knowledge, and truth (*R.* I. 467). Beni accepts this commonplace argument, and uses it in a trenchantly puritanical way to agree with Plato that all arts whose aim is *luxus* or *deliciae* should be banned (*R.* I. 209). Similarly, while Aristotle suggests that physical size and stature contributes to a man's happiness (*The 'Art' of Rhetoric*, p. 55), Beni avers that it is not physical but 'animi magnitudo' which counts (*R.* I. 234): perhaps he was pleading his own cause! Aristotle's suggestion that 'idleness, carelessness, amusement, recreation and sleep' (*The 'Art' of Rhetoric*, p. 115) are pleasurable draws from Beni the shocked reply that idleness can never be good, and that hard work is the thing (R. I. 444–6). Temperance is graphically described (R. I. 383); and Beni loses no opportunity of recommending it where Aristotle did not (see R. II. 39 for example). Finally, adopting a more overt Christian standard, Beni shows, not how to deal practically with envy, or how to wreak vengeance, but instead how to avoid and ignore both (R. II. 141; I. 157 and 395). Aristotle had said that 'revenge is pleasant' (The 'Art' of Rhetoric, p. 121); Beni comments that 'qui Christiana praecepta imbiberit altius, vindictam refugiat, iniuriis etiam (quod difficilius videri potest) gaudeat cum iucunditate' (R. I. 457).

A further group of observations within the moral field relate to the emotions. Like many of his contemporaries, Beni shows a particular interest in the definition and function of the emotions; and he feels that Aristotle gave them inadequate treatment in the Rhetoric. He attempts, with his knowledge of human nature and his classical learning, to fill in the gaps left by Aristotle. He provides a definition of affectio (R. II. 16) which goes beyond Vettori's evasive comment on the same passage (see Vettori, Commentarii (1548), pp. 238–9). Beni also shows an interest in the workings of the reader's or the audience's emotions (R. II. 68–9; III. 88), and he examines many physical effects of emotion (R. II. 95–8).

The second most important group of asides centre on literary style. In most cases these also point in a moral direction. It is fully to be expected that Beni should lament the decline in Ciceronian Latin (R. I. 10), and that he should advise philosophers and logicians to study rhetoric in order to improve their Latin style (R. I. 48; III. 8). But that a supposed champion of Secentismo should cast a shadow over the value of elocutio is amazing. And yet it is true. Beni argues strenuously that elocutio should not become an end in itself and that it should not be indulged at the expense of the proper end of eloquence (R. III. 59).

It is worth noting in this connection that Beni does not show particular interest in ornament and metaphor in this commentary (and there was of course plenty of scope in the Rhetoric for indulging such interest). Beni never goes beyond the dutiful explanation of Aristotle's ideas on the subject. Indeed, Beni's dislike of obscurity leads him to prefer clear definitions to delightful metaphors (R. II. 226–7). In all his other linguistic works he repeats the need for clarity (especially in prose), and here he fully endorses Aristotle's plea for *perspicuitas* in the *Rhetoric* (R. III. 14 and 15; II. 205).

Beni believed that rhetoric (like everything else) required a balance between art and nature (R. I. 20); and, with this ideal balance in mind, he was always quick to warn against any unnatural use of ornament. On the use of antithesis, for instance, he adds to what Aristotle had said a moderating word of warning:

Interim illud monuerim eiusmodi contraria quae contentionem habent, illustrare quidem orationem, sed non esse in eam exquisito studio conferenda, ne ars emineat et immoderatum artificium coarguatur. Quod si Natura ipsa fere duce se se inferant in orationem, non excludenda. Potius in illud incumbendum ut elocutio ex ratiocinationum pondere, quae probabilitatis habeant plurimum, splendorem ac vim accipiant: vis enim ac pondus ratiocinationum nervos continet orationis, ita ut alioquin vacua ac verbis redundans merito videri possit (R. III. 58).

His clearly non-Baroque advice is evident also in his treatment of *parisosis/paramoiosis* (R. III. 60–1) and of *proemia* (R. III. 108). This notion of an ideal balance between nature and art lies at the back of a very significant comment on contemporary Italian literature, and it is rendered the more significant by being virtually his only reference to the subject in this commentary. Like Aristotle he realized that the rules for *elocutio* in the *Rhetoric* applied mainly to prose writing (R. III. 11; see *The 'Art' of Rhetoric* p. 349), and, again like Aristotle, he stressed that prose should not be too poetical in its use of artifice. This rule inspired Beni to make an exceptional criticism of modern Italian prose writing which (he implies) had derived too much from Boccaccio:

Atque hoc diligenter observandum esset iis qui soluta oratione italice scribunt: sunt enim permulta qui epitheta, numeros, flosculos, stylum denique a poetis aut his similibus derivantes, poetice potius, quam oratorie aut historice scribunt [. . .]. Id quod factum est quia curiosi, atque ociosi dum inde capiunt voluptatem ob fabulas, per inscientiam elocutionem imbibunt: quae tamen hoc tempore a melioribus scriptoribus spernitur qui Isocrateo more turgidum illud dicendi genus respuentes, temperatum ac facile, moderateque ornatum amplectuntur sermonis genus (R. III. 11).

This criticism is nothing new in Beni's writings: the very same thoughts run through the linguistic works, as we have seen. What is new is that Beni's criteria for prose writing are taken, with some justification, from the *Rhetoric*. Furthermore, far from using Aristotle (as some modern critics have suggested) as a justification for Secentistic stylistic fireworks, Beni uses him precisely to criticize such displays. This is strikingly evident when, again in a digression, Beni transfers Aristotle's criteria of clarity and naturalness in prose to modern Italian verse, and states that Italian poetry reached its peak in Tasso and thereafter declined by virtue of its quest for novelty:

Carmen eo progressum est, ut ad summum pervenerit, ac propterea verendum sit ne in posterum a perfectione sensim dilabitur: dum novitati studentes multi, perfectum desuerunt stylum: id quod Ciceronis ac Virgilii tempore contigit, a quibus posteriores degenerarunt, stylum supra quam dici possit ad extremum infuscantes. Hoc igitur subvereor hoc tempore de Italico carmine, quod sigillatim a Torquato ad summum perductum est (R. III. 11).

Again it is evident, as it was in the commentary on the *Goffredo*, that Beni does not see Tasso in a seventeenth-century and novel light, but in a classically balanced one; and, as we saw in his writings on Tasso, Beni showed no interest in the novelty of Tasso's ornaments and style, and tried instead to show that everything Tasso wrote had some previous authority. This is Beni's modernism: it stops with Tasso (not the Tasso that looks ahead to the seventeenth century, but the Tasso that looks back to Petrarch and Virgil). It is a modernism quite different from Tassoni's, much less anti-authoritarian in the literary field, much more staid, more sober. Beni did not provide any justification for Secentismo in his theoretical writings, and far less did he provide any sustained practical demonstration of it.[17] The passage quoted above from his commentay on the *Rhetoric* shows the opposite: namely, that towards the end of his life he

---

[17] This is at least true of Beni's own poetry, though not perhaps of some isolated prose passages. Yet this does not diminish the fact that Beni did not provide any theoretical justification for the phenomenon. And the number of such prose passages (P. 4, for instance) in his work is exceedingly small.

felt uneasy about the novel direction in which Italian poetic style was moving. And no one familiar with his linguistic and literary theories could expect anything else from him.[18]

In a third category of asides—which concern the relative merits of the three branches of rhetoric—Beni again appears backward-looking in his preference. He feels that Aristotle said too little about judicial oratory and, using Cicero and the *Ad Herennium*, Beni fills in the details (R. I. 566). He does this because he knows that for his seventeenth-century readers the judicial was the most important and frequently used branch of oratory, while the deliberative and the demonstrative were (according to him) in decline or obsolete (R. I. 412–16). At this point Beni does not express approval or disapproval of this modern state of affairs. But later, towards the end of his commentary, he confesses that, of the three branches, he prefers the demonstrative (R. III. 100), a preference which is more in line with early sixteenth-century practice than with the seventeenth century.[19] Beni also groups under demonstrative oratory certain forms of preaching, such as he had used (R. III. 99).

A further series of digressions could be classed as aesthetic. They show Beni trying to define, where Aristotle had not defined, terms such as beauty (R. I. 269–70), the relationship between grace and beauty (R. II. 105–10), *voluptas*, and *ingenium* (R. I. 315; III. 158). For Beni beauty has three components: symmetry, size, and *coloris decus*, but, of the three, size is not essential (Plato did not include it in his definition of beauty). Both beauty and grace are apprehended by the senses and are difficult to explain, but grace is more difficult to define than beauty because it appears only in movements and gestures while beauty appears in quiet, still, static subjects. Finally, *ingenium* is described as a natural phenomenon, the opposite of art; the *ingeniosus* is 'a Natura potius quam arte fictus [. . .] ad leporem et elegantiam' (R. III. 158). This again shows, as in the commentary on the *Poetics*, that when Beni used the word *ingenium* or its

[18] See above, Chapters 11 and 12.
[19] See Baldwin, *Renaissance Literary Theory and Practice*, 39 where it is said that most published oratory of the Renaissance was of the demonstrative type (by 'Renaissance' he seems to mean the first half of the sixteenth century since he quotes as evidence F. Sansovino's collection of contemporary orations).

derivatives he meant something different from the faculty which creates artifice.[20]

There remain two groups of asides which are of far less importance. Beni's political asides are mainly of personal and local interest: he praises Venetian laws and the freedom of the Venetian Republic (R. I. 397); and he bases his political views on Venetian practice. He thinks little of democracy or monarchy, and opts instead for oligarchy (R. I. 353–6).[21]

Finally, a group of digressions give practical advice: on feeding large numbers of the population spread over a wide area (R. I. 207–9), on the benefits of travel (restricted by Beni to Christian countries) (R. I. 219–21), on the place of women in the home (R. I. 254), on how to preserve health in old age (R. I. 279), and so on. What is remarkable in all these examples is the way in which he combines a modicum of practical experience with a good deal of classical learning: as always with him, his practical rules for living, for the here and now, are adapted from ancient authorities; and the impression is that he lived in and through the past (except, of course, it is the past seen through Christian eyes). This was always Beni's way, in theory at least.

Enough has now been said to give an idea of the content and tone of the commentary on the *Rhetoric*. Before it can be situated in its historical context, it is necessary to look briefly at one of the companion works, the *Oratoriae disputationes seu rhetoricae controversiae*.

VI

It is a group of five dialogues which aim to clarify some of the major doubts which arose in the commentary. When he began writing the commentary he did not seem to have conceived this companion work (see, for example, R. I. 28), but it is not long before he mentions a projected work containing ten dialogues (R. I. 73). In fact, the *Oratoriae disputationes* were published with

---

[20] See above, Chapter 13, Section VI.

[21] See also the summary of his unpublished (and possibly now lost) 'Discorsi politici' in BB 107–10, where it is shown that *Aristocratia* is the best form of government and that its epitome was to be found in Beni's day in the Venetian Republic. This praise of Venice is also to be linked with Beni's other pro-Venetian writing, and especially with his treatise 'Della veneta libertà'.

Book One of the commentary in 1624, and had only five dia-
logues. These are set in the past and purport to be based on
Beni's personal experience of learning about rhetoric with
Marc-Antoine Muret (for whom he worked in and around 1577),
Carlo Sigonio, and Achille Stazio in Rome when he was young
(*OD, Ad lectorem*). Beni creates the scene (Muret's house in
Rome in 1577), and introduces the interlocutors (Muretus himself, Sigonius, Statius, and the young Benius) in the introduction (*OD* 3).[22] All three scholars were by that time deeply
involved in the theory and practice of rhetoric; and all made
more or less significant contributions to it.[23]

The first dialogue asks whether the orator should be permitted to stir up the emotions. Nothing important is said which
was not said in the commentary, except that here more detail is
presented, and the various arguments are divided between the
speakers. Benius, modest and humble and over-awed, proposes
the doubts, but does not take part in the debate, and the dialogue ends with Muretus promising to decide next day between
the two sides of the proposed argument (a promise he never ful-
fils). This dialogue was first published as a separate volume,
dedicated to Cardinal Benedictus Iustinianus, in 1594.[24] It is
essentially the same as the first of the *Oratoriae disputationes*,
except that the earlier version puts more stress in the introduction on the Christian aspect of the problem. This can be seen
from a comparison of two parallel passages in the two versions:

1594. nihil antiquius habui quam ut pervestigarem quid ingenuo Oratori ac Christiano praesertim, in hac esset controversia sentiendum:
quae moderato viro ac frugi probanda ac retinenda sententia (p. 4);

1624. nil antiquius habui quam ut pervestigarem quid ingenuo Oratori
in hac esset controversia sentiendum: quae moderato viro et frugi
probanda ac retinenda sententia (p. 1).

Though Beni may seem to have diluted the religious element in

---

[22] For the full quotation of this passage, see above, pp. 27–8.

[23] All three scholars produced copious oratorical treatises and works. Muret's
production and range were prodigious.

[24] *Disputatio. In qua quaeritur an sive actori, sive reo, et in universum oratori
ingenuo; liceat in iudiciis et concionibus affectus concitare: ac iudicum animos flectere et permiscere* (Rome, 1594). For the context of this work, see above, Chapter
1, Section IV.

the later version (where his personal circumstances make religious concerns less momentous than during his fateful Jesuit years), yet (as we shall see) there remains in these later *disputationes* at least a residual interest in Christian oratory and its problems.

The second dialogue again treats a subject which had been fully aired in the commentary: the 'goodness' of the orator, and the differences on the subject between Aristotle and Plato. Benius again poses the question, but now plays a greater part in the debate. Both sides are well argued, and the conclusion is reached that inner goodness and apparent goodness are both necessary in the orator. However, there is a development here which is not evident in the commentary: the theological or Christian implications of the question are discussed. If, as they all agree, an evil orator is still worthy of the name of orator, does it follow that the evil Christian orator (preacher) is also worthy of such a name? The answer is 'Yes'. This dialogue is interesting for two reasons: it shows Beni moving from theories of classical rhetoric to moral and theological questions which concern a Christian society in and after the Counter-Reformation. Secondly, there is an attempt to unite Aristotle and Plato rather than to see them at loggerheads in this dialogue.

The third dialogue has Benius as its principal speaker. In it he develops his doubts about the relative status in rhetoric of *rationes, mores,* and *affectiones,* and concludes (with the aid of the other speakers) that a combination of all three is desirable. But he cannot decide which is the most important. At this point the scene changes. Deciding that it is time to call in the Ancients for illumination, Muretus leads them into his garden and introduces them to his guest (Mercury), who is sitting under a clump of laurels. Muretus asks him to travel to the underworld and fetch the shades of Carneades, Demosthenes, Plato, Aristotle, Cicero, and others, if possible. He departs on his mission.

The fourth dialogue predictably introduces some new faces. Mercury returns with Cicero (first in line, significantly), Aristotle, Plato, and Demosthenes. Benius addresses the shade of Aristotle with great respect, and raises ten doubts about his (Aristotle's) definition of rhetoric, which Aristotle has no difficulty in answering satisfactorily.

In the final dialogue it is proposed that Statius should question Plato and that Muretus should then question Cicero. Statius takes Plato through the two definitions of rhetoric which he offered in the *Phaedrus* and the *Gorgias*. Plato does not emerge here as hostile to rhetoric; and Benius is pleased with his replies. Benius is surprised to realize how close Plato and Aristotle are on this subject: they both agree on the status of rhetoric; they both reduce rhetoric to persuasion through speech; though Aristotle opts for verisimilitude, and Plato for truth, yet even this difference is not substantial for Beni; they both condemn the dishonest and morally bad orator (though Plato is made to say that such an orator should not retain the name of orator); they both agree on the breadth of rhetoric's subject-matter, and so on. Benius concludes from this comparison that Aristotle learned a good deal from his teacher, Plato, that he elaborated on what he learned, and sometimes reached different conclusions. (This contrasts with the idea in the commentary that Aristotle was inspired by envy of Plato (*R.* III. 50).) This dialogue ends with Plato suggesting that Benius should compose a *Rhetorica Platonis*, which the latter duly did (it is published with the dialogues and briefly repeats what had already been stated in the commentary and the dialogues themselves). No time remains for Muretus to question Cicero; and the work ends, like so many of Beni's, not properly finished.

The importance of these dialogues is threefold. First, they show that the sort of questions Beni found most important and difficult in rhetorical theory were principally moral and philosophical rather than stylistic or literary. Secondly, they show that he was more concerned with discovering (not altogether convincingly) a consensus between Aristotle and Plato than in accentuating their differences (something he could easily have done when he had them both present in the same room, so to speak). And finally, they show that his respect for the authority of the Ancients in rhetorical matters was very strong: Plato and Aristotle are the ultimate authorities: their opinions are made to appear in the dialogues superior to and more reliable than those of Muretus, Sigonius, and Statius, all first-class contemporary authorities.

VII

How did Beni's work on rhetoric fit into the pattern of other work produced in the sixteenth and early seventeenth centuries? Using what are no doubt over-simplifications, the following trends in the study of rhetoric can be seen in this period. First, there is a movement towards the fusion of rhetoric and poetry. This tended to reduce rhetoric to *elocutio*, and to treat it as an ornamental adjunct to poetry rather than an art in itself. Such a treatment can be traced back to the Paduan Accademia degl'Infiammati, and to Speroni and Tomitano (see Roaf, thesis, p. 262; Trabalza, p. 134; Vickers, 'On the Practicalities', pp. 136–7). Secondly, there was an increased interest in the passions and emotions: and, of the three sub-aims of rhetoric (*docere*, *movere*, and *delectare*), *movere* became the most important (Vickers links this trend with the first—'On the Practicalities', p. 137). Thirdly, close links were forged between rhetoric and the art of preaching in the second half of the sixteenth century: these grew and flourished exceedingly in F. Panigarola's posthumous and influential *Predicatore* of 1609 (where, however, it was the artificial and stylistic aspect that most appealed to the seventeenth century) (Trabalza, pp. 134, 145–6, 293–8). Finally, there was a tendency to reconcile Aristotle and Plato: the latter's critique of rhetoric was reduced in stature by amalgamating the different views expressed in the *Phaedrus* and the *Gorgias* (Kristeller, 'Philosophy and Rhetoric', p. 254; Weinberg, i. 297 and 315).

It is clear where Beni fits in here. He is typical of his age in three ways: he showed greater interest in the passions and emotions than Aristotle had shown (but he does not allow his interest in these to dictate an exclusive interest in *elocutio*, *pace* Vickers in his general point); secondly, Beni reaches a position in the *Oratoriae disputationes* where he prefers to unite Aristotle and Plato; and, finally, he begins tentatively to deal with the links between the preacher and the orator (though here again it is not the stylistic but the moral aspect which interests him).

But in other ways Beni moves far from the general trends. First, he is a scholar with no axe to grind. His work is to be seen as part of the noble line of works which includes Maioragius' and Vettori's: it is dedicated to the elucidation and exemplification of Aristotle's text. Moreover, the fact that Beni chose to comment on a text such as Aristotle's (which, compared with Cicero's or Quintilian's, is limited in its treatment of style and ornament) and the fact that he chose to write a commentary, rather than a work with a freer more individual form, indicate that Beni was prepared to obey the restrictions imposed by Aristotle's treatment of the subject. Secondly, Beni shows little interest in contemporary Italian writing, and is very far from reducing rhetoric to *elocutio*. His comments on style and language run counter to what we know of seventeenth-century trends: his interest is firmly in the ancient past, and his place in the *Querelle des anciens et des modernes*, where he is customarily grouped with Tassoni, is (once again in this study) called into question by his retrospective attitude and his unmistakable respect for ancient authority. Thirdly, Beni is distinguished in his time by being more concerned than most with the broad philosophical and moral problems raised by the *Rhetoric*. He tries throughout to Christianize the function and content of rhetoric; and, in this sense, one could describe him as a Modern who attempted to bring Christian illumination to many of Aristotle's implicitly pagan attitudes. In this way, one of Beni's last works looks back to and echoes one of his first, the commentary on the *Timaeus*, which was significantly subtitled *Aristotelis et Platonis Theologia*.

CONCLUSION

It would be absurd to pretend that this study has presented a full portrait of the private life of Beni: such an aim, even with seemingly unlimited documentation, is always questionable, for how can anyone know (let alone describe, in whatever medium) the essence of another separate unique being? Yet the near-impossibility of the task should not prevent us from attempting it, especially when (as in the present case) the result is a clearer understanding of the development and work of a writer who has previously been barely understood, and often perversely misunderstood.

In his early life Beni showed a desire to escape from the security of his family home into the outside world of learning and religion. He did everything possible to secure this escape, which finally came about when he entered the Jesuit novitiate in 1581. Having once become a Jesuit, however, he began to look back to that from which he had escaped, and tried, with disastrous consequences, to retrieve his financial and familial status and rights. What seemed like an escape thus became a prison; and his behaviour towards his family led almost inevitably to his dismissal from the Jesuits. Thereafter he floundered for a while, trying to discover a new identity in Rome in the 1590s, until, after 1600, he settled down in Padua, and cultivated his learning (now tinged with a good deal of residual Christianity). The security he found in Padua did not, however, blot out from his consciousness the security and status within his family which he had lost; and his final years were desperately employed in the sad attempt to regain that lost security and status.

In the course of these vicissitudes one cannot help but admire the courage, resilience, fervour, and energy which Beni showed again and again in the face of disaster and in the aftermath of disappointment. But what is most striking, and what largely accounts for all his moral and other strength, is the obsessive, neurotic impulse which drove him, which forbade him to accept things or to leave them alone. In his personal life this evinced itself in his insecurity about money and in his ugly struggles against his family to retrieve what he considered his due inheritance. And the same applies even to what was the constant (from as early as 1566) of his life and work, namely his humanism (his quest for learning and scholarship). There is something neurotic (even by the standards of his age) in the continual threat of *adversarii* in his work, in the weight of hypothetical counter-arguments, in the incredible number of words and works, in the massive artillery produced again and again in order to scotch a mouse, in the complete absence of humour, and in the pedantic lack of judgement about how far to take a point. These are not necessarily defects: in some ways they are the merits of Beni's work, which, neurotic though it might be, is thorough, accurate, scrupulous, selfless, scholarly. Beni had (and had clearly from a tender age) a mind quick to grasp facts and issues, quick to react to them logically and reasonably. The quality of his mind was matched by an equally prodigious memory, a linguistic facility, and the productive energy of several men. These talents made it possible for him to absorb, synthesize, and add to the considerable body of knowledge which had accumulated throughout the Renaissance on such topics as the arts of history, rhetoric, and poetry, natural philosophy, theology, Tasso, the Italian language, and so on.

The neurotic impulse in him did not therefore lead to self-portrayal or self-preoccupation in the works. He kept himself mostly very much out of the way. Indeed, his frequent impersonal moralistic admonitions in his work are at times so at odds with what we know of his private life that there is more than a suspicion of hypocrisy (of a kind, no doubt, which was very common in his society and which is only too understandable in any age, given the immense difficulty of practical 'goodness'). However, this impulse led to a startlingly energetic even frenzied rate of production, to a desire to publish at all costs (literally), and to a desire to improve on all previous work. In Beni humanism becomes its own end; and, even within his own production, there is a remarkable divergence between theory and practice.

Where does this leave his reputation as a Modern? We have seen more than once in this study that such a reputation is far from justified. Even in the linguistic field (where he was more a Modern than anywhere else) he was by no means anti-authoritarian (for he merely opted for a different set of authorities from the Crusca, and in fact valued Tasso's language as the embodiment of the best of fourteenth-century usage). In rhetoric and history he did not follow all seventeenth-century trends; and he was in no way responsible for a Baroque deformation of Aristotle in poetic matters. He stands apart from Marino, Tassoni, Campanella, and others who challenged authority, with humorous or tragic consequences. He looks forward more to the French classicists, who clearly knew his work. Even his far from ineffectual championship of Tasso is better explained by reference to his humanistic and religious ideals than by reference to his supposed Baroque modernism: for Beni, Tasso was good as an epic poet because he combined the best of both humanistic and religious worlds. And Beni's undoubted love of Tasso is far from providing the dominant motive for all his literary activities, and it does not even spill over into his far more weighty Latin works.

If Beni is not a Modern who obeyed our *ex post facto* views about the development of Italian culture, he is important as a scholar and thinker who shared the same cultural background with (amongst others) the author of the *Liberata*. Tasso's letters (to mention only a small part of his prose works) are filled with preoccupations identical to Beni's: the *Timaeus*, the *Poetics*, the Italian language, the authority of Dante, Petrarch, and Boccaccio, the relationship between history and poetry, rhetoric, the Inquisition, religion: Tasso and Beni certainly would agree on which questions ought to be asked, even though they may have disagreed (slightly) about the answers. To read Beni is therefore to enter the same intellectual world as Tasso inhabited, but, in Beni's case, that world is undiluted, essential, rarefied. And not only with Tasso did Beni share, and in some ways best represent, the same literary, cultural, academic, and religious world, a world which perhaps understandably is all too often overlooked in our view of that age.

BIBLIOGRAPHY

This Bibliography is divided into two parts. The first contains Beni's writings in three sections: published work, with a note on his *Opera omnia*; MS works; and a chronological reference list of his (mostly unpublished) letters. The second part contains all other works consulted, MS and printed.

WORKS BY PAOLO BENI

A. Printed Works (Excluding Letters)

Here are included all works which I have seen in libraries in England, Italy, and Paris, arranged according to date of publication of first editions. All subsequent reissues and reprints are listed after details of the relevant first edition. I make a distinction throughout between 'reprinted' and 'reissued' for reasons which are fully explained in 'A Note on Paolo Beni's *Opera omnia*' at the end of this section.

Panegirico nel felice dottorato dell'illustre, et eccellentissimo signor Gioseppe Spinelli, dignissimo rettor de legisti, et cavalier splendidissimo. Raccolto da Giovanni Fratti gentil'huomo veronese, et academico animoso (Padua, L. Pasquati, 1575), fos. 20–4 and 31ᵛ–32ʳ (for Beni's poems).

Disputatio. In qua quaeritur, an sive actori, sive reo, et in universum oratori ingenuo; liceat in iudiciis et concionibus affectus concitare: ac iudicum animos flectere et permiscere (Rome, ex typographia Gabiana, 1594).

In Platonis Timaeum sive in naturalem omnem atque divinam Platonis et Aristotelis philosophiam decades tres (Rome, ex typographia Gabiana, 1594). First decade only.

Oratio habita in sacro Clementis IIX. Pont. Max. et Amplissimorum S.R.E. Cardinalium consessu. Feria IV. Cinerum. In B. Sabinae Templo (Rome, ex typographia Gabiana, 1594). Reprinted as 'Oratio Prima' in *Orationes quinque et septuaginta* (1625), pp. 1–4.

De Ecclesiasticis Baronii Cardinalis Annalibus disputatio (Rome, apud Impressores Camerales, 1596). Reprinted in C. Baronio, *Epistolae et opuscula*, ed. by Raymundus Albericius, 2 vols. (Rome, 1759), ii. 1–45.

Discorsi sopra l'inondation del Tevere alla santità di nostro sig. Clemente VIII dove oltr'il disputarsi e risolversi in questa materia varii e diversi dubbii non men'utili che curiosi, si va mostrando con particolar diligenza, quali siano state le vere cagioni di tal'inondatione, e quai siano i sicuri et efficaci rimedii (Rome, G. Facciotto, 1599).

De humanitatis studiis oratio. In qua ostenditur huiusmodi studia tum esse difficillima, ac multarum magnarumque artium scientia indigere, tum iucunditatis esse plenissima, et pulcherrima animi ornamenta continere. Quibus omnibus perfectus humanitatis doctor describitur ac fingitur. Habita Patavii in publico Gymnasio xvii. Kal. Aprilis Anno MDC. (Padua, F. Bolzetta, 1600). Reprinted as 'Oratio Secunda' in *Orationes quinque et septuaginta* (1625), pp. 4–13.

Disputatio in qua ostenditur praestare comoediam atque tragoediam metrorum vinculis solvere: nec posse satis, nisi soluta oratione, aut illarum decorum ac dignitatem retineri; aut honestam inde voluptatem solidamque utilitatem percipi (Padua, F. Bolzetta, 1600). Reprinted in *Trattati di poetica e retorica del '500*, ed. by B. Weinberg, 4 vols. (Bari, 1970–4), iv (1974), 345–95.

Risposta alle Considerationi o dubbi dell'eccellentissimo signor dottor Malacreta academico ordito sopra il Pastor fido, con altre varie dubitationi tanto contra detti dubbi e considerationi, quanto contra l'istesso Pastor fido. Con un discorso nel fine per componimento di tutta l'opera (Padua, F. Bolzetta, 1600). Reprinted in G. B. Guarini, *Opere*, 4 vols. (Verona, 1737–38), iv. 123–278.

Discorso nel qual si dichiarano e stabiliscono molte cose pertinenti alla Risposta data a' Dubbi e considerationi dell'eccellentissimo signor dottor Malacreta sopra il Pastor fido. Et alle Dubitationi mosse inoltre tanto contro le dette Considerationi, quanto contro l'istesso Pastorfido (Venice, P. Ugolino, 1600). Reprinted in Guarini, *Opere*, iv. 279–300.

Qua tandem ratione dirimi possit controversia quae in praesens de efficaci Dei auxilio et libero arbitrio inter nonnullos Catholicos agitatur (Padua, L. Pasquati, 1603).

Comparatione di Homero, Virgilio e Torquato. Et a chi di loro si debba la palma nell'heroico poema (Padua, L. Pasquati, 1607). Reprinted in T. Tasso, *Opere colle controversie sopra la Gerusalemme liberata*, 6 vols. (Florence, 1724), vi. 365–491. (See also 2nd, enlarged, edn. and its reprints under 1612.)

De historia libri quatuor [sic] (Venice, apud I. Vincentium, 1611). Reprinted in Venice, apud Io. Gueriglium, 1622.

L'Anticrusca: overo il paragone dell'italiana lingua: nel qual si mostra chiaramente che l'antica sia inculta e rozza: e la moderna regolata e gentile (In casa et a spese dell'Autore, B. Martini, 1612). Reissued, again in Padua, in 1613.

Comparatione di Torquato Tasso con Homero e Virgilio insieme con la difesa dell'Ariosto paragonato ad Homero, 2nd, enlarged edn. (Padua, in casa e a spese dell'Autore, B. Martini, 1612). Reprinted (1) in T. Tasso,

Opere (Venice, 1722–42), viii (1738), 335–534 (Discorsi i–vii) and xi (1740), 411–525 (Discorsi viii–x); and (2) in *Opere di Torquato Tasso colle controversie sulla Gerusalemme*, ed. by G. Rosini, 33 vols. (Pisa, 1821–32), xxi (1828) (Discorsi i–iv) and xxii (1828) (Discorsi v–x).

In Aristotelis Poeticam commentarii in quibus ad obscura quaeque decreta planius adhuc dilucidanda, centum poeticae controversiae interponuntur et copiosissime explicantur (Padua, in Beniana, F. Bolzetta, 1613). Reprinted in Venice, apud Io. Gueriglium, 1622, and reissued in 1623 and 1624.

Orationes quinquaginta (Padua, in Beniana, F. Bolzetta, 1613).

Il Cavalcanti: overo la difesa dell'Anticrusca: di Michelangelo Fonte. Al serenissimo e generosissimo Granduca di Toscana Cosimo II. Opera piacevolissima, et a studiosi di purgato e vago italiano stile utilissima (Padua, F. Bolzetta, 1614). (See next item.)

Rime varie del signor Paolo Beni. Raccolte e date in luce dal Cavalcanti (Padua, F. Bolzetta, 1614). This is the third part of *Il Cavalcanti*, the second part being an edn. of Salviati's famous *Orazione* of 1564. All parts are separately paginated.

Il Goffredo, overo la Gierusalemme liberata, del Tasso, col commento del Beni. Dove non solamente si dichiara questo nobil poema, e si risolvono vari dubbi e molte oppositioni, con spiegarsi le sue vaghe imitationi, et insomma l'artificio tutto di parte in parte; ma ancora si paragona con Homero e Virgilio, mostrando che giunga al sommo: e perciò possa e debba riceversi per essempio et Idea dell'heroico poema (Padua, F. Bolzetta, 1616).

Benianae lucubrationes sive Pauli Benii Eugubini ad historiam, ad poesim, ad eloquentiam, perspicua et omnibus absoluta numeris institutio (Padua, B. Martini, 1622).

In P. Virgilii Maronis Aeneidem commentarii. Quibus authoris sententia explanatur et illustratur passim, heroici poematis artificium agnoscitur, et cum aristoteliae poeticae praeceptis coniungitur. Eiusdem poematis condendi ratio, legibus ac documentis ex ordine promulgatis, ostenditur. Aeneis cum Odyssea et Iliade comparatur: simulque demonstratur quantopere Homerum Virgilius superaverit. Quibus accessit Platonis poetica (Venice, apud Io. Gueriglium, 1622). Reissued in 1623.

In Sallustii Catilinariam commentarii. In quibus proposita historia sic explicatur et uno eodemque tempore historica praecepta tradantur, et cum exemplis et usu coniungantur. Denique ratio ac via ostenditur, qua historia tum intelligenter evolvi, tum recte diiudicari, tum pro dignitate scribi, tum ad publicam privatamque utilitatem referri, possit . . . His additur Iugurthinum Bellum: cui Annuae Literae quaedam subiiciuntur, ut annalibus quoque scribendis extet exemplum (Venice, apud Io. Gueriglium, 1622). Reissued in 1624.

Trattato dell'origine et fatti della famiglia Trissina (Padua, in casa dell'auttore, 1624). (Contains only the first of two books.) Reprinted as *Trattato dell'origine, et fatti illustri della famiglia Trissina* (Milan, M. Malatesta, 1626).

In Aristotelis libros Rhetoricorum commentarii. In quibus aristotelea de arte dicendi praecepta non solum copiose declarantur, verum etiam centum oratoriis controversiis interpositis illustrantur: cum Platone, etiam in decretis multis, cum M. Tullio in toto dicendi artificio, conferuntur. Accessit Platonis rhetorica ex eius monumentis excerpta (Venice, apud Io. Gueriglium, 1624).

Oratoriae disputationes seu rhetoricae controversiae. In quibus cum veterum multorum, tum maxime Aristotelis de ratione dicendi praecepta explanantur, et cum Platonis Ciceronisque decretis conferuntur. Hic praeter ea, quae in aristoteliae rhetoricae commentariis, e controversiis dubitantur, ut aristotelica de arte dicendi praecepta declarentur, et cum Platone, et M. Tullio conferantur, controversiarum vela panduntur explicatius. Et Platonis rhetorica subiicitur, ex variis eius locis excerpta (Venice, apud Io. Gueriglium, 1624). Reissued in 1625.

Platonis et Aristotelis theologia (Padua, typis Io. Baptistae Martini, et Livii Pasquati, 1624). (Contains the first two books of the second decade of the commentary on the *Timaeus*.)

In Aristotelis libros Rhetoricorum secundum, et tertium commentarii. In quibus aristotelea de arte dicendi praecepta non solum copiose declarantur, verum etiam centum oratoriis controversiis interpositis illustrantur: cum Platone, etiam in decretis multis, cum M. Tullio in toto dicendi artificio, conferuntur (Venice, apud Io. Gueriglium, 1625).

In M. T. Ciceronis Orationem Pro Lege Manilia commentarii. Ut autem cum theoria et praeceptis coniungatur praxis et usus, sic explicatur nobilis haec Oratio, ut uno eodemque tempore eloquentiae praecepta observentur, et Cicerone authore ac duce, cum usu coniungantur. His omnibus, ut in quolibet orationis genere praeclara extent exempla, subiicitur Oratio Pro Archia Poeta, Pro M. Marcello, et in L. Pisonem (Venice, apud Io. Gueriglium, 1625).

Orationes quinque et septuaginta . . . His accesserunt epistolae et praefationes . . . necnon . . . elogia, epitaphia et carmina quaedam (Venice, apud Io. Gueriglium, 1625).

L'Anticrusca: parte II, III, IV, ed. by G. Casagrande (Florence, 1982).

A NOTE ON PAOLO BENI'S 'OPERA OMNIA'

It is generally assumed that Beni's unfinished *Opera omnia*, published in Venice by G. Guerigli between 1622 and 1625, comprised five folio volumes (see Mazzacurati, art. cit., 500 and Casagrande, ed. cit., p. xvii); and Casagrande has stated (ibid.) that there were ten books spread amongst the five volumes (though he has not particularized them). This last task has been attempted by E. Landoni, who, basing her research wholly on the Beni published holdings of Padua's Biblioteca Universitaria, has offered a detailed description of the contents of all five volumes (art. cit., 32). Briefly her scheme is as follows:

vol. i (1622)   commentaries on Sallust;
vol. ii (1623)   commentary on *Aeneid*; *De historia*;
vol. iii (1624)   commentary on *Rhetoric I*;
vol. iv (1625)   commentary on *Rhetoric II* and *III*; *Oratoriae disputationes*;
vol. v (1625)   commentaries on Cicero; commentary on the *Poetics*; *Platonis poetica.*

It will be immediately obvious that this scheme is not in accord with the publication dates of several works listed in my Bibliography: according to my findings the *De historia* was published in 1622 (not 1623), and the commentary on the *Poetics* certainly appeared in this Venetian edition well before 1625 (in 1622, 1623, and 1624 in fact). More importantly, it is not at all certain that only five volumes had appeared before Beni's death. For, at the end of his *In M. T. Ciceronis Orationem Pro Lege Manilia commentarii* (1625), p. 236, there is a printed note: 'Finis totius voluminis sexti' which can leave us in no doubt that the *Opera omnia* had reached (at least) six volumes by 1625.

Taking in perhaps a wider selection of libraries and books than Landoni, I have been able, through the assistance of similar indications about volume numbers and their contents (on the original spines or at the end or in the colophons of Beni's later works), to establish for myself the following scheme for the projected *Opera omnia*:

vol. i   *De historia* (1622); commentary on the *Poetics* (1622);
vol. ii commentary on the *Aeneid* (1622); commentaries on Sallust (1622);
vol. iii——
vol. iv——
vol. v commentary on *Rhetoric I, II* and *III* (1624–5); *Oratoriae disputationes* (1624);
vol. vi commentaries on Cicero.

No certain details have emerged of what was in volumes iii and iv. The *Orationes quinque et septuaginta* (1625) most probably formed part of volume v or vi. The problem is aggravated, also, by the fact that the publication dates on the title-pages have frequently been altered for the purpose of reissuing identical editions. Thus the commentary on the *Poetics*, first published by Guerigli in 1622, has been altered in some copies to 1623 (Oxford, Bodley, M. 1. 21. Art.) or 1624 (Padua,

Universitaria, 54 b. 41; Oxford, Exeter College, AAL 64 u) by the simple
addition of one or two 'I's to the date of publication. This is also the
case with the commentary on the *Aeneid* which, in some copies, carries
the date 1622 (Oxford, Bodley, M. 1. 22. Art.; Paris, Bibliothèque nationale, Z. 677), and in others that of 1623 (Padua, Universitaria, 54 b. 38);
and the same applies to the commentaries on Sallust which exist in two
identical issues: 1622 (Oxford, Codrington, SR. 14. f. 3; Paris, Bibliothèque nationale, Z. 671) and 1624 (Oxford, Bodley, M. 1. 22. Art.). In
establishing my own admittedly unsatisfactory scheme I have attended
only to the first date of publication in Guerigli's Venetian edition (and
it is easy to see where the dates have been altered). As for the contents
of volumes iii and iv, it seems most likely that they contained (for
whatever reasons) reissues of works which had already appeared in
volumes i and ii. This also explains perhaps why we find that three of
the four works in the first two volumes were reissued shortly afterwards with altered dates.

B. Manuscript Works (Excluding Letters)

There are several possible orders. The most satisfactory would perhaps
be chronological, but this is not possible on our present state of knowledge: for it is impossible to assign every work to a definite date or
period. Furthermore, many of the works (especially those in the Archivio Segreto Vaticano) exist in several autograph drafts and are clearly
the result of work produced over a long period. Beni tended to revise
and refine his works (especially his learned Latin commentaries) right
up to the moment of publication; and many of the works which he
completed very late in life (such as the commentary on the *Rhetoric*)
have their genesis far back in the early days of his career.

Another attractive order is according to the different types of work
(poetic, rhetorical, political, etc.), but this would be difficult and artificial because most of Beni's works overlap in subject-matter and genre,
and far too many would naturally fall into a grey miscellaneous
category.

The only solution was to adopt an order according to library or
archive. This is not so haphazard and unwieldy as it might at first
seem, for Beni's MSS are mostly concentrated in a handful of regions.
In particular, the massive and most important concentration of his MSS
in the Archivio Beni of the Archivio Segreto Vaticano can be clearly
seen from my order: none of these MSS is signalled in any other published catalogue and all of them have been presumed lost. My hopes
are that this presentation will provide a starting-point for further
research into this important and hitherto unnoticed Vatican collection.

In the descriptions which follow I have used the word 'autograph' to designate MSS either in whole or in part (signature or corrections, etc.) in Beni's hand. All MSS are unpublished unless otherwise indicated.

GUBBIO, ARCHIVIO DI STATO

MS Fondo Armanni, II. D. 27: Beni's will of 1 October 1621 'in mano dell'Illustrissimo Vescovo d'Ugubbio che lo conserva'. 11 fos. 17C.

MILAN, BIBLIOTECA AMBROSIANA

MS R. 102. Sup., fos. 432–7: Letter and *Discorso* to Pope Clement VIII on the flooding of the Tiber, dated 9 February 1601. Early 17C. copy. See also Bibl. Vat., MS Vat.lat. 6557 (prima parte), fos. 1–6.

PADUA, BIBLIOTECA UNIVERSITARIA

MS 412: 'Della veneta libertà Paolo Beni al Serenissimo Prencipe et Eccelso Consiglio Veneto'. 364 pp. Autograph (early 17C.). Described wrongly in the catalogue as early 18C. Kristeller repeats this (*Iter italicum*, ii. 13) as does E. Landoni (art. cit., 34). Curiously, Landoni sees in this MS only one (copyist's) hand (ibid.); but there are at least two: that of the scribe and that of Beni (mostly in neat corrections and headings). See also Paris, BN, MS 324 for Beni's other autograph version of this work.

MS 911: 'Due discorsi di P. B. [sic] sopra l'impresa di Ferrara, et altre occorrenze per tutto l'Anno Santo del Giubileo. Alla Santità di N. S. Clemente VIII'. 86 pp. (Late 16C.). See also Bibl. Vat., MS Vat.lat. 6557 (parte seconda), fos. 203ʳ–33ᵛ.

PARIS, BIBLIOTHÈQUE NATIONALE

MS 324: 'Della veneta libertà Paolo Beni al Serenissimo Prencipe et Eccelso Consiglio Veneto'. 283 fos. Autograph (early 17C.). See also Padua, Universitaria, MS 412.

PARMA, BIBLIOTECA PALATINA

MS Pal. 555 (66): Four-line *carmen* 'De Nive Exquilia'. Not autograph. 16C. (?). Beni printed it in 'Epitaphia et elogia' in *Orationes quinque et septuaginta* (1625), 64 to show that he had cultivated the 'Latinas Musas'.

VENICE, BIBLIOTECA NAZIONALE MARCIANA

MS Lat. IX. 52 (=3167). IX, pp. 122–51: 'Pauli Benii Eugubini sacrae theologiae doctoris De Ecclesiasticis Baronii cardinalis Annalibus disputatio'. Copy made in the 18C. by Andrea Galland for a three-volume edn. of Baronio's works. Originally published in 1596 and reprinted in 1759.

MS Lat. XIII. 87 (=3998): 'Beniana bibliotheca'. 300 pp. Pp. 233–44 contain the printed *Benianae lucubrationes* (Padua, 1624 (the date has been altered by hand from 1622, probably by Beni for the projected publication of the present MS in the *Opera omnia*)). Autograph (17C.).

VICENZA, BIBLIOTECA BERTOLIANA

MS G. 21. 11. 20* (=2830), pp. 1–37: 'Trattato dell'origine della famiglia Trissina, libro secondo'. 19C. copy.

VATICANO (CITTÀ DEL), BIBLIOTECA APOSTOLICA VATICANA

MS Urb.lat. 1206, fos. 26ʳ–27ᵛ: 'Difesa del Cavalcanti'. Undated (but before 24 January 1614). 17C. copy.

MS Vat.lat. 6557 (parte prima), fos. 1–6: Letter and *Discorso* to the pope on the flooding of the Tiber, dated 9 February 1601. 17C. copy. See Bibl. Ambrosiana, MS R. 102. Sup., fos. 432–7.

MS Vat.lat. 6557 (parte seconda), fos. 203ʳ–33ᵛ: 'Due discorsi sopra la recupera di Ferrara'. Late 16C. or early 17C. copy, wrongly attributed to P. Paruta in a catalogue. See also Padua, Universitaria, MS 911.

MS Vat.lat. 7065: Commentary on the first decade (ten books) of the *Timaeus*. 448 fos. + some unfoliated fragments. Autograph (16C.).

VATICANO (CITTÀ DEL), ARCHIVIO SEGRETO VATICANO

MS Archivio Beni, 36: Thirty-two autograph letters and a will, dated 23 June 1623, copied by Conte Luca Beni in the 17C. (12 fos.).

MS Archivio Beni, 69: Philosophical 'Disputationes'. Unfoliated. Autograph.

MS Archivio Beni, 70: 'Physicae disputationes, habitae in Almo Urbis Gymnasio Anno MDLXXXXIIII'. Seven booklets (A–G). Unfoliated. Autograph.

MS Archivio Beni, 71: Unpublished Paduan *Digressiones, Disputationes, Praefationes*, and *Orationes* (some in several versions and drafts). Unfoliated. Autograph.

MS Archivio Beni, 77: 'Platonis poetica'. Autograph. Unfoliated. Incomplete. Published in full in 1622, etc.

MS Archivio Beni, 81: 'Exemplum vetus commentarii in secundum Rhetoricorum Aristotelis'. Unfoliated. Incomplete, Autograph. Published in 1625.

MS Archivio Beni, 82: Fragments (chapters 3–5) of the commentary on the *Rhetoric*, I. Unfoliated. Autograph. Published in 1624.

MS *Archivio Beni, 83*: Fragments (chapters 7–10) of the commentary on *Rhetoric*, I. Unfoliated. Autograph. Published in 1624.

MS *Archivio Beni, 84*: 'Fragmenta quaedam in librum I et II Rhet [oricorum] Ar[istoteli]s'. Unfoliated. Autograph. Published in 1624–5.

MS *Archivio Beni, 85*: Fragments of the commentary on the *Rhetoric* in various booklets. Unfoliated. Autograph. Published in 1624–5.

MS *Archivio Beni, 86*: 'In M. Tullii Orationem Pro Lege Manilia, seu de Pompeio Imperatore deligendo, commentarii'. 43 fos. at the beginning, then unfoliated. Autograph. Published in 1625.

MS *Archivio Beni, 87*: 'M. Tullii Ciceronis Pro Lege Manilia, seu de Pompeio Imperatore deligendo, ad populum Oratio'. Unfoliated. This is a contemporary MS copy of Cicero's text with marginal notes in Beni's hand. The first folio also contains notes by Beni on Roman history 'Anno ab Urbe condita 661' to 689.

MS *Archivio Beni, 88*: Fragments of the commentary on the *Pro Lege Manilia*. Unfoliated. Autograph. Published in 1625.

MS *Archivio Beni, 89*: 'In Aristotelis libros De moribus ad Nicomachum commentarii'. Unfoliated. Two small printed booklets (containing the Greek text and the Latin translations of other writers) have been broken up by Beni and interspersed here and there in the MS to provide the basic text and translations. Reconstituted, these printed sections contain respectively pp. 81–416 and fos. 22–187. A scribe has also transcribed some of the text and translations. Autograph.

MS *Archivio Beni, 90*: 'Aristotelis Moralium Nicomachiorum'. Unfoliated. Fragments of the commentary. See previous entry. Autograph.

MS *Archivio Beni, 91*: 'In Aristotelis Politicam commentarii'. Unfoliated. Two small printed booklets (containing the Greek text and the Latin translation) are broken up and interspersed here and there in the MS. Reconstituted, the printed sections contain respectively pp. 21–160 and fos. 2–79. Autograph.

MS *Archivio Beni, 95*: Alphabetical index for the commentary on the first decade of the *Timaeus*. Unfoliated. Autograph. Published in 1594.

MS *Archivio Beni, 97*: 'In Platonis Timaeum, sive in naturalem omnem atque divinam Platonis et Aristotelis philosophiam, decadis secundae liber tertius' (pp. 1–127) and 'liber quartus' (pp. 129–344). Autograph. At the end (pp. 343–4) there is the *Nulla Osta* from the Paduan Censors, dated 1607.

MS *Archivio Beni, 98*: 'In Platonis Timaeum . . . decadis secundae liber quintus' (pp. 344–581) and 'liber sextus' (pp. 1–200). At the end (p. 200) there is the *Nulla Osta*, dated 1608.

MS Archivio Beni, 99: 'In Platonis Timaeum . . . decadis secundae liber septimus'. 260 pp. Autograph. At the end there is the *Nulla Osta*.

MS Archivio Beni, 100: 'In Platonis Timaeum . . . decadis secundae liber octavus' (pp. 1–367) and 'liber nonus' (pp. 368–950). Autograph.

MS Archivio Beni, 101: 'In Platonis Timaeum . . . decadis secundae liber decimus'. 460 pp. At the end there is the *Nulla Osta*. Autograph.

MS Archivio Beni, 102: 'In Platonis Timaeum . . . decadis secundae liber quartus'. Unfoliated fragmentary booklets. Autograph. See MS Archivio Beni, 97.

MS Archivio Beni, 103: 'In Platonis Timaeum . . . decadis secundae liber quintus'. Many unfoliated fragmentary loose booklets. Autograph. See MS Archivio Beni, 98.

MS Archivio Beni, 104: 'In Platonis Timaeum . . . decadis secundae liber septimus'. Unfoliated fragmentary booklets. See also MS Archivio Beni, 99. Autograph.

MS Archivio Beni, 105: 'In Platonis Timaeum . . . decadis secundae liber octavus'. Unfoliated fragmentary booklets. Autograph. See also MS Archivio Beni, 100.

MS Archivio Beni, 106: 'In Platonis Timaeum . . . decadis secundae liber nonus'. Unfoliated fragmentary booklets. Autograph. See also MS Archivio Beni, 100.

MS Archivio Beni, 107: 'In Platonis Timaeum . . . decadis secundae liber decimus'. Unfoliated fragmentary loose booklets. Autograph. See also MS Archivio Beni, 101.

MS Archivio Beni, 108: 'In Platonis Timaeum . . . decadis tertiae liber primus'. Unfoliated. Complete. Autograph.

MS Archivio Beni, 109: 'In Platonis Timaeum . . . decadis tertiae'. Books 2–10. Complete. At the end there are some further fragments of Book II of the commentary on the *Timaeus*. All unfoliated. Autograph.

MS Archivio Beni, 110: 'Procli Diadochi in Timaeum, sive in naturalem philosophiam commentarii, Paulo Benio Eugubino interprete. Liber primus et secundus'. Unfoliated. Autograph.

MS Archivio Beni, 111: 'Procli Diadochi commentariorum in Platonis Timaeum, liber secundus'. 136 fos. Dated 6 August 1593. Autograph.

MS Archivio Beni, 112: 'Liber secundus de primo motore Deo' and 'Liber tertius, in quo Deus cum intelligentiis reliquis comparatur'. In seven unfoliated booklets. Autograph.

MS Archivio Beni, 113: Three lectures on Aristotelian natural philosophy. They were all originally delivered in the Sapienza and are dated respectively 1596, 1597, and 1599. Unfoliated booklets. Autograph.

MS Archivio Beni, 115: 'Pauli Benii Eugubini in Somnium Scipionis commentarii'. In two incomplete versions (one with an alphabetical index). Unfoliated. Autograph.

MS Archivio Beni, 116: 'In Platonis Euthyphronem, sive in dialogum de sanctitate, copiosa commentaria: in quibus etiam ad platonicos dialogos reliquos sic introducitur et instruitur lector . . . authore Paulo Benio Eugubino'. There is an index at the end. 243 pages + some others. Between pp. 219 and 220 a MS booklet 'De Platonis philosophia' or 'De Platonis methodo' has been stitched in. Autograph.

MS Archivio Beni, 117: 'Qua tandem ratione dirimi, ac tuto definiri possit controversia quae de efficaci Dei auxilio inter religiosas Dominicanorum Jesuitarumque familias agitatur . . . authore Paulo Benio'. Dated 1603. 202 pp. + some others. Autograph.

MS Archivio Beni, 118: 'Actio constantiana'. Drama in five acts, partly in prose, partly in verse, partly in Italian, partly in Latin. In three versions. Unfoliated. Autograph.

MS Archivio Beni, 119: 'Homeri, Virgilii, Torquati in heroico poemate comparatio, in qua etiam heroici poematis condendi ratio ac via demonstratur'. Contains only 2 *Disputationes* and an index at the end. 124 pp. + some others. Autograph. See also the Italian *Comparatione* (published in 1607 and 1612).

MS Archivio Beni, 120: another version of first half of MS Archivio Beni, 119.

MS Archivio Beni, 123: 'Discorso intorno alla riforma dello Studio di Padova'. In several drafts and fair copies. Unfoliated. Autograph.

MS Archivio Beni, 124: 'Risposta alle considerationi o dubbi dell'Academico Innaspato sopra il Pastor fido, con altre varie dubitationi tanto contra l'Innaspato, quanto contra l'istesso Pastor fido. Dell'Academico Tessuto [*Paolo Beni*]'. Paduan *Nulla Osta* and *Imprimatur* dated 21 August 1600 at end. Incomplete. Unfoliated. Autograph. Published in 1600.

MS Archivio Beni, 125: 'Apologetico del Beni agli eccellentissimi dottori Faustin Summo e Lucio Scarano' or 'Apologia della comedia e tragedia in prosa, dove si risponde all'invettiva degli avversari'. Almost all unfoliated. Autograph.

MS Archivio Beni, 126: Fragmentary drafts, only partially foliated, in preparation for MS Archivio Beni, 125. Autograph.

MS Archivio Beni, 128: 'Delle bellezze della filosofia. Dialogo primo'. Unfoliated booklet. Autograph.

MS Archivio Beni, 129: 'Avertimenti [*sic*] per la lingua italiana nella prosa e nel verso. Al signor [*BLANK*]. Signor tanto per lo splendor del sangue e gloria de' Maggiori, quanto per generosità d'animo e soavità de costumi, e per ingegno insieme e nobili dottrine chiarissimo. Ai quali Avvertimenti si aggiunge un Trattato della memoria locale: in cui brevemente si spiega il modo facile per acquistarla'. Unfoliated. Autograph.

MS Archivio Beni, 130: 'Modo di riformare e ridurre a perfettion l'arte della stampa'. In two drafts. Unfoliated. Autograph.

MS Archivio Beni, 131: 'Paolo Beni. Bozze delle sue opere'. Unfoliated bundle of unconnected fragments. Autograph.

MS Archivio Beni, 132: (amongst other things about Beni) 'Pauli Benii Eugubini, sacrae theologiae et philosophiae doctoris, quique quatuor iam ac viginti annos eloquentiam in prima patavini Gymnasii sede profitetur, miscellanea sive opuscula varia'. This consists of Beni's own comments and annotations on what he considered to be his miscellaneous writings. Unfoliated. Autograph.

C. Chronological Reference List of Beni's Letters

All letters are autograph (or original) and unpublished unless otherwise stated. The following abbreviations have been used: ASVB=Archivio Segreto Vaticano, Arch. Beni; MA=Milan, Ambrosiana; ME=Modena, Estense; MT=Milan, Trivulziana; PO=Pesaro, Oliveriana; VA=Vaticana; VB=Vicenza, Bertoliana; VC=Venice, Correr. Letters marked with an asterisk are the work of a different 'Paulo Beni'.

No.	Place	Date	Addressee	MSS or Pr. edn.
1	Perugia,	15.1.1566	Paulus Manutius	(a) VA Vat.lat. 3435, fo. 44
				(b) ME It. 1827=Beta 1. 3. 1. c, fos. 71ᵛ–72ʳ (16C. copy)
				(c) in *Inedita manutiana 1502–1597*, ed. cit., pp. 255–7
* 2	Rome,	3.iv.1574	G.B. Borromeo	MT N. 1. 127. 14
* 3	Rome,	17.iv.1574	G. B. Borromeo	MT N. 1. 127. 14
4	Pesaro,	4.ii.1580	Baldo Beni	ASVB 36
5	Rome,	10.xi.1581	Francesco Beni	ASVB 36
* 6	Rome,	2.vii.1583	Carlo Borromeo	MA F. 164. Inf., fos. 9–10
* 7	Rome,	6.viii.1583	Carlo Borromeo	MA F. 164. Inf., fo. 237
* 8	Rome,	13.viii.1583	Carlo Borromeo	MA F. 164. Inf., fo. 282
* 9	Rome,	10.ix.1583	Carlo Borromeo	MA F. 165. Inf., fo. 81
* 10	Rome,	8.x.1583	Carlo Borromeo	MA F. 165. Inf., fo. 386
* 11	Rome,	28.i.1584	Carlo Borromeo	MA F. 89. Inf., fos. 294–5
* 12	Rome,	4.ii.1584	Carlo Borromeo	MA F. 89. Inf., fo. 298
* 13	Rome,	11.ii.1584	Carlo Borromeo	MA F. 89. Inf., fo. 300
* 14	Rome,	19.v.1584	Carlo Borromeo	MA F. 89. Inf., fo. 301
15	Rome,	24.viii.1596	Giacomo Beni	ASVB 36
16	Rome,	23.x.1596	Giacomo Beni	ASVB 36
* 17	Madrid,	18.vi.1599	Camillo Caetano	ASV, Fondo Borghese, Serie I, 649, fo. 278

No.	Place	Date	Addressee	MSS or Pr. edn.
18	Padua,	9.ii.1601	Clement VIII	(a) MA R. 102. Sup., fo. 432ʳ (17C. copy)
				(b) VA Vat.lat. 6557 (parte prima), fo. 1ʳ (17C. copy)
19	Padua,	3.viii.1607	Giacomo Beni	ASVB 36
20	Padua,	19.ii.1610	M. A. Bonciario	in *Lettere . . . a M. Antonio Bonciario*, op. cit., pp. 11–14
21	Padua,	30.vii.1613	G. B. Fazi	PO 429, Fasc. xiv, fos. 53ʳ–56ᵛ
22	Padua,	5.xi.1614	Nicolò Contarini	VC MS Correr 1375, pp. 655–7
23	Padua,	15.vii.1616	Francesco Beni	ASVB 36
24	Padua,	9.viii.1616	Giulio Brunetti	PO 429, Fasc. xiv, fos. 54ʳ–55ᵛ
25	Padua,	10.iii.1617	Francesco Beni	ASVB 36
26	Padua,	15.iv.1618	Camillo Giordani	PO 1594, Fasc. ii
27	Padua,	16.viii.1618	Francesco Beni	ASVB 36
28	Padua,	20.xi.1618	Camillo Giordani	PO 1594, Fasc. ii
29	Padua,	10.viii.1620	Andrea Dandolo	ASVB 129
30	Padua,	14.viii.1620	Andrea Dandolo	ASVB 129
31	Padua,	25.viii.1620	Andrea Dandolo	ASVB 129
32	Padua,	27.viii.1620	Andrea Dandolo	ASVB 129
33	Padua,	29.viii.1620	Andrea Dandolo	ASVB 129
34	Padua,	3.ix.1620	Andrea Dandolo	ASVB 129
35	Padua,	6.ix.1620	Andrea Dandolo	ASVB 129
36	Padua,	8.ix.1620	Andrea Dandolo	ASVB 129
37	Padua,	10.ix.1620	Andrea Dandolo	ASVB 129
38	Padua,	20.ix.1620	Andrea Dandolo	ASVB 129
39	Padua,	22.x.1620	Francesco Beni	ASVB 36
40	Padua,	2(?).xii.1620	Andrea Dandolo	ASVB 129
41	Padua,	12.xii.1620	Unnamed poet	VB G. 5. 1. 4 (17). E. 139
42	Padua,	16.xii.1620	Andrea Dandolo	ASVB 129
43	Padua,	19.ii.1621	Francesco Beni	ASVB 36
44	Padua,	5.iii.1621	Francesco Beni	ASVB 36
45	Padua,	30.iv.1621	Francesco Beni	ASVB 36
46	Padua,	2.vii.1621	Francesco Beni	ASVB 36
47	Padua,	2.x.1621	Francesco Beni	ASVB 36
48	Padua,	20.v.1622	Francesco Beni	ASVB 36
49	Padua,	18.viii.1623	Urban VIII	VA Barb.lat. 6458 (L. xxiv. 4), fo. 39. 17 C. copy
50	Padua,	19.viii.1623	Camillo Giordani	PO 1594, Fasc. ii.
51	Padua,	c.15.xii.1623	Felice Beni	ASVB 36
52	Padua,	15.xii.1623	A cardinal	ASVB 36
53	Padua,	22.xii.1623	A cardinal	ASVB 36
54	Padua,	22.xii.1623	Francesco Beni	ASVB 36
55	Padua,	5.i.1624	Francesco Beni	ASVB 36
56	Padua,	26.i.1624	Felice Beni	ASVB 36
57	Padua,	16.ii.1624	Felice Beni	ASVB 36
58	Padua,	5.iv.1624	Francesco Beni	ASVB 36
59	Padua,	26.iv.1624	Francesco Beni	ASVB 36

No.	Place	Date	Addressee	MSS or Pr. edn.
60	Padua,	3.v.1624	Francesco Beni	ASVB 36
61	Padua,	25.vii.1624	Francesco Beni	ASVB 36
62	Padua,	16.viii.1624	Francesco Beni	ASVB 36
63	Padua,	31.xii.1624	Francesco Beni	ASVB 36
64	Padua,	24.i.1625	Francesco Beni	ASVB 36
65	Padua,	30.i.1625	Giacomo Beni	ASVB 36
66	Padua,	21.ii.1625	Francesco Beni	ASVB 36

This list does not include dedicatory and prefatory letters, of which there are of course many; nor does it include letters printed by Beni in his *Orationes quinque et septuaginta* (1625), many of which are reprints of dedicatory and prefatory letters.

OTHER WORKS CONSULTED

A. Manuscript Material

GUBBIO, ARCHIVIO DI STATO

MS Fondo Armanni, I. B. 12: 'Memorie' concerning Gubbio by Giovanni Battista Primoli, a disciple of V. Armanni. 17C.

MS Fondo Armanni, I. B. 13: Medieval documents (1282–1312), some concerning the Beni family.

MS Fondo Armanni, I. B. 14: Medieval documents, some concerning the Beni family.

MS Fondo Armanni, I. B. 15: *Memorie* extracted from the archives of Francesco Beni by Giovanni Battista Primoli. 17C.

MS Fondo Armanni, I. C. 13. Fasc. 9: 'Prammatica o istanza del Comune nel vestire delle donne e degli uomini (An. 1561)'. 16C.

MS Fondo Armanni, I. D. 3, fos. 82ʳ–83ᵛ: 'Vita di Pauolo Beni da Gubbio'. First half of 17C. Forms part of collection entitled 'Scrittori della città di Gubbio raccolti dal signor Vincenzo Armanni'. 17C.

MS Fondo Armanni, I. F. 2: Genealogical trees, one of the Panfili family.

MS Fondo Armanni, I. F. 3: Gubbian coats of arms: Beni (fo. 10ʳ, no. 39); Panfili (fo. 44ʳ, no. 176).

MS Fondo Armanni, I. F. 10: Huge miscellany, some of which concerning Beni family.

MS Fondo Armanni, I. F. 11: A bundle of papers, including (fos. 8–11) two genealogical trees of the Beni family with details of civic offices which they held.

MS Fondo Armanni, II. A. 17: Contains a few muddled papers concerning the Beni family. 17C.

MS Fondo Armanni, II. D. 10: Contains two genealogical trees of the Beni family. 17C.

MS Fondo Armanni, II. D. 31, pp. 41–97: Material on the history of the

Beni family collected by Marcello Franciarini, mostly but not exclusively taken from V. Armanni. Early 18C.

MS Fondo Armanni, II. E. 9, Section 145: Later copy of the life of Beni in MS Fondo Armanni, I. D. 3, fos. 82ʳ–83ᵛ.

MS Fondo Armanni, III. D. 19, pp. 94–8: Life of Beni, very influenced by Mazzuchelli. 18C.

MS Fondo Armanni, III. D. 29: List of baptisms 1549–71.

MS Fondo Armanni, III. E. 10: Life of Beni. Derivative and erroneous. 18C.

MS Fondo Notarile, 554, fos. 141–5: contemporary (the notary's) copy of Francesco Beni's will, dated 3 July 1586.

GUBBIO, ARCHIVIO DELLA BIBLIOTECA DEL CONVENTO DI S. FRANCESCO

MS 17. G. 7. pp. 46–8: Life of Giacomo Beni. Probably 18C.

MS Unclassified: A bundle of 52 original documents relating to the Beni family. 16–17C.

MILAN, BIBLIOTECA AMBROSIANA

MS G. Inf., 160/60, fo. 118ʳ: Letter (Gubbio, 18 February 1593) from Giacomo Beni to Federico Borromeo in Milan. Autograph.

MS R. 102. Sup., fos. 358ʳ–59ᵛ: Antonio Scaino's judgement on Beni's *Disputatio* of 1600. Early 17C.

MILAN, BIBLIOTECA TRIVULZIANA

MS N. 1. 127. 20: Letter (12 January 1581) from Carlo Borromeo to the pope about the Jesuits and Cesare Speciano. 17C. copy.

OXFORD, BODLEIAN LIBRARY

MS D. Phil. d. 2231, 2: E. C. M. Roaf, 'Bartolomeo Cavalcanti, 1503–62: A Critical and Biographical Study'. Unpublished thesis, July 1959.

PADUA, BIBLIOTECA DELL'ACCADEMIA PATAVINA DI SCIENZE, LETTERE, ED ARTI

MS: 'Atti dell'Accademia dei Ricovrati', Giornale A.

PESARO, BIBLIOTECA OLIVERIANA

MS 384, Fasc. XXI, fo. 61ʳ: notes on G. B. Fazi.

MS 458. II. Mis. 101: notes on C. Giordani, *seniore*.

MS 781, fo. 22ʳ⁻ᵛ: Undated (but 1616) letter from the Duke of Urbino to Paolo Beni. 17C. copy. See also Bibl. Vat. MS Vat.lat. 10975, fo. 17ʳ.

MS 1063 (under letter 'G'): notes on C. Giordani, *seniore*.

ROME, ARCHIVUM ROMANUM SOCIETATIS JESU

References to the following were kindly supplied in detail by the late
Father Georges Bottereau, SJ, Assistant Archivist:
MS Rom. 14. I; *MS Rom. 14.* II; *MS Rom. 53.* I; *MS Rom. 171.* A; *MS Rom.
171.* C; *MS Ven. 37*; *MS Med. 20*; *MS Hist.Soc. 54.*

VATICANO (CITTÀ DEL), BIBLIOTECA APOSTOLICA
VATICANA

MS Urb.lat. 1206, fos. 22ʳ–24ᵛ: Letter from the *Arciconsolo, e Accademici
della Crusca* to Curzio Picchena, dated 24 January 1614, on the subject
of Beni and his *Cavalcanti*. 17C. copy. Printed from the original in [D.
Moreni], op. cit., pp. 149–73.
MS Vat.lat. 8225 (parte seconda): (1) fos. 315ʳ–17ᵛ: Notes on Beni's *Qua
tandem* (virtually undecipherable); (2) fos. 318ʳ–19ʳ: Notes on Beni's
life and works culled from standard 17C. printed authorities;
(3) fo. 320ʳ: An account of a document concerning Beni's election as
one of the best theologians of his age (dated 17 May 1622).
MS Vat.lat. 10975, fo. 17: Undated letter (but 1616) from the Duke of
Urbino to Paolo Beni. A partial 17C. copy. See also Bibl. Oliveriana,
MS 781, fo. 22ʳ⁻ᵛ.

VATICANO (CITTÀ DEL), ARCHIVIO SEGRETO VATICANO

MS Archivio Beni, 7: 'Hic est liber Francisci Benii suorum amicorumque
ad usum'. Unfoliated. Autograph. 17C.
MS Archivio Beni, 25: Bundle of documents and genealogical trees concerning the Beni family. Unfoliated. 17 and 18C.
MS Archivio Beni, 31: Original documents (1601–10) concerning Giacomo Beni. Unfoliated. 17C.
MS Archivio Beni, 35: 5 documents concerning Paolo Beni: (1) copy of
the papal contract awarding him his *cavalierato pio*; (2) copy of
C. Aquaviva's permission for him to make a will; (3) illegible booklet
containing minutes of a legal case; (4) tenancy agreement (original);
(5) publishing agreement with F. Bolzetta (original). Unfoliated. 16
and 17C.
MS Archivio Beni, 68: 'Raccolta di memorie di Paolo Beni, famoso letterato di Gubbio, tirate dalle opere di più autori'. Unfoliated. 18C. A
very full and comprehensive list (copiously illustrated with quotations) of published works which deal with Paolo Beni. Most of
them are erroneous however.
MS Archivio Beni, 132: Contains (amongst other things) 'Catalogo delle
opere stampate di Paolo Beni, che si ritrovano in casa Beni'. Unfoliated. 18C. original.

B. Printed Material

ACCADEMIA DELLA CRUSCA, *Vocabolario degli Accademici della Crusca* (Venice, 1612).

[ALLEGRI, A.], *Fantastica visione di Parri da Pozzolatico, poderaio moderno in Piandigiullari* (Lucca, 1613).

[——], *Lettere di Ser Poi pedante nella corte de Donati a M. Pietro Bembo, M. Giovanni Boccacii, & M. Francesco Petrarca* (Bologna, 1613).

[Anon], *Raccolta de libri prohibiti* (Milan, 1624).

[——], *Notizie intorno alla vita di Primo del Conte milanese della Congregazione di Somasca teologo al Concilio di Trento* (Rome, 1805).

ARCUDI, B. A., 'The Author of the *Secchia* Does Battle with Pietro Bembo's School', *Italica*, 44 (1967), 291–313.

—— 'A Seicento Reappraisal of Trecento Language', *Italian Quarterly*, 15, No. 58–59 (1971), 3–15.

—— 'Alessandro Tassoni and the Accademia della Crusca', *Forum Italicum*, 6, No. 3 (Sept. 1972), 378–92.

ARGELATI, Ph., *Bibliotheca scriptorum mediolanensium*, 2 vols. (Milan, 1745).

ARISI, F., *Cremona literata*, 3 vols. (vols. i and ii: Parma, 1702–26) (vol. iii: Cremona, 1741).

ARISTOTLE, *On the Art of Poetry*, a revised text with critical introduction, translation and commentary by Ingram Bywater (Oxford, 1909).

—— *The 'Art' of Rhetoric*, trans. by J. H. Freese (Loeb Classical Library: Cambridge, Mass. and London, 1926).

ARMANNI, V., *Delle lettere*, 3 vols. (Rome, 1663–74).

—— *Della famiglia Bentivoglia* (Bologna, 1682).

ARMOUR, P., 'Galileo and the Crisis in Italian Literature of the Early Seicento', in *Collected Essays on Italian Language and Literature Presented to Kathleen Speight*, ed. by G. Aquilecchia *et al.* (Manchester, 1971), 143–69.

ASOR-ROSA, A., 'Allegri, Alessandro', in *Dizionario biografico degli Italiani*, ii (1960), 477–8.

—— 'Aromatari, Giuseppe degli', in *Dizionario biografico degli Italiani*, iv (1962), 292–4.

ASPASIO, C., *La biblioteca aprosiana passatempo autunnale di Cornelio Aspasio Antivigilmi trà Vagabondi di Tabbia detto l'Aggirato* (Bologna, 1673), 256–8 (on Beni).

BAILLET, A., *Jugemens des savans sur les principaux ouvrages des auteurs*, 7 vols. (Paris, 1722), iii. 294–5 (on Beni).

BAISI, C., 'Congregatio de Auxiliis divinae gratiae', in *Enciclopedia cattolica*, iv. 339–40.

—— 'Molinismo', in *Enciclopedia cattolica*, viii. 1223–4.

BALDWIN, C. S., *Ancient Rhetoric and Poetic* (New York, 1924).

—— *Medieval Rhetoric and Poetic* (New York, 1928).

—— *Renaissance Literary Theory and Practice* (New York, 1939).

BARON, H., 'The *Querelle* of the Ancients and the Moderns as a Problem for Renaissance Scholarship', *Journal of the History of Ideas*, 20 (1959), No. 1, 3–22.

BAROTTI, G. A., 'Difesa degli scrittori ferraresi composta dal dottor Giovannandrea Barotti', in *Esami di vari autori sopra il libro intitolato l'Eloquenza italiana di Monsignor Giusto Fontanini* (Roveredo, 1739), pp. 35, 44, 45, etc. (on Beni).

BATTAGLIA, R., 'Dalla lingua dell'*Armadigi* a quella della *Conquistata*', *Cultura neolatina*, 1 (1941), 94–115.

—— 'Note sul dissolversi della forma rinascimentale', *Cultura neolatina*, 2 (1942), 174–90.

BAYLE, P., *Dictionaire* [sic] *historique et critique*, 1st edn., 2 vols. (Rotterdam, 1697); 2nd ed., 3 vols. (Rotterdam, 1702).

BELLONI, A., 'Il pensiero critico di Torquato Tasso nei posteriori trattatisti italiani dell'epica', in *Miscellanea di studi critici pubblicati in onore di Guido Mazzoni dai suoi discepoli*, ed. by A. della Torre and P. L. Rambaldi, 2 vols. (Florence, 1907), ii. 5–79.

—— 'Un professore anticruscante all'Università di Padova', *Archivio veneto-tridentino*, 1 (1922), 245–69.

—— 'Beni, Paolo', in *Enciclopedia italiana*, vi (1930), 640.

—— 'Il pensiero di Galilei sopra la natura e i modi dell'arte', *Giornale storico della letteratura italiana*, 103 (1934), 82–92.

—— *Il Seicento* (Milan, 1947).

BEMBO, P., *Prose della volgar lingua*, ed. by M. Marti (Padua, 1955).

BENI, G., *De privilegiis I[uris] consultorum* (Venice, 1602).

—— *Statuta civitatis Eugubii, auctoritate Serenissimi Francisci Mariae II Ducis nostri confirmata, et edita* (Gubbio, 1624).

BERTONI, G., *Giovanni Maria Barbieri e gli studi romanzi del sec.XVI* (Modena, 1905).

BOBBIO, A. A., 'Beni, Paolo', in *Enciclopedia dantesca*, i (1970), 586–7.

BOLAFFI, E., *Sallustio e la sua fortuna nei secoli* (Rome, 1949).

BOLGAR, R. R., *The Classical Heritage and Its Beneficiaries* (Cambridge, 1954).

BONINI, F. M., *Il Tevere incatenato: overo l'arte di frenar l'acque correnti* (Rome, 1663).

BOURNET, L., 'Auxiliis (Congrégation de)', in *Dictionnaire d'histoire et de géographie ecclésiastiques*, ed. by A. Baudrillart, A. de Meyer, and Ét. Cauwenbergh (1912–), v (1931), 960–70.

BOUWSMA, W. J., 'Three Types of Historiography in Post-Renaissance Italy', *History and Theory*, 4 (1964–5), 303–14.

BRAND, C. P., 'Stylistic Trends in the *Gerusalemme Conquistata*', in *Ita-*

lian Studies Presented to E. R. Vincent, ed. by C. P. Brand, K. Foster, and U. Limentani (Cambridge, 1962), pp. 136–53.

BRODRICK, J., SJ, *The Origin of the Jesuits* (London, 1940).

BROWN, P. M., 'The Historical Significance of the Polemics over Tasso's *Gerusalemme liberata*', *Studi secenteschi*, 11 (1970), 3–23.

—— *Prose or Verse in the Comedy: A Florentine Treatment of a Sixteenth-Century Controversy* (Hull, 1973).

—— *Lionardo Salviati: A Critical Biography* (Oxford, 1974).

BUDD, F. E., 'A Minor Italian Critic of the Sixteenth Century: Jason Denores', *Modern Language Review*, 22 (1927), 421–34.

BULLOCK, W. L., 'Italian Sixteenth Century Criticism', *Modern Language Notes*, 41 (1926), 254–63.

BURKE, P., 'A Survey of the Popularity of Ancient Historians, 1450–1700', *History and Theory*, 5 (1966), 135–52.

BUSSOLINI, G. F., 'Giulio Ottonelli e le *Annotazioni al Vocabolario degli Accademici della Crusca* (1698)', *Lingua nostra*, 31 (1970), 5–12.

CAMPANELLA, T., 'Historiographiae liber unus iuxta propria principia', in *Tutte le opere*, ed. by L. Firpo (Milan–Verona, 1954), 1221–55.

CANTIMORI, D., 'Rhetoric and Politics in Italian Humanism', *Journal of the Warburg and Courtauld Institutes*, 1 (1937–8), 83–102.

CAPPONI, A. G., *Catalogo della Libreria Capponi* (Rome, 1747), 54–5 (on Beni).

CARTA, F., 'La scrittura di Alessandro Tassoni', in *Miscellanea tassoniana*, ed. by T. Casini and V. Santi (Bologna–Modena, 1908), 178–207.

CASAGRANDE, G. A., 'Le parti inedite dell'*Anticrusca* di Paolo Beni', *Giornale storico della letteratura italiana*, 155 (1978), 224–9.

—— 'Introduzione', in P. Beni, *L'Anticrusca parte II, III, IV* (Florence, 1982), pp. ix–lxxiv.

CASTELVETRO, L., *Ragioni d'alcune cose segnate nella Canzone di Messer Annibal Caro: 'Venite a l'ombra de gran gigli d'oro'* (Venice, 1560).

—— *Correttione d'alcune cose del Dialogo delle lingue di Benedetto Varchi, et una giunta al primo libro delle Prose di M. Pietro Bembo dove si ragiona della vulgar lingua* (Basel, 1572). The *Correttione* was reprinted in B. Varchi, *L'Ercolano* (Florence, 1846), 535–647.

—— *Poetica d'Aristotele vulgarizzata et sposta* (Basel, 1576).

CASTOR, G., *Pléiade Poetics: A Study in Sixteenth-Century Thought and Terminology* (Cambridge, 1964).

CAVALCANTI, B., *Lettere edite e inedite*, ed. by C. Roaf (Bologna, 1967).

CHARLTON, H. B., *Castelvetro's Theory of Poetry* (Manchester, 1913).

[CHARNES, J. A. de], *La Vie du Tasse* (Paris, 1690).

CHIAPPELLI, F., *Studi sul linguaggio del Tasso epico* (Florence, 1957).

CINELLI CALVOLI, G., *Biblioteca volante continuata dal dottor Dionigi Andrea Sancassani*, 2nd edn., 4 vols. (Venice, 1734–47).

COCHRANE, E., *Historians and Historiography in the Italian Renaissance* (Chicago and London, 1981).

COLDAGELLI, U., 'Armanni, Vincenzo', in *Dizionario biografico degli Italiani*, iv (1962), 222–4.

COOPER, L., *The Poetics of Aristotle: Its Meaning and Influence* (London–Calcutta–Sydney, 1924).

—— and Gudeman, A., *A Bibliography of the Poetics of Aristotle* Cornell Studies in English, 11 (New Haven, 1928).

COSMO, U., 'Le polemiche tassesche, la Crusca e Dante sullo scorcio del cinque e il principio del seicento', *Giornale storico della letteratura italiana*, 43 (1903), 112–60.

—— *Con Dante attraverso il Seicento* (Bari, 1946).

COZZI, G., *Il Doge Nicolò Contarini: ricerche sul patriziato veneziano agli inizi del Seicento* (Venice–Rome, 1958).

CRANZ, F. E., *A Bibliography of Aristotle Editions 1501–1600* (Baden-Baden, 1971).

CRASSO, L., *Elogii d'huomini letterati*, 2 vols. (Venice, 1666).

CROCE, B., *Storia della età barocca in Italia* (Bari, 1929).

CURTIUS, E. R., *European Literature and the Latin Middle Ages*, trans. by W. R. Trask (London and Henley, 1953).

DÉJOB, C., *Marc-Antoine Muret: un professeur français en Italie dans la seconde moitié du XVIe siècle* (Paris, 1881).

DELL'AQUILA, M., *La polemica anticruscante di Paolo Beni* (Bari, 1970).

DIFFLEY, P. B., 'A Note on Paolo Beni's Birthplace', *Studi secenteschi*, 24 (1983), 51–5.

—— 'Paolo Beni's Commentary on the *Poetics* and Its Relationship to the Commentaries of Robortelli, Maggi, Vettori and Castelvetro', *Studi secenteschi*, 25 (1984), 53–100.

DIONISOTTI, C., 'Introduzione', in P. Bembo, *Prose e rime* (Turin, 1960), 9–56.

—— 'Bembo, Pietro', in *Enciclopedia dantesca*, i (1970), 567–8.

DIONYSIUS OF HALICARNASSUS, 'La Composition stylistique', in *Opuscules rhétoriques*, trans. and ed. by G. Aujac and M. Lebel, iii (Paris, 1981).

DOGLIO, M. L., 'Beni, Paolo' in *Dizionario critico della letteratura italiana*, ed. by V. Branca, 3 vols. (Turin, 1973), i. 273–8.

DUCCI, L., *Ars historica* (Ferrara, 1604).

FACCIOLATI, I., *Fasti Gymnasii patavini* (Padua, 1757).

FAITHFULL, R. G., 'Teorie filologiche nell'Italia del primo Seicento con particolare riferimento alla filologia volgare', *Studi di filologia italiana*, 20 (1962), 147–313.

FARRELL, A. P., SJ, *The Jesuit Code of Liberal Education: Development and Scope of the 'Ratio Studiorum'* (Milwaukee, 1938).

FAVARO, A., *Galileo Galilei e lo Studio di Padova*, 2 vols. (Florence, 1883).

FELLER, F. X. de, 'Beni, Paul', in *Dictionnaire historique ou histoire abrégée*, 2nd edn., 8 vols. (Liège, 1797), ii. 152.

FERRAI, E., *L'ellenismo nello Studio di Padova* (Padua, 1876), 51 (on Beni).

FERRARI, L., *Onomasticon: repertorio biobibliografico degli scrittori italiani dal 1501 al 1850* (Milan, 1947).

[FIORETTI, B.], *Proginnasmi poetici di Udeno Nisiely da Vernio, accademico apatista*, 5 vols. (Florence, 1620–39).

FLICK, M., 'Congruismo', in *Enciclopedia cattolica*, iv. 355–7.

FOFFANO, F., *Ricerche letterarie* (Livorno, 1897).

—— 'Il catalogo della biblioteca di Paolo Beni', *Giornale storico e letterario della Liguria*, 2 (1901), 327–36.

FONTANINI, G., *Notizia de' libri rari nella lingua italiana divisa in quattro parti principali* (London, 1726).

FRANCE, P., *Rhetoric and Truth in France: Descartes to Diderot* (Oxford, 1972).

FRANZONI, D., *L'oracolo della lingua d'Italia* (Bologna, 1641).

FRATI, C., *Dizionario bio-bibliografico dei bibliotecari e bibliofili italiani dal sec. XIV al XIX raccolto e pubblicato da A. Sorbelli* (Florence, 1933). See also Parenti, M.

FRATTAROLO, R., *Studi su Dante dal Trecento all'età romantica*, i (Ravenna, 1970).

FREHERUS, D. P., *Theatrum virorum eruditione clarorum*, 2 vols. (Nuremberg, 1688).

FRIZZI, A., *Memorie per la storia di Ferrara*, 2nd edn., 5 vols. (Ferrara, 1847–50).

GALILEI, G., *Scritti letterari*, ed. by A. Chiari, 2nd edn. (Florence, 1970).

GARIN, E., 'Note su alcune retoriche rinascimentali', in *Testi umanistici su la retorica* (Milan, 1953), 7–55.

GENNARI, G., 'Saggio storico sopra le accademie di Padova', in *Saggi scientifici e letterari dell'Accademia di Padova*, 3 vols. (Padua, 1786–94), i (1786), pp. xiii–lxxi.

GHILINI, C., *Teatro d'uomini letterati*, 2 vols. (Venice, 1647).

GRAYSON, C., *A Renaissance Controversy: Latin or Italian?* (Oxford, 1960).

—— 'Dante and the Renaissance', in *Italian Studies Presented to E. R. Vincent*, ed. by C. P. Brand, K. Foster, and U. Limentani (Cambridge, 1962), 57–75.

—— Review of B. Weinberg's *A History of Literary Criticism in the Italian Renaissance*, *Romance Philology*, 17 (1963–4), 490–6.

—— 'Le lingue del Rinascimento', in *Il Rinascimento: aspetti e problemi attuali*, ed. by V. Branca *et al.* (Florence, 1982), 135–52.

GRIFFITH, T. G. *Italian Writers and the 'Italian' Language* (Hull, 1967).

GUALDO, P., *Vita Ioannis Vincentii Pinelli, patricii genuensis* (s.l., 1607).

GUARINI, G. B., 'Il Verrato ovvero difesa di quanto ha scritto Messer Jason Denores contra le tragicommedie, e le pastorali, in un suo discorso di poesia', in *Opere*, 4 vols. (Verona, 1737–8), ii (1737), 209–308.

HALL, R. A., jun., *The Italian Questione della Lingua: An Interpretative Essay* (Chapel Hill, 1942).

HATHAWAY, B., *The Age of Criticism* (Ithaca–New York, 1962).

—— *Marvels and Commonplaces: Renaissance Literary Criticism* (New York, 1968).

HERRICK, M. T., *Tragicomedy: Its Origin and Development in Italy, France, and England* (Urbana, 1955).

HOUSE, H., *Aristotle's Poetics: A Course of Eight Lectures*, revised, with a preface, by C. Hardie (London, 1956).

IMPERIALE, G., *Musaeum historicum et physicum* (Venice, 1640).

JACOBILLI, L., *Bibliotheca Umbriae sive de scriptoribus Provinciae Umbriae alphabetico ordine digesta* (Foligno, 1658), pp. 216–17 on Beni.

JANNACO, C., 'Critici del primo Seicento', in *La critica stilistica e il barocco letterario: Atti del II Congresso Internazionale di Studi Italiani* (Florence, 1958), 219–44.

—— *Il Seicento* (Milan, 1963).

[JESUITS], *Constitutiones Societatis Jesu cum earum declarationibus* (Rome, 1583).

—— *Annuae litterae Societatis Jesu anni M.D.LXXXV* (Rome, 1587).

—— *Litterae Societatis Jesu duorum annorum M.D.LXXXVI et M.D.LXXXVII* (Rome, 1589).

JOYCE, G. H., SJ, *The Catholic Doctrine of Grace*, 2nd edn. (London, 1930).

KREBS, Io. PH., *Vitam Caroli Sigonii . . . ad imitandum iuventuti exposuit . . . Io. Phil. Krebsius* (Weilburgi, [1837]).

KRISTELLER, P. O., *Renaissance Thought: The Classic, Scholastic and Humanist Strains* (New York, 1961).

—— 'Philosophy and Rhetoric from Antiquity to the Renaissance', in *Renaissance Thought and Its Sources*, ed. by M. Mooney (New York, 1979), 211–59.

—— *Renaissance Thought and the Arts* (Princeton, 1980). First publ. in 1965.

LADVOCAT, Mr. L'Abbé, *Dictionnaire historique portatif*, new edn., 2 vols. (Basel, 1758), i. 150 (on Beni).

LANDONI, E., 'A proposito della vita e delle opere di Paolo Beni (1552–1625)', *Rendiconti dell'Istituto lombardo*, 113 (1979), 27–34.

LEO, U., *Torquato Tasso: Studien zur Vorgeschichte des Secentismo* (Berne, 1951).

—— *Lettere d'uomini illustri, che fiorirono nel principio del secolo decimosettimo, non più stampate* (Venice, 1744).

LETTERE, V., 'Costantini, Toldo', in *Dizionario biografico degli Italiani*, xxx (1984), 304–6.

LEWIS, C. S., *English Literature in the Sixteenth Century* (Oxford, 1954).

—— *Studies in Words* (Cambridge, 1960).

—— *The Discarded Image: An Introduction to Medieval and Renaissance Literature* (Cambridge, 1964).

LIMENTANI, U., *The Fortunes of Dante in Seventeenth Century Italy* (Cambridge, 1964).

—— 'La fortuna di Dante nel Seicento', *Studi secenteschi*, 5 (1965), 3–49.

LOMBARDELLI, O., *Fonti toscane* (Florence, 1598).

—— 'Discorso intorno a i contrasti, che si fanno sopra la Gerusalemme liberata di Torquato Tasso', in *Opere di Torquato Tasso*, vi (Florence, 1724).

LUCARELLI, O., *Memorie e guida storica di Gubbio* (Città di Castello, 1888).

LUGLI, G., and FROSINI, P., 'Tevere' in *Enciclopedia italiana*, xxxiii (1937), 750–4.

MAGGI, V., and LOMBARDI, B., *In Aristotelis librum de poetica communes explicationes* (Venice, 1550).

MAIORAGIUS, M. A., *Orationes, et praefationes omnes* (Venice, 1582).

MALACRETA, G. P., 'Considerazioni intorno al Pastorfido dell'Eccellentissimo Signor Dottor Giovanni Pietro Malacreta', in G. B. Guarini, *Opere*, 4 vols. (Verona, 1737–8), iv (1738), 1–122.

MARTINELLI, L., *Dante* (Storia della critica, 4) (Palermo, 1966).

MAYLENDER, M., *Storia delle accademie d'Italia*, 5 vols. (Bologna, 1926–30).

MAZZACURATI, G., *La crisi della retorica umanistica nel Cinquecento (Antonio Riccoboni)* (Naples, 1961).

—— 'Beni, Paolo', in *Dizionario biografico degli Italiani*, viii (Rome, 1966), 494–501.

MAZZUCHELLI, G. M., *Gli scrittori d'Italia* (Brescia, 1760).

MIGLIORINI, B., 'Lessicografia', in *Enciclopedia italiana*, xx (1933), 966–7.

—— 'La questione della lingua', in *Questioni e correnti di storia letteraria*, ed. by A. Momigliano (Milan, 1949), 1–76.

—— *Che cos'è un vocabolario?*, 2nd edn. (Florence, 1951).

—— *Storia della lingua italiana* (Florence, 1960).

—— and GRIFFITH, T. G., *The Italian Language* (London, 1966).

MONTI, V., 'Al Signor Marchese D. Gian Giacomo Trivulzio', in *Proposta di alcune correzioni ed aggiunte al Vocabolario della Crusca*, 3 vols. and 1 vol. (Appendix) (Milan, 1817–26), i (1817), pp. iii–lix.

[MORENI, D.], *Illustrazione storico-critica di una rarissima medaglia rappresentante Bindo Altoviti opera di Michelangelo Buonarroti* (Florence, 1824).

MORERI, L., *Le Grand Dictionaire historique ou le mélange curieux de l'histoire sacrée et profane*, 2nd edn., 2 vols. (Lyons, 1681); later edn., 10 vols. (Paris, 1759).

MORPURGO TAGLIABUE, G., 'Aristotelismo e barocco', in *Retorica e barocco: Atti del III Congresso Internazionale di Studi Umanistici*, ed. by E. Castelli (Rome, 1955), 119–95.

MORSOLIN, B., *Giangiorgio Trissino: monografia d'un gentiluomo letterato nel secolo XVI*, 2nd edn. 'corretta e ampliata' (Florence, 1894).

MULTINEDDU, S., *Le fonti della 'Gerusalemme liberata'* (Turin, 1895).

MURATORI, L. A., 'Vita Caroli Sigonii mutinensis', in C. Sigonius, *Opere omnia*, 6 vols. (Milan, 1732–7), i (1732), pp. i–xxii.

——— 'Vita di Alessandro Tassoni', in (=after) Tassoni, *La secchia rapita* (Venice, 1739), pp. i–xlviii.

MURETUS, M. A., *Pontificum Rom. epistolae xxx . . . Epistolae xxv m. Antonii Mureti et ad Muretum . . .* (Rome, 1758).

MURPHY, J. J., *Renaissance Rhetoric: A Short-Title Catalogue of Works on Rhetorical Theory from the Beginning of Printing to A.D.1700* (New York and London, 1981).

NARDI, B., 'Platonismo', in *Enciclopedia cattolica*, i (1952), 1614–23.

NEGRI, G., *Istoria degli scrittori fiorentini* (Ferrara, 1722).

NEGRI, R. and FUBINI, M., 'Tasso, Torquato', in *Enciclopedia dantesca*, v (1976), 526–8.

NICERON, J. P., *Mémoires pour servir à l'histoire des hommes illustres dans la république des lettres, avec un catalogue raisonné de leurs ouvrages*, 44 vols. (Paris, 1729–45).

NICCOLAI, F., *Pier Vettori (1499–1585)* (Florence, [1912]).

OLIVIERI, O., 'I primi vocabolari italiani fino alla prima edizione della Crusca', *Studi di filologia italiana*, 6 (1942), 64–192.

ONGARO, A., *L'Alceo: favola pescatoria* (Ferrara, 1614).

OTTONELLI, G., *Discorso sopra l'abuso del dire sua santità, sua maestà, sua altezza* (Ferrara, 1584).

[———] *Annotazioni sopra il Vocabolario degli Accademici della Crusca* (Venice, 1698).

PANIGAROLA, F., *Modo di comporre una predica con l'aggiunta di un trattato della memoria locale* (Padua, 1599).

——— *Il predicatore overo parafrase, commento, e discorsi intorno al libro dell'elocutione di Demetrio Falerio* (Venice, 1609).

PAPADOPOLI, N. C., *Historia Gymnasii patavini*, 2 vols. (Venice, 1726).

PAPARELLI, G., 'Paolo Beni e l'*Anticrusca*', in *Da Ariosto a Quasimodo* (Naples, 1977), 48–59.

PARENTE, P., 'Grazia', in *Enciclopedia cattolica*, vi (1951), 1019–28.

PARENTI, M., *Aggiunte al Dizionario bio-bibliografico dei bibliotecari e bibliofili italiani di Carlo Frati*, 3 vols. (Florence, 1952–60).

PATRIZI, F., *Della historia diece dialoghi* (Venice, 1560).

—— *Della retorica dieci dialoghi* (Venice, 1562).

—— *Della poetica la deca disputata: nella quale, e per istoria, e per ragioni, e per autorità de' grandi antichi, si mostra la falsità delle più credute vere opinioni, che di poetica, a dì nostri vanno intorno* (Ferrara, 1586).

PELLEGRINO, C., 'Il Carrafa, o vero della epica poesia', in *Opere di Torquato Tasso colle controversie sulla Gerusalemme*, ed. by G. Rosini, xviii (Pisa, 1827).

PERELLA, N. J., *The Critical Fortune of Battista Guarini's Il Pastor fido* (Florence, 1973).

PESCETTI, O., *Risposta all'Anticrusca del molto rev. et eccellentiss. sig. D. Paolo Beni pubblico lettore nello Studio di Padova* (Verona, 1613).

PHILLIPS, H., *The Theatre and Its Critics in Seventeenth-Century France* (Oxford, 1980).

PIGNORIA, L., 'L. P. Balthassari Bonifacio archi-diacono tarvisino, viro reverendissimo. Epist. XLIV', in *Symbolarum epistolicarum liber* (Padua, 1628), 174–90.

PINCHERLE, A., 'Baronio, Cesare', in *Dizionario biografico degli Italiani*, vi (1964), 470–8.

PITTORRU, F., *Torquato Tasso: l'uomo, il poeta, il cortegiano* (Milan, 1982).

PORTENARI, A., *Della felicità di Padova* (Padua, 1623).

PRAZ, M., 'Secentismo', in *Enciclopedia italiana*, xxxi (1936), 274–6.

—— *Studies in Seventeenth-Century Imagery*, 2 vols. (Warburg Institute, 1939).

PULIATTI, P., *Bibliografia di Alessandro Tassoni*, 2 vols. (Florence; 1969–70).

—— 'Introduzione' in A. Tassoni, *Scritti inediti* (Modena, 1975).

—— 'Le letture e i postillati del Tassoni', *Studi secenteschi* 18 (1977), 3–58.

PULLAPILLY, C. K., *Caesar Baronius: Counter-Reformation Historian* (Notre-Dame and London, 1975).

QUADRIO, F. S., *Della storia e della ragione d'ogni poesia*, 4 vols. (and 1 vol. Index) (Bologna, 1739–52) (i. 403–4 and 303; iv. 317; vi. 568 and 675 ff. on Beni).

RAPIN, R., *Les Réflexions sur l'éloquence, la poétique, l'histoire, et la philosophie*, 2 vols. (Paris, 1684), (ii. 84 on Beni).

RENAZZI, F. M., *Storia dell'Università degli studi di Roma*, 4 vols. (Rome, 1803–6).

RENDA, U., 'Alessandro Tassoni e il *Vocabolario della Crusca*', in *Miscel-*

lanea tassoniana di studi storici e letterari, ed. by T. Casini and V. Santi (Bologna–Modena, 1908), 277–324.

REYNOLDS, M. A., 'The *Considerazioni al Tasso* of Galileo Galilei', *Italian Quarterly,* 80 (1980), 11–28.

RICCIO, C. M. *Memorie storiche degli scrittori nati nel regno di Napoli* (Naples, 1844).

RICCOBONI, A., *Orationes decem* (Padua, 1573).

—— *Poetica Aristotelis latine conversa* (Padua, 1587).

RISTINE, F. H., *English Tragicomedy: Its Origins and History* (New York, 1910).

ROBORTELLI, F., *De historica facultate, disputatio* (Florence, 1548).

—— *In librum Aristotelis de arte poetica, explicationes* (Basel, 1555).

ROSSI, G., *Studi e ricerche tassoniane* (Bologna, 1904).

ROSSI, L., 'Brunetti, Giulio', in *Dizionario biografico degli Italiani,* xiv (1972), 580.

ROSSI, V., *Battista Guarini ed il Pastor fido* (Turin, 1886).

—— 'La biblioteca manoscritta del senatore veneziano Iacopo Soranzo', in *Scritti di critica letteraria: dal Rinascimento al Risorgimento* (Florence, 1930), 251–71.

RUGGIERI, R. M., 'Presecentismo tassesco', in *La critica stilistica e il barocco letterario: Atti del II Congresso Internazionale di Studi Italiani* (Florence, 1958), 327–34.

—— 'Aspetti linguistici della polemica tassesca', *Lingua nostra,* 6 (1944–5), 44–51.

—— 'Latinismi, forme etimologiche e forme 'significanti' nella Gerusalemme liberata', *Lingua nostra,* 7/4 (1946), 76–84.

Saggio di rime di diversi buoni autori che fiorirono dal XIV fino al XVIII secolo (Florence, 1825).

SALVIATI, L., *Orazione nella quale si dimostra la fiorentina favella e i fiorentini autori essere a tutte l'altre lingue, così antiche come moderne, e a tutti gli altri scrittori di qual si vuol lingua di gran lunga superiori* (Florence, 1564).

—— *Dello Infarinato Accademico della Crusca Risposta all'Apologia di Torquato Tasso* (Florence, 1585).

—— 'Degli Accademici della Crusca difesa dell'Orlando furioso dell'Ariosto contra 'l Dialogo dell'epica poesia di Cammillo Pellegrino. Stacciata prima', in *Opere di Torquato Tasso colle controversie sulla Gerusalemme,* ed. by G. Rosini, xviii (Pisa, 1827).

SANSONE, M., 'Le polemiche antitassesche della Crusca', in *Torquato Tasso: comitato per le celebrazioni di T. T., Ferrara, 1954* (Milan, 1957), 527–74.

SCARANO, L., *Scenophylax dialogus, in quo tragaediis, et comaediis anti-*

quus carminum usus restituitur, recentiorum quorundam iniuria intercep-
tus. Et de vi, ac natura carminis agitur (Venice, 1601).

SERASSI, P. A., *Vita di Torquato Tasso* (Rome, 1785).

SIGONIUS, C., *Historiarum de Occidentali Imperio libri xx* . . . (Bologna, 1577).

SOLERTI, A., 'Bibliografia delle edizioni delle opere complete di T. Tasso', in *Appendice alle opere in prosa di T. Tasso* (Florence, 1892) (pp. 12–13 on Beni).

—— *Vita di Torquato Tasso*, 3 vols. (Turin–Rome, 1895).

SOZZI, B. T., 'La fortuna letteraria del Tasso', *Studi tassiani*, 4 (1954), 37–45.

—— *Studi sul Tasso* (Pisa, 1954).

—— 'Il Tasso estimatore del Petrarca', *Studi tassiani*, 11 (1961), 45–8.

—— 'Lingua, Questione della', in *Dizionario critico della letteratura italiana*, ed. by V. Branca, 3 vols. (Turin, 1973), ii. 432–41.

SPAMPANATO, V., *Sulla soglia del Seicento* (Milan–Rome–Naples, 1926) (pp. 195–8 on Beni: first published in *Giornale critico della filosofia italiana*, 5 (1924), 118–21).

SPECIANO, C., *Proposizioni morali e civili*, ed. by N. Mosconi (Brescia, 1961).

SPERONI, S., 'Dialogo dell'historia', in *Dialoghi del sig. Speron Speroni* (Venice, 1596).

SPINGARN, J. E. *A History of Literary Criticism in the Renaissance*, 2nd edn. (New York, 1908).

SPINI, G., 'I trattatisti dell'arte storica nella Controriforma italiana', in *Contributi alla storia del Concilio di Trento e della Controriforma* (Florence, 1948), 109–36.

—— 'Historiography: The Art of History in the Italian Counter Reformation', in *The Late Italian Renaissance 1525–1630*, ed. by E. Cochrane (London, 1970), 91–133.

STOREY, G., *A Preface to Hopkins* (London and New York, 1981).

SUMMO, F., *Discorsi poetici* (Padua, 1600).

—— *Discorso in difesa del metro nelle poesie, e ne i poemi, et in particolare nelle tragedie, & comedie* (Padua, 1601).

TARDUCCI, D. A., *De' vescovi di Cagli* (Cagli, 1896).

TASSO, T., *La Gerusalemme liberata di T. T. con le annotationi di Scipion Gentili, e di Giulio Guastavini. Et li argomenti di Oratio Ariosti* (Genoa, 1617).

—— *Le lettere*, ed. by C. Guasti, 5 vols. (Florence, 1852–5).

—— *Prose*, ed. by E. Mazzali (Milan–Naples, 1959).

—— *La raccolta tassiana della Biblioteca Civica 'A Mai' di Bergamo* (Bergamo, 1960).

TASSONI, A., *Parte de Quisiti del S. Alessandro Tassoni modonese* [sic].

Dati in luce da Giulian Cassiani e dedicati a gli illustrissimi signori accademici della Crusca (Modena, 1608; 2nd, enlarged, edn. Modena, 1612).

—— *La tenda rossa* (Frankfurt, 1613).

—— *Le considerazioni rivedute e ampliate alle rime di Francesco Petrarca*, ed. by L. A. Muratori (Modena, 1711).

—— *La secchia rapita*, ed. by L. A. Muratori (Modena, 1744).

—— 'Postille scelte . . . alla Divina commedia di Dante Alighieri' (Estratto dall'*Enciclopedia contemporanea* edita in Fano. Vol. iii. Dispensa 4a.) (Reggio, 1826).

—— 'Postille all'*Ercolano*', in B. Varchi, *L'Ercolano* (Florence, 1846), 1–528.

—— 'Le postille . . . alla *Divina commedia*', ed. by G. Rossi, in *Studi e ricerche tassoniane* (Bologna, 1904), 369–406.

—— *Prose politiche e morali*, ed. by G. Rossi (1930), reprint ed. by P. Puliatti, 2 vols. (Bari, 1978).

—— *Scritti inediti*, ed. by P. Puliatti (Modena, 1975).

TAVANI, G., *Dante nel Seicento: saggi su A. Guarini, N. Villani, L. Magalotti* (Florence, 1976).

TAYLOR, A. E., *Platonism and Its Influence* (London, [1925]).

TESSADRI, E., *Il grande cardinale Cristoforo Madruzzo* (Milan–Rome, 1953).

TIRABOSCHI, G., *Storia della letteratura italiana*, 8 vols. (Modena, 1787–94).

TOFFANIN, G., *La fine dell'Umanesimo* (Milan–Turin–Rome, 1920).

—— *Il Cinquecento*, 6th edn. (Milan, 1960).

TOMASINI, I. PH., *Illustrium virorum elogia iconibus exornata* (Padua, 1630).

—— *T. Livius patavinus* (Padua, 1630).

—— *Bibliothecae patavinae manuscriptae publicae et privatae* (Udine, 1639) (pp. 81–2 on Beni).

—— *Gymnasium patavinum* (Udine, 1654).

TRABALZA, C., *La critica letteraria* (Milan, 1915).

VALLONE, A., *L'interpretazione di Dante nel Cinquecento*, 2nd edn. (Florence, 1969).

VARCHI, B., *L'Ercolano dialogo . . . con la Correzione di Lodovico Castelvetro e la Varchina di Jeronimo Muzio con le note di G. Bottari e di G. A. Volpi aggiuntevi ora alcune postille inedite, tratte dalla Biblioteca Parmense, alcune di Vittorio Alfieri e molte di Alessandro Tassoni* (Florence, 1846).

VARESE, C., 'Torquato Tasso', in *I classici italiani nella storia della critica*, ed. by W. Binni, i (Da Dante al Tasso) (Florence, 1954), 461–516.

VECCHIETTI, F., and MORO, T., *Biblioteca picena: o sia notizie istoriche delle opere e degli scrittori piceni*, 5 vols. (Osimo, 1790–6).

VEDOVA, G., *Biografia degli scrittori padovani*, 2 vols. (Padua, 1832–6).

VETTORI, P., *Commentarii in tres libros de arte dicendi* (Florence, 1548).

—— *Commentarii in primum librum Aristotelis de arte poetarum* (Florence, 1560).

VICKERS, B., (ed.) *Rhetoric Revalued: Papers from the International Society for the History of Rhetoric* (Binghampton, New York, 1982).

VIGLIANI, L., 'Beni, Paolo', in *Grande dizionario enciclopedico Utet*, 3rd edn. (Turin, 1966–75), ii (1966), 894–5.

VISDOMINI, F., *Lettere del signor Francesco Visdomini*, 2 parts (Venice, 1626) (ii/352 has an undated letter to Beni).

VITALE, M., 'Il Vocabolario degli Accademici della Crusca', in *Le prefazioni ai primi grandi vocabolari delle lingue europee*, ed. by A. Viscardi *et al.* (Milan–Varese, 1959), 25–74.

—— *La questione della lingua*, new edn. (Palermo, 1978).

VIVALDI, V., *Storia delle controversie linguistiche in Italia da Dante ai nostri giorni* (Catanzaro, 1925).

VOLPI, G., *La libreria de' Volpi, e la stamperia cominiana* (Padua, 1756), (pp. 21–2 on Beni).

WALKER, J. C., *Memoirs of Alessandro Tassoni* (London, 1815) (p. 40 on Beni).

WEINBERG, B., *A History of Literary Criticism in the Italian Renaissance*, 2 vols. (Chicago, 1961).

—— (ed.) *Trattati di poetica e retorica del Cinquecento*, 4 vols. (Bari, 1970–4).

WILLIAMS, N. P., *The Grace of God* (London, 1930).

WILLIAMS, R. C., 'Italian Critical Treatises of the Sixteenth Century', *Modern Language Notes*, 35 (1920), 506–7.

YATES, F. A., *The Art of Memory* (Chicago and London, 1966).

ZONTA, G., 'Rinascimento, aristotelismo e barocco', *Giornale storico della letteratura italiana*, 104 (1934), 1–63 and 185–240.

INDEX